A beautifully written account of a childhood
all, the tastes of a particular world are lyrica
although Mathias rightly celebrates the ric
through this magical remembrance of things past a skein of sadness that makes
it haunting. It's lovely!

Francesca Kay, *An Equal Stillness*

With *Rosaries, Reading and Secrets,* Anita Mathias invites us into a totally
absorbing world of past and present marvels. She is a natural and gifted
storyteller who weaves history and biography together in a magical mix.
Erudite and literary, generously laced with poetic and literary references
and Dickensian levels of observation and detail, *Rosaries* is alive with
glowing, vivid details, bringing to life an era and culture that is unfor-
gettable. A beautifully written, important and addictive book.'

Jenny Lewis, *Gilgamesh Retold*

A dazzling, vibrant tale of the childhood of "the naughtiest girl in school"
whose sweet tooth is exceeded only by her insatiable appetite for language and
stories. Mathias conjures 1960s India, and her extended family in uproarious
and heartbreaking detail.

Erin Hart, *Haunted Ground*

Joining intelligent winsomeness with an engaging style, Anita Mathias writes
with keen observation, lively insight and hard-earned wisdom about navigating
the life of thoughtful faith in a world of cultural complexities. Her story bears
witness to how God wastes nothing and redeems all. Her words sing of a spirit
strong in courage, compassion and a pervasive dedication to the adventure of
life. As a reader, I have been challenged and changed by her beautifully told and
powerful story - so will you.

Carolyn Weber, *Surprised by Oxford*

Anita Mathias's memoir is a remarkable account of a Catholic childhood in India. A treasure chest of sights, sounds and scents, it is full of food (always food),
books (always books), a family with all its alliances and divisions, and many
glimpses of a world which is at once exotic and familiar. A feat of memory and
remembrance of a moment in Indian culture, still tinged by the English presence, which yet has universal qualities.

Philip Gooden, *The Story of English*

Anita Mathias's beautiful childhood memoir reflects the rich complexities of
India's myriad minorities – in her case the Catholics of Jamshedpur, built by

the Tata family, the first planned industrial city in India. The Church figures prominently; one of her childhood tortures is family rosary-saying. Secondly, this is a book about "food, always food," described in mouth-watering detail. Anita's reading is hugely wide-ranging (from the Panchatantra and Shakespeare to Dickens) and whenever there is trouble with her parents she plunges into her book. Gossip and social scandals run throughout the book, while at school, she indulges in characteristic naughtiness (locking her class into their classroom, for example). India's wretched wealth-poverty polarisation forms a backdrop to her story. Tormented, passionate and often sad, this book is immensely readable.

Trevor Mostyn, *Coming of Age in The Middle East*

Rosaries takes us into the psyche of place, from an insider who has lived and breathed India yet stands at a distance from it, both as a constantly alert observer of the human condition, and as a Catholic negotiating a Hindu culture. This subtle balance of insider and outsider means we are treated to fascinating insights and angles on life in India – its tastes and smells, its quirks and eccentricities, preoccupations and prejudices, told with glorious detail, precision and humour. Mathias reveals her evolution from naughty girl to writer: how she is shaped by inner and outer worlds to become the independent spirit and artist of language so deliciously demonstrated in this memoir.

Professor Jane Spiro, *Testimony of Flight*

Born of extraordinary parents and raised in an Indian steel town, Anita Mathias was blessed with no shortage of brains. She spent her first nine years putting them to endless, delightful mischief, but not without making room for some very advanced learning. With an unprecedented appetite for reading, Anita tore through libraries and every volume she could lay her tiny hands on before leaving for boarding school at nine – which incidentally she adored. Her middle class homelife was a rich array of experiences: the copious quantities of gastronomic delicacies – oh the food! – a strict and strong creative mother, a learned and caring father, a close younger sister, and the large hinterland of an impressively accomplished family. Anita was undoubtedly a dazzling star in the red earth firmament of the industrial landscape of Jamshedpur, and her pluck and charm shine through every page of this beautifully crafted, comprehensive, and erudite memoir.

We wait impatiently for the next episode – which will cover her continued rebellions at a Catholic boarding school before her own religious conversion and entry into Mother Teresa's convent as a novice.

Ray Foulk, *Picasso's Revenge*

A fascinating description. Anita Mathias is an accomplished writer.

Merryn Williams, *Six Women Novelists*

Rosaries, Reading and Secrets:

A Catholic Childhood in India

by

Anita Mathias

BENEDICTION CLASSICS

ISBN: 978-1-78943-348-7.

Gratefully dedicated to my families:

Noel and Celine Mathias and Shalini Cornelio

and

Roy, Zoe, and Irene Mathias

For inspiration, and endurance.

When such as I cast out remorse

So great a sweetness flows into the breast

We must laugh and we must sing,

We are blest by everything,

Everything we look upon is blest.

          W. B Yeats, *A Dialogue of Self and Soul*

I can with one eye squinted take it all as a blessing."

          Flannery O'Connor

"We shall not cease from exploration

And the end of all our exploring

Will be to arrive where we started

And know the place for the first time.

          T.S. Eliot, *Little Gidding*

CONTENTS

In the Beginning:
You Woke and Heard the Birds Cough

I was made in India, in Jamshedpur, in Bihar then, Jharkhand now, where the great Gangetic plains lope up to the foothills of the Himalayas.

The Buddha achieved enlightenment there in Bihar, six centuries before Christ; Mahavira, founder of Jainism, was born there. But I was an accidental pilgrim in this birthplace of religions. I was born in Jamshedpur because of steel.

The soil was red-ochre, flecked with tiny balls of *murram*, iron ore, visible signs of the hidden lodes which, in 1907, drew Zoroastrian industrialist, Jamshedji Nusserjani Tata, to Bihar to found Jamshedpur, The Steel City.

In Jamshedpur, blast furnaces belched grimness into the bleared skies as iron ore was refined to shining steel by The Tata Iron and Steel Company, one of the world's largest steel companies, which, in 1952, lured my father, a Chartered Accountant, from still-racist London. ("Our accountant is Indian; is that a problem?" his boss had to ask. Sometimes it was.) Now he was the Controller of Accounts at Tata's—and after he visited Pittsburgh in the sixties and introduced the first computers to TISCO, monsters which hogged a wall, he also became Manager of Data Processing, as I told everyone proudly. And "What is that?" they asked.

My father married late, aged thirty-eight. I was born after seven years of infertility and the death of their infant first-born son, Gerard, three days old. My mother never overcame her disappointment that I, born the year after

Gerard, was a mere girl, while my father, who'd mournfully say that girls were a terrible thing, expected me to be every bit as extraordinary as the boy who never lived would undoubtedly have been.

Within hours of my birth, I fell ill with dysentery, which had killed my elder brother. My father vowed he would go to Mass every Friday for ten years if I lived. I did; he did. And so, in an emergency baptism with hastily-blessed hospital water, in Jamshedpur, at the heart of the Hindu heartland, I was christened Anita Mary Mathias, daughter of Noel Joseph Mathias and Celine Mary Mathias, the European surname given to our family when the Portuguese occupied my ancestral town of Mangalore on the coast of the Arabian Sea in 1510, converting the population to Roman Catholicism with the carrot of government jobs, and the stick of the Inquisition—Counter-Reformation fires reaching the tropics.

Which explains why a child born in the Hindu heartland had grandparents called Piedade Felician Mathias and Josephine Euphrosyne Lobo, Stanislaus Coelho and Molly Rebello, and great-grandmothers called Gracia Lasrado Mathias, Julianna Saldanha Lobo, Alice Coelho Rebello and Apolina Saldanha Coelho, though, on my mother's side, everyone was a Coelho, for Coelhos, as the thirteen branches of that family observe proudly, Coelhos, whenever possible, only marry Coelhos.

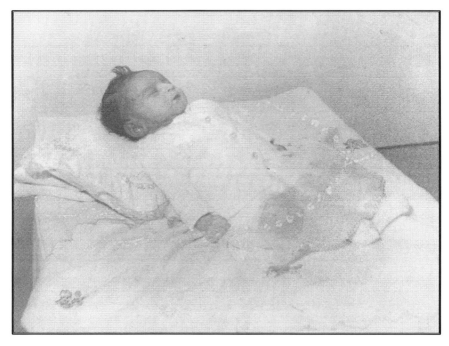

Last picture of my elder brother, Gerard Mathias, who died, three days old

Anita

Rosaries at the Grotto

During May, "The Month of our Lady," Father Jesus Calvo, the Spanish parish priest, corralled the entire Catholic community of Jamshedpur at the grotto of St. Mary's Church: a cave constructed of rocks and mortar, over-planted with rambling roses, built because the Virgin appeared to Bernadette at a grotto in Lourdes. There we recited the rosary.

"Hail Mary," "Holy Mary," the words rose and fell, hypnotic as the sea, fifty repetitions of Hail Marys punctuated by the mini-relief of the Glory Be, and, at last, the Memorare, signalling the glorious end: *"Remember, Oh most gracious Virgin Mary, that never was it known that anyone who fled to thy protection, implored thy help, or sought thy intercession was left unaided."*

My mother bowed over her rosary, her long-lashed eyes closed, an image of fervour. My father prayed rapidly, head down, frowning, as if his rapidity would hasten the conclusion. I suspected he disliked saying the rosary as much as I did.

Decades later, adults reminded me of when I slipped away, climbed to the top of the grotto, and squatted there, like a wise monkey, surveying the crowd. Giggles rose.

On hearing the giggles, my father looked for me. It was a reflex. And there I was, on top of the grotto, the eyes of every Catholic in Jamshedpur on me.

"Anita, come down," my father hissed. I remained there, grinning. Despite my bravado, I was terrified of heights.

"Anita come down,' he stage-whispered between clenched teeth as children giggled and adults chanted, laughter in their voices. Finally, my dignified father, senior management in that company town, fifty-two years old to my six, squeezed through the crowd, past the amputee Mrs Watkins, past Mr D'Costa, who owned Boulevard Hotel, and Mrs D'Cruz, who owned a nursery school, scaled the grotto, then inched down, half-carrying me, while around us the chuckle-flecked rosary rose and fell, *"Hail Mary, full of grace."*

* * *

Catholic social life in Jamshedpur revolved around the Parish Church of St. Mary's, the Mangalorean-Goan Association, and the Catholic Family Movement, introduced to Jamshedpur by an American Jesuit, appropriately called Father Love. It brought together Catholics of the same socio-economic class, an insular tight-knit group.

There were the Fernandezes, the Saldanhas, and the Diases, who had six children whose names all started with D—Denise, Dany, Diane, Dougie, Denzil, and David. There was an Anglo-Indian family, the Thompsons, whose green-eyed daughter, Paula, my sister Shalini adored down to her freckles, lily-white skin, and long, brown ringlets. My father claimed Shalini's private litany went "Paula most pure, Paula most amiable, Paula most admirable!" (And when I misbehaved, my father would say of Paula's handsome brother (who later became a priest), "Anita, Anita, if you're so naughty, Jeff will never marry you, but he would marry Shalini *instantly.*")

The adults gathered for spiritual instruction, about which we felt *no* curiosity, while the children played in the host child's bedroom until everyone clustered around the potluck, an innovation of the American priests. The Indian way would have been for the hostess to say, "Oh, *please* don't worry about bringing food. I'll just prepare a little something," and then spend a week planning,

shopping for, and magicking a lavish near-banquet; most women prided themselves on their generosity, hospitality, and culinary repertoire.

Everyone competed to produce the most delectable dishes, savoured the
offerings, and then asked for the recipe, ultimate compliment. Unless the dish
was brought by Blanche, wife of the local Mangalorean doctor, Bert Lasrado,
who, like my father, had been to England for his professional education.
Blanche was the first woman in town with a free-standing freezer; its potential
exhilarated her. While other women brought freshly cooked aromatic dishes,
she gleefully announced the provenance of her offerings–prawn *balchow*: three
months old; chicken *indad*: six months old; pork *vindaloo*: eight months old. And
appetites withered.

The adults had Bloody Marys, while we had "Virgin Marys"–tomato
juice, after which what we considered "western food" was served. As a student
in England, to my surprise, I rarely found the supposedly Western food I had
grown up with: "potato chops," mashed potato croquettes stuffed with spicy
minced beef, pan-fried in a batter of egg and breadcrumbs, or "cutlets," large,
flat burgers, cooked with onions, green chillis, coriander and mint; or "meat
puffs," crisp hot filo pastry stuffed with spicy curried minced lamb.

After dinner, Dougie Dias or Benny Fernandez produced guitars and
led us in "Jamaica Farewell," "Old Man River," "Banana Boat Song," or "Polly-
Wolly-Doodle." How we loved them–"Oh my darling Clementine," "Silver
Dollar," "Country Roads", or "Una Paloma Blanca." The lyrics were mysterious, but we sang along, *Hang down your head, Tom Dooley,/ Poor boy you're gonna die;
John Brown's body is a-mouldering in the grave,* or with greater gusto, *Oh bloodee, oh
blood-dah,* that chorus striking us as deliciously naughty. *The sun so hot, I froze to
death; Susannah, don't you cry.* What did the lyrics mean? Who knew? But it all felt
magical…*Daylight come, and I wanna go home.*

* * *

We once rented a beach house in Puri, Orissa, with the Diases, Thompsons, and other CFMers, one of whom brought his gun and shot doves, pigeons, and even sparrows, which we roasted over an improvised fire of bricks and sticks; the deliciousness lingers in memory. Their young son was allowed to use the shotgun, and I, aged six, seeing it left unattended, picked it up, looked through the sight, and, inspired by books and movies, pulled the trigger. The safety catch was off: Bang! I was startled and thrilled, though I did not shoot a bird (or myself). The father ran out and cuffed his son, and I felt scared, sad, and guilty, for it had all been my fault.

* * *

The Catholic Diocese of Jamshedpur was a missionary project of the Jesuit Maryland Province in Baltimore; it was run by hearty, good-hearted Irish American priests: Father McGauley, Fr. MacFarland, Fr. Guidera, Fr. Keogh, Fr. Moran, and Fr. O'Leary. There were other priests from the worldwide fraternity of the Jesuits--Father Durt, a Belgian who built St. Mary's Hindi School for underprivileged children, and, on loan from the Spanish Gujarat Mission in Ahmedabad, Father Arroyo and Father Jesus Calvo, a kindly Spanish priest, who helped me develop a magnificent stamp collection by asking all the Europeans he knew to send me stamps.

The Jesuits were respected, even loved, by Jamshedpurians, both Catholic and non-Catholic, for they ran Loyola School, which turned out achieving boys, as well as the prestigious local Business School, Xavier Labour Relations Institute, XLRI, at which my father later taught, which had sought-after courses in Business Management and Industrial Relations which drew students from all over India, Asia, and the Middle East.

We had the American Jesuits over for meals and parties and were invited to dinners at the Jesuit residence. My father was amused to be told that, among Irish-American Catholics, one son became a priest, one became a cop, and one a criminal! My father marvelled when Father O'Brien told us of his father, the butcher, who distilled and sold moonshine in Baltimore during Prohibition. "Can you imagine, Anita? Father O'Brien is *a butcher's son!*" (Indian Jesuits were, then, largely upper-middle or middle-class). "And his father, though a pious Catholic, had *no compunction* about breaking the law and making bootleg liquor!"

* * *

The priests returned from furlough with American brands—packets of Campbell's Chicken Noodle soup, Smarties, Betty Crocker cake mixes, Danish Butter Cookies, squeezable tubes of icing sugar, or flavoured Primula cheese, coveted because foreign. These they gave their favourite Catholic housewives who compared their bounty, apparently carelessly, "Oh Father MacFarland is so sweet; he got me lovely Devil's Food Cake mix,"–happy if their loot was the most bountiful and secretly cross about Lola or Deidre's Angel Food Cake.

From America, too, came boxes of lightly used clothes collected for "the poor in India." These the priests sold at jumble sales to middle-class Catholics, using the proceeds for the poor. Some of my favourite clothes came via America—my fuchsia winter coat and a red plaid coat with a fur collar for my Himalayan boarding school; a shimmering white silk blouse with pearl buttons that I passed off as boarding school uniform; a pale blue silk dress, and red goloshes.

From boxes of donated books shipped from America, I acquired books which, in my late teens, changed the course of my faith–and life: Catherine Marshall's *Beyond Ourselves* and *Something More*, David Wilkerson's *The Cross and the Switchblade*, and Nicky Cruz's *Run, Baby Run*. The American priests, inexplicably, gave us boxes of old American magazines: *Chatelaine, McCall's, Family Home Circle,* and *Good Housekeeping,* in which we found the recipe for brownies, chewy, cocoa-laden, and bursting with walnuts, adding a new much-imitated item on the party circuit. I leafed through the glossy pages, coveting dolls that walked and talked, dollhouses, and walkie-talkie radios that one could receive by just sending in a postcard–glossy magazines of dreams, never gratified, though my Jesuit Uncle, Father ₜₕₑₒ Mathias, always bought me a Barbie doll on his annual trip to the States even into my early teens, when makeup was more exciting than dolls!

* * *

Goa and Mangalore, seacoast communities, were colonised by the Portuguese. Four hundred years later, traces endure--in the names: Mathias, Coelho, Lobo, Rebello, Pinto, Saldanha, Mascarenhas; the imported religion: Catholicism; and the language, Konkani: only spoken by Goans and Mangaloreans, a patois of Portuguese and the Kannada and Marathi spoken by the indigenous communities before colonisation. (I have never learnt Konkani, nor did my father who, as the son of an upwardly mobile surgeon in British India, was only taught English.)

Goan-Mangalorean food is distinctive--*sarpatel*, archetypal Mangalorean delicacy, small pieces of pork beneath inches of fat and chewy, rubbery rind, simmered in a sauce of spices, wine and the pig's own blood and liver, eaten with *sannas*: fluffy steamed rice cakes, fermented in toddy. *Kube*, a curry of clams or cockles, was breakfast at my paternal grandmother's house. Fish cooked in coconut milk was ubiquitous while, at afternoon tea, people ate *patolio* and *patrade*, dumplings and pancakes stuffed with fresh grated coconut and *jaggery*, unrefined brown sugar, and steamed in plantain leaves.

At the Mangalorean-Goan Association dinners, people danced the waltz, *one-two together, one-two together,* we murmured under our breaths, or the foxtrot and polka to Engelbert Humperdinck, Elvis Presley, or Jerry Lewis. If I spotted my parents waltzing together, I flung myself between them in a frenzy of jealousy, trying to drag my father away. They continued waltzing…laughing.

Mangaloreans and Goans of every social class, from Goan manual workers at the factory to TISCO executives, met at Mangalorean-Goan Association meetings. I held hands with a child from the large Andrade family, who all moved to Jamshedpur from Goa, drawn by the jobs in TISCO. "Why are your hands so rough?" I asked. "Because I help my mother wash clothes," she explained. My mother had an *ayah, a* maid, to do the laundry, as I naively supposed *everyone's* mother did. It never occurred to me that *children* might do the washing. "*You help your mother wash clothes?*" I asked, genuinely shocked. Sabrina, embarrassed, avoided me for the rest of our childhoods; her mother never forgave me, and neither did mine.

The Catholics from Mangalore, Goa, and Bombay traditionally visited all their Catholic friends during the twelve days between Christmas Day and the sixth of January, the feast of the Epiphany, the official end of the season.

Weeks before Christmas, my mother began creating traditional Christmas treats, *kushwar* in Konkani, offered to visitors, and given in little boxes to my father's colleagues, nuns, teachers, priests, and friends. We made chocolate *nankatis*, mouth-meltingly soft, buttery, sugary cookies; light, crisp meringues; and crunchy coconut, chocolate, or cashew nut macaroons. *Kulkuls* were another Mangalorean speciality, dough curled on the tines of a comb into shells, deep-fried, then dropped into a thick, simmering sugar syrup, which lumpily congealed around them. Sitting together around the dining table, we hand-crafted marzipan fruits and moulded "milk toffee," made from condensed milk, sugar, and butter in our buttered red rubber seashell mould to create wentletrap, shrimp, cockles, mussels, seahorses, oysters, and snails.

* * *

How foreign Christmas was when I was a child, how imported! We lopped the top off one of the two scraggly fir trees in our garden, hauling it indoors to deck it with cotton wool or popcorn snow, topped with a little pine-cone angel with a wooden mothball face, flaxen hair, a gold wire halo, and little gold paper wings that I brought back from boarding school in Nainital, in the Himalayas. (And each year, my mother said of this durable angel, "I can't believe you paid five rupees at the Fun Fair for that rubbish some child made.")

We sent each other Christmas cards of robins in snowy fields and sleighs in an entranced Snow Queen landscape, though the wintry sun shone all December, as it might have done in Bethlehem. We carolled outside all Catholic homes: "Rudolf the Red-nosed Reindeer;" "Freddy, the Little Fir Tree;" "Little Drummer Boy," and "Jingle Bells"—a Nordic Christmas transplanted to the tropics.

At midnight mass, congregations, not all of whom spoke fluent English, sang a full-bodied *Gloria in Excelsis Deo* in Latin. I shivered with pleasure. And then we returned home to eat Christmas fruit cake, crammed with crystallised cherries, candied peel, raisins, and nuts, and to drink the very sweet homemade wine made from *Jamun* berries and mulberries from our garden that we never considered alcoholic.

And what did all this have to do with the sweet, humble birth in a manger? Generations of Europeans had transported the husk of Christmas to Indian homes while its glory lay obscured here as elsewhere. Still, *Glor-ooo-ooo-ooo-reeaa in ex-cel-sis Deo,* we sang lustily, though we might have been nonplussed if asked to translate.

.

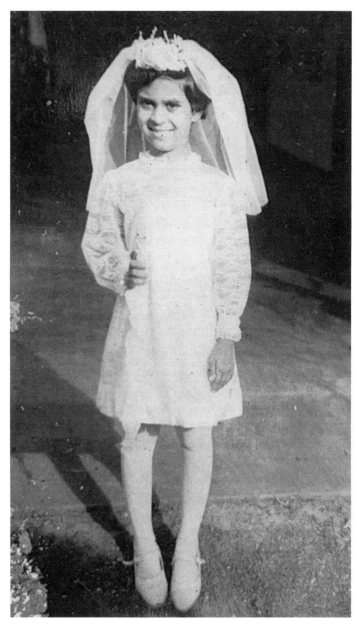

My First Holy Communion

Shalini and me with our Easter Eggs

My Uncle Father Theo Mathias, S. J., my sister Shalini, me and my father

Visiting: When People were Entertainment (and Family Secrets)

The latch on the green steel front gates clanked. The cook or *ayah* ran to open the gate for the car; Shalini, Rover the dog, and I ran to the veranda to check out the visitor, while my mother ran in to replace her "house-coat," a buttoned cotton dressing gown which most Mangalorean housewives wore all day, with a saree, and to slap on the lipstick and rouge without which she said she felt naked.

Visits were unannounced. To say you were coming was considered rude, for the hostess would then be expected to stay home and to provide respectfully elaborate food, whereas if you just showed up, you took their manger or mansion as you found it and would be served a tray of delicious snacks—of which we always had a pantry full, which the hostess would present, apologetically and self-deprecatingly, and you would effusively praise.

Most upper-middle-class women did not work. For a woman to have a job implied that her husband was ill-paid and could not provide for his family—or so my father and his brothers believed. Domestic help was affordable; we had three servants for a family of four, comfortable but not extraordinary. So, women had time for sociability and the bonding ritual of gossip. Housework supervised, they jumped into the car on an impulse, alone, or with their husband and children in the evenings, to see who was in. There was no television in Jamshedpur during my childhood. *People* were entertainment. Dougie and Daphne Dias and Denise and Dany, Joe and Lulu Saldanha and Nina and

Debby, Bill and Pat Thompson and Jeff and Paula, Benny and Ramona Fernandez and Marcheta and Benita, Thrassie and Marie Domingo and Ozzy, David and Kathleen Oliver and Nicolette, Lancy and Iris Rebello and their seven children, Joe and Hermie Rebello, Pam and Arnold Mathias, the Pintos, the Athaides, people who visited us on bicycles, scooters, motorcycles and cars as they moved up the economic ladder, the background cast of my childhood, friends seen so often they felt like relatives.

If we were bored or liked the visitor, my sister and I sat in the living room during the visit, reducing the women to sharing information in a code of widened or rolled eyes, innuendoes, "you know who's", and "You *know* how so-and-so is..." My sister and I listened with heightened attention—our first introductions to the adult world.

"I sat behind her in church," Lola said, "and poor thing, poor thing, you could see the dirt behind her ears!" "*Who?*" I asked. "Nobody," both ladies said hastily and improbably. "I touch my toes a hundred times every morning," continued sexy, buxom Lola, changing the subject. "And *that's* how I keep slim."

And then they were back at it. "His Beatles haircut...and he took drugs at St. Stephen's in Delhi and fried his brain." Little spies, we listened in. "Sssh, Big Ears," adults sometimes whispered, though they generally pretended we were the proverbial monkeys who'd hear, speak, and understand no evil. Ha! I listened, I listened, decoding, analysing, mentally recording those adult mysteries, as I now do with my pen.

* * *

And again, the latch on the gate clanged. My mother darted in for lipstick, saying, "Oh, I just hope it's not Mrs Domingo," a plump, kindly, good-natured woman, and her best friend. "She stays forever."

Well, well, well, guess who it was?

My mother emerged smiling, fresh lipstick, fresh saree. "Oh, *Marie Domingo*!!" she said, "How *lovely* to see you. I was *hoping* it was you."

What?

* * *

In Catechism class, Sister Laeticia explained the difference between mortal and venial sins. "White lies," for instance, were venial sins, harmless (as opposed to "black lies," I suppose). Missing Mass was a mortal sin. If we died before we confessed it, we would go straight to hell (the teaching which, fifteen years later, triggered led me to leave Catholicism forever).

I stopped studying Sister Laeticia's hands, swollen, empurpled, clawed, and misshapen with rheumatoid arthritis.

"When my mother says, 'I do hope it's not Mrs Domingo,' and then says, 'Oh Marie, how *wonderful* to see you,' is that a white lie?" I asked.

And do you know what that kindly nun did, she who used to smile at me so fondly and laugh at and repeat all my sayings (though I usually could not figure out what was so funny)?

Mrs Domingo appeared again. "Be careful what you say in front of her, Celine," she warned. "She tells Sister Laeticia *everything*. She said…"

Ah, the serpent's-tail of betrayal!

"Family Secrets," my mother now hissed whenever my father said any -thing faintly interesting in front of me, as if I were not part of the family. "Don't tell family secrets in front of her. She'll blab."

But forbidden fruit—I merely listened more carefully

* * *

After some chitter-chatter, my mother excused herself. If she explained her errand, the guest would insist, "Oh no, we've *just* eaten; *please* don't worry. *Please* stay and talk to us. We've come to see *you*." The guests, abandoned, talked to us children brightly, kindly, patronisingly, until my mother reappeared with a tray laden with *nimbu pani*, fresh-squeezed lemonade, and snacks, which varied according to the status of the guest, and whether it was imperative to impress them—or not!

People who visited us out of gratitude for past favours–a job my father hired or recommended them for–or in the hope of future favours were served a tray with *bought food* (a housewifely failure, a minor insult)—*chaklees or murkus,* deep-fried spirals of spiced flour; *sev, chura,* or *ghatias,* delicious deep-fried, yellow spicy lentil snacks, *til laddoos,* black sticky sesame balls, or ginger or Marie biscuits which none of us liked, and so could safely be saved for unexpected visitors.

If the visitor was wealthier, or uneasily suspected of being classier than us, or just a very good friend—then, oh, those trays! From the recesses of her roomy walk-in pantry, my mother produced homemade goodies–a rainbow of halwas, pedas, and *burfis,* rich, fudge-like sweets whose basic recipe was simmer milk, sugar, and ghee with either fruit, vegetables, or nuts. There were diamonds or rectangles of russet guava halwa, red beetroot burfi, pink coconut burfi, bright green pistachio burfi, or carrot halwa with nuts and raisins. There were plates with slices of cold meats we'd cured ourselves: "corned beef;" pink salt pork, or tongue, served with tiny dabs of precious imported Colmans's mustard, which we adored. There were little triangular plates of "cheeslings," little airy cheese crackers, expensive and "guest food;" light, airy cheese straws, or salty Monaco biscuits, served with a dainty topping of imported goodies brought back by friends who lived overseas: little black grains of caviar, or slices of Laughing Cow or Baby Bell cheese, topped with pimento olives, with their cheerful red core.

A successful recipe made a woman famous—Daphne Dias's chocolate fudge, Mrs Domingo's Midnight Chocolate Cake, or Mrs D'Costa's *nankatis,* melt-in-the-mouth butter cookies. My mother was known for her kidney toast: chopped lamb's kidneys fried with tomatoes and onions, served on deep-fried toast, and sprinkled with grated Amul cheese. When guests asked for a recipe—

your mint juleps, your Christmas cake, please--the hostess was sometimes re-luctant, hesitant, and evasive. My father suspected the recipes were deliberately garbled in transmission so that your version never tasted as good as the original, and each woman continued to be renowned for her distinctive dishes.

* * *

One year, my mother reinvented Coca-Cola (which had shut down its Indian operations in 1977 after the government required it to be fifty-one per-cent controlled by Indian investors). Following a national competition to name its substitute, Double Seven, 77 was introduced, commemorating the year the nationalist Janata government came to power. However, my mother, secretly believing she could do whatever the government did and better, tried to crack the formula of Coca-Cola. She experimented, served it, experimented again and again, and once "successful," guarded her recipe as carefully as the original for-mula, famously secured in a vault in Atlanta. Her "Coca-Cola" was a dark viscous brew of sugar, coffee, vanilla, lime, orange essence, cinnamon, and nut-meg she served in soda water, and when I arrived home from boarding school in December 1977, she was proudly asking me and our guests, "Would you like *my* Coca-Cola?" It may not have tasted *exactly* like Coke; there was none to compare it with anyway, but it *was* good.

* * *

Our hearts sank when we saw "Masterji" shuffle up the driveway, an elderly, turbanned Bihari gentleman who had taught my parents Hindi when they moved to Jamshedpur, in the Hindi-speaking heartland, from Bombay and Bangalore in the South. (The second language in their pre-Independence Eng-lish-medium schools had been French, not Hindi).

One Christmas, my parents offered "Masterji" our homemade marzipan fruits, our most expensive, time-consuming delicacy, served only to honoured guests—hand-painted reddening apples, blushing peaches, toothpick-dented strawberries, miniature apricots with defined cleavage, oranges with toothpick dimples, pears with a lovingly painted tint of cerise food colouring, and bright cherries, dewy with glistening sugar. We'd handcrafted them out of ground almonds and confection's sugar, a miracle of verisimilitude right down to the little wooden stem, and a cloth leaf bought from a confectioner in Calcutta and re-used each year.

We watched, transfixed, as Masterji's large, gnarled palm swept up a handful, and stuffed them in his mouth, wooden twig, cotton leaf and all. Had we been Queen Victoria, she who on who seeing her guest, the Shah of Persia, drink from a finger bowl, followed suit with inerrant courtesy, we would have done the same, but being ourselves, we stared aghast, collapsing in laughter after he left.

Masterji once arrived just as we returned from the market with a massive bunch of lychees, sold freshly plucked off the tree, costly coveted juicy fruits, which had just entered their brief season. My mother hurriedly put the bunch on a plate and offered them to him, expecting him to detach a few. My sister and I watched helplessly as he took the entire bunch as tribute when he left, shuffling away with it. We burst into tears, for we loved lychees. "We'll buy you more," my father promised ineffectually.

* * *

Since families moved in packs, children were dragged along on visits. My mother, who hated anything unusual, forced me to go too, even when I begged to stay home and read.

During dull patches in the conversation, or while my mother once again, brightly, told the same stories, we made repeated compulsive trips to our hostess's centre table laden with snacks. When she thought no one was looking, my mother frowned, made her face small and disapproving, and shook her head emphatically, which meant: "Stop."

Her grimaces and vehement headshakes were replaced by a broad, fixed smile when the hostess looked her way. She could not tell us aloud not to have third helpings of the fudge because the social contract required the hostess to say, *"Oh, let her,"* and then, effusively and forcefully, to offer it to me herself. Generosity, natural or feigned, was an expected and admired social virtue.

"Oh, you ate so much fudge," my mother reproached me back in the car, heaping on the shame. "I am sure she was very sad. You could see her face fall as she watched."

* * *

During these visits, parents bragged about their genius children, prodigies all, who could sing, dance, paint flowers on water glasses, barbecue, and were *so brilliant* (if they would *only* work harder) and "stood first in class," each of them, all of them (if the parents could plausibly get away with the claim). Above-average was never good enough.

The other parents listened with broad, admiring smiles, murmured praise, and passive-aggressive encouragement. "Anita writes well? Perhaps she will win the Noble Prize." "Your son can do mental maths. Perhaps he will win the Fields Medal." "She's good at Bharat Natyam. Well, she should tour Europe!" they said. Were they encouraging you or crushing you by suggesting unachievable ambitions? Who knew!

And our guests earned every diamond of their "milk toffee" as we, in turn, earned ours at their homes as we listened to them boast about their prodigy children, boasting until busted by adulthood when the golden boy or girl was revealed as perfectly ordinary, a fairy tale in reverse.

Parents of only children were particularly galling. The life and conversation of the Oliphants, David and Kathleen, Anglo-Indians, revolved around their pretty Nicolette, an only child. Admire Nicolette's handwriting; read the beautiful letters she'd written home; admire her light skin, her freckles, and curls… We did so, annoyed, while secretly suspecting that we were cleverer.

My mother breathlessly detailed every single accomplishment of my younger sister, "Shalini plays the drum in the school band; she acts, she sings, she paints," while I sat there, seething, for being three years older, I always had, of course, more bragging rights--prizes for General Knowledge, English, debating, Quiz, Elocution, published pieces of writing, President of the Debating Club, leader of the literary group, secretary of the social service league, none of which she mentioned, as if I were a stepchild.

My father did not join the general showing off. "I've achieved much more than Shalini or these children in her school, and you never mention it," I'd grumble. He shrugged. "I just don't like to show off," he said quietly. His eight years in England had heightened his natural reticence.

When I got bored, I pointedly looked at my watch every few minutes.

"Poor thing, she wants to go," the hostess eventually said, probably entirely of one mind with me on the subject.

* * *

And then the dread moment—to everyone, except the parents of the performing child. "Oh, Shalini, do you want to do your Bharat Natyam dance for the Fernandezes and Diases?" my mother would say. "Yes, *dooo,*" the victims urged with feigned enthusiasm, *"Do!"*

And, if we were at home, my sister put on her *gungaroos,* jingly belled anklets, poised her legs in the traditional diamond pose, joined her forefinger and thumb, other fingers splayed, and flinging out her arms, danced Bharat Natyam, the ancient temple dance, *thaam-thut-thaam; thaay-thut-thaay; thaam-thut-thaam; thaay-tut-thaay;* adopting the traditional large, bright, fixed smile; making ritualised seductive eye-movements, pupils swerving left to right. She danced without music, or music heard so deeply that it was not heard at all.

"Oh, Shalini sings and plays her guitar *so well,*" my mother announced, and Shalini took out her guitar and sang "Hotel California," or a sentimental Paul Anka song, "Papa."

Shalini, not having gone to boarding school, had acquired feminine accomplishments, painting, batik, singing, dancing, and playing the guitar. I did not sing, I did not dance, I did not paint, but I *did* recite. And aged eleven--the year I began to passionately memorise Shakespeare—with only the slightest encouragement, I recited, joyfully, "Oh pardon me, thou bleeding piece of earth," a speech from *Julius Caesar* that my father had introduced me to, or "Is this a dagger I see before me?" from *Macbeth*, words which have become part of my internal music, a buried word-hoard within me.

* * *

Since my sister's birthday was eight days after mine, and just before Christmas, we had a joint birthday party, lest (so said our proud, sensitive parents) people might resent appearing at our house twice in a festive month and with two sets of presents.

All Catholic children's birthday party photographs were interchangeable: the same children in party hats, tugging at gaudy crackers. The same games– Here we go round the Mulberry Bush, Ring-a-ring-a-roses, Musical Chairs, and Passing the Parcel—games adults supposed children enjoy, which we played with determined hilarity, tinged with fierce longing for the prize. With the forced merriment of the observed, we wove in and out of the circle, singing with the expected joyousness, "*In and out the sparkling bluebells, I am the leader. Rat-tat-tat-tat, on the window.*" "The farmer's in the dell," we sang, except we said *den*, not knowing what *dell* was. We never ever played such games ourselves, settling instead for jacks.

Games, we went through for the prizes. But the exciting, heart-racing part of the party was the table covered with *laddoos*, sweet orange globes comprised of hundreds of microscopic sugary balls; crisp, thin-skinned samosas filled with spicy beef, and *parthecums,* deep-fried spicy banana chips. My mother made triple-decker tricolour sandwiches for our parties, a green layer of mint chutney, a saffron layer of tomato creamed with butter, and a yellow layer of egg in mayonnaise. And you wanted to eat *everything*, all at once, in multiples, and triple-heaped your small plate, and then absolutely couldn't finish it, and the hostess said in feigned amusement, "Her eyes are bigger than her stomach." For the birthday girl, however, the thrill of the evening was the pile of brightly wrapped presents (my mother: "*Open them carefully, don't rip the paper, let's save it to reuse, and the ribbon too*"), wild improbable dreams of the haul subsiding into everyday content.

* * *

But the moon has its dark side, and the sun casts shadows. Sometimes Chinese whispers coursed through the two phone lines most families had, destroying reputations. Amid the homogeneity of the town—the Anglo-Indian ladies in their fitting knee-length dresses, short hair puffed and teased over their heads in the style of the time; the rest in sarees or churidar kameez, their long hair in buns, padded with false hair arranged in elaborate, artful curls; the girls in their extravagantly flared bell bottoms, there were a few who, by their eccentricities, became the sacrificial lambs gossiped about at the endless rounds of social visits, whose very weirdness and strangeness made everyone else, the poor, the failed, the ugly, feel better about themselves.

I arrived home from boarding school when I turned fourteen to hear that a new girl, a couple of years older, had joined the tight-knit circle of Catholic families in town. Her name was Geraldyne, but, being obsessed with the skinny British model, she'd say airily, "Call me Twiggy." She was indeed dramatically thin, all lankness and angles, hip bones protruding through her tight-fitting bell-bottom trousers.

Since we were somewhat related, as all Mangaloreans of a certain class usually are, my parents took me to visit her.

"Who is your favourite writer?" I asked, as we sat on the veranda, amid the evening chorus of the cicadas, one of the common first twenty questions among intellectually aspirant young people. "Victor Hugo," she said, while other girls our age would have said Georgette Heyer or Victoria Holt. I was impressed. "George Eliot," I said.

Had I been in love, she asked. "No!!" Had she? "Oh, many times!"

Did I believe in God? "No." She? "No!"

Did I want to get married? "*NO*." Did she? "Of course!"

We talked, revealing not our real selves, whoever *they* were, but imagined romantic selves, sophisticated, intellectual, complex, multi-layered selves, creating them even as we spoke–Anita Tulliver, Geraldyne Bovary.

It wasn't just other girls who gossiped about Geraldyne; adults did too. "The poor thing's boy-crazy," my father said. "Boys think girls like that are fun, but no one will ever *marry* her, of course. Lola Sequeira said," he continued, "that Geraldyne sits on her veranda in the evening, surrounded by boys from Loyola School. And she invited *only boys* for her birthday party" (unheard of in a culture in which, then, boys and girls did not hang out one-on-one, and rarely even in groups, and most marriages were arranged).

"Hugo and Prissy must be crazy to let her do that. There are girls men play with and girls they marry."

"How do *you* know, Pa?"

"I know."

"You are a square peg in a round hole," my father often mourned. And now, for the first time ever, here was someone squarer. And when we met, I said, like the prissy, proper child I was not, "Geraldyne, you should not be reckless. If you only hang out with boys and give birthday parties to which only boys are invited, then, my father says, they'll come, but you'll become *that* girl whom every boy talks about, but no boy will marry." (I had meant to diplomatically use the generic pronoun "one," but not for the last time, the English language betrayed me, and I said "you," which, of course, was both what I meant—and how Geraldyne took it.)

(Of course, we intellectual girls declared that we *never ever* wanted to get married– "Married! Who'd want to get *married?*"–but still, the thought of *never* ever getting married, a spinster, an old maid, "on the shelf," held some of the horror that widowhood held for our mothers' generation.

The next day, a clanging at the gate and two grim, tense figures sat in our living room, Hugo and Prissie Pereira, Geraldyne's parents. I left to read a Restoration novel in the guest room, in which fops and dandies carried little pomanders of oranges studded with cloves to ward off the nauseating odours of London streets into which human waste was chucked from high windows.

And then heard…

"Anita just came down from Nainital last week," Prissy said, "And she is already saying our Geraldyne only hangs out with boys and invited only boys to her birthday party!! Who did she hear that from?"

"Hmm. We've never heard that! Girls' chatter! Anita must have been teasing her. A birthday party with only boys?" my father asked disingenuously.

Prissie's lips tightened. "May we speak to Anita?" they asked.

I burst in, for I had been listening, astonished.

"But Paaaa, you told me…," I said.

"What rubbish!" he said, turning red, his voice sounding throttled. "As if! I have never heard of all this nonsense."

"But *Pa*," I exclaimed, not realising that it was now *I* who was the sacrificial lamb, "*Remember?* You said Lola Sequeira told you?"

"Of course not!" my father stammered, but the Pereiras were already leaving, battle fire in their eyes.

Late that evening, we got a hysterical phone call from Lola, who had been "yelled at."

"I was so embarrassed," she said. "I nearly died. They kept saying, 'Why are you spreading rumours about Geraldyne? Why are you spoiling her name? What have we ever done to you?"

"I told them, 'But this is the first time I've heard about this birthday party! How could *I* have heard?' They said, 'The Mathiases said you told them.'"

"Why did you tell them?" Lola wailed.

"We didn't," my parents said lamely.

Warm-hearted, generous Jeff and Lola Sequiera, givers of beautiful hardback editions of my favourite classics, four at a time, who had been our close family friends for twenty years, never spoke to us again; we never entered their house again, nor they ours; ditto with the Pereiras. The Sequieras had a dizzy social ascent after Lola became unofficial social secretary to the Company's Managing Director, Russi Modi, while we were frozen out of Mangalorean-Goan social life, which my mother claimed was because of this episode, though perhaps my parents, uber-proud and super-sensitive, imagining that they were being frozen out, froze themselves out.

Certainly, when I returned home from boarding school the next winter, we had moved across town to Xavier Labour Relations Institute, XLRI, the Business School at which my father now taught; we visited none of our old friends, the kindly cast of characters of my childhood, and no one visited us. We went to Sunday Mass at Xavier Institute with the priests and students, not at the parish church. We were invited to no Catholic parties and only invited my father's colleagues and students to ours. I never saw the Catholic families of my childhood again, all of whom we had called Aunty and Uncle. And this freezing out, for my mother for whom social life and acclamation was flesh, blood, bones, spirit, life, everything, was an ever-suppurating wound. She never forgave or forgot the incident. "All because of you!" my mother said bitterly for years after that. "We lost all our friends!" (though, in retrospect, I wonder if I was just the scapegoat, and there were other reasons).

"Family secrets, family secrets," my mother hissed whenever my father mentioned anything remotely interesting in frantic attempts to exclude me, which, of course, merely sharpened my antennae for juicy gossip.

One sentence. Repeated, repeated. And the echoes! Echoes travelling...

And two oddball, blue-stocking girls who could and should have become friends did not. Geraldyne taught English literature at St. Agnes College in our ancestral hometown, Mangalore, where everyone knew everyone and in which my father refused to retire, for he claimed, "If you sneeze at one end of the town, your cold will be discussed at the other." And there she was still called Twiggy, or Call-me-Twiggy, and still known for her men friends, decreasing each year as their parents found them nondescript wives who were *not* called Twiggy. She never did marry as my father had long ago predicted—*the girls men play with, the girls they marry*--an Indian Madame Bovary, doomed to live in towns too small for her dreams and with dreams too big for the towns.

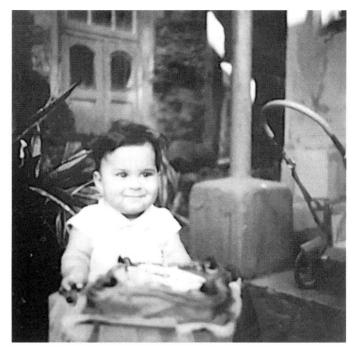

First Birthday Party

Second Birthday Party

Top L Denise Dias, Anne Cherian, Bottom L Anita, Dany Dias

Treasure Islands: Childhood Reading

In the snapshots of memory, learning to read was a heuristic leap. I sat in our oversized, green wicker armchair with a picture book my grandmother sent me: A for Apple, B for Ball, looking at the shiny red apple, its gleaming sides, then the word beneath the picture, somehow putting it together…reading.

And then I was six, my mother reading me Enid Blyton's *Claudine at St. Clare's,* and I was immersed in its drama. And then, she stopped. "Continue reading!" I exclaimed. "Ye-es," she said absently, continuing to speed-read. "It's *my* book," I snatched it and climbed into my beloved gnarled *champak*, a frangipani tree with its delicate white and yellow flowers, discovering that I could read a long book that was all print and no pictures and that it was not boring, as I imagined. A misconception withered. I was reading, sailing away to a private treasure island…waiting, always waiting. I had discovered a way of escape.

* * *

Those were the days of enchantment: I read and reread the fairy tales my father had first read me, Grimm, Andersen, Perrault, and Andrew Lang's rainbowed Fairy books--Jack Frost painting the windows with exquisite snowflakes. *Fee-fih-foh-fum, I smell the blood of an Englishman.* A little man dancing in the light of the flames: *Rumpelstiltskin is my name. What big teeth you have, Granny. Mirror, mirror on the wall, who's the fairest of us all? Rapunzel, Rapunzel, let down your hair.* Snow White, Cinderella, and Sleeping Beauty overcome, despite thwarting elders; against all odds, the meek inherit the earth. The girl who wanted just a rose gets everything.

And a cold wind blew from the North. The Norse myths in an old book my grandparents gave me felt to me like a native language. I loved the very sound of the words—*Asgard*, the land of the Gods; *Jotunheim*, realm of the giants; *Niflheim*, abode of mist, frost giants and treasure-hoarding Nibelungs; the Valkyrie, beautiful warrior maidens flying through the heavens, escorting dead warriors to Valhalla, where fallen heroes feast and repose; the wolf Fenrir tricked by the Gods and bound with Gleipnir, a dwarf-forged chain, thin as silk, stronger than iron, forged from impossible things. And so Fenrir writhed until *Ragnarok*, the day of destruction, in which all the nine worlds convulse, and the glorious Gods are annihilated.

Oh, the strange beauty, the if-onliness of the tales: Freya gets every created thing to promise not to harm her son, the golden God Balder, ignoring only the puny mistletoe. And with hubris—so dangerous in myth—the Gods hurl deadly things at Balder, which bounce until malevolent Loki guides the blind God Hodor to slay Balder with an arrow-of mistletoe. But: a second chance! Hel will spring Balder from the underworld if everything in all creation weeps, and all creation *does* weep--except Loki, disguised as a wizened giantess. And Balder stays dead.

* * *

But nothing enchanted me, enchanted me so much that it became a part of me, as Greek mythology did, three-thousand-year-old tales, ancient shell-trapped seas, singing songs I instantly loved.

How they speak to us, cautionary tales: The giant Procrustes who ensured that every visitor fit on his bed, whether he amputated their legs or stretched them on a rack: the chilling price of conformity. Icarus, drunk with the joy of achievement, soaring only to plummet into the ocean. Arachne turned into a spider as punishment for showing off. The giant Antaeus, son of Gaia, who gained strength as he touched the earth, fortified by his origins. Tantalus, beneath a low-hanging vine whose grapes receded as he strained for them;

Sisyphus, forced to endlessly roll a boulder uphill, which no sooner summited than it crashed. It was as if they, too, dwelt in an unending powerless childhood.

Three vain goddesses covet the tricksy golden apple inscribed *Te Kalliste*, *For the Most Beautiful*, which Paris--spurning Juno's offer of power and Minerva's of wisdom--gave Aphrodite, who had bribed him with the most beautiful woman in the world: Helen, whose face launched a thousand ships and the Trojan war which reverberates through Greek myths. The wooden gift horse clanks into Troy, from which enraged soldiers emerge at night to set the city ablaze, a chiaroscuro scene I remember from my father's retelling. And that voyage home, past interminable seas heaving with sirens; past Circe's isle where men turn swinish; past islands whose inhabitants live in a time-and-world-for-getting dreamy reverie. Odysseus blinds Polyphemus, who demands his name. "Nobody," says Odysseus, and Polyphemus howls, "Father Poseidon, Nobody has blinded me."

The most dramatic stories: The Gorgon Medusa, the ugliest woman in the world, whose hair was writhing serpents, a glimpse of whom literally petri-fied her beholder, decapitated by Perseus, flying with Hermes' winged sandals and an invisibility helmet. A fateful head, potent in death—turning the sea mon-ster to stone, helping him win Andromeda. Romance, Greek-style.

The bright lavish illustrations, like the stories, wove themselves into memory: Beautiful Psyche, prodded by her jealous sisters, gazes by the light of an oil lamp at her slumbering secret lover, which he'd forbidden--and, oh, he's no monster, but the golden God of love, Cupid himself, who vanishes. And then, his mother, Venus, punitively makes her sort a jumbled heap of barley, maize, rice and millet in a single night, though kindly ants rescue her. There's Achilles, invulnerable but for his heel; Persephone, who would have escaped Hades…but she had eaten six fateful pomegranate seeds; Orpheus, maker of music, whose melodies enchanted Pluto, who granted him Eurydice if he did not glance back until the sunlit world, but he did, of course, he did, needing to check if she had followed, and so he lost his beloved once more and forever… Those tales full of the wrenching consequences of careless words and deeds captivated me, perhaps because my own life felt as chaotic and arbitrary, as full of God, angels, demons, gorgons, cyclops, capricious trouble and injustice, and blaming, shaming mothers and teachers.

My hobby, when I was eleven, was "collecting" every detail I could find about Greek mythology, recording them in my brown hardback TISCO diary, a page per character: Atlas, tricked into hefting the entire world on his shoulders; Jason sowing dragon's teeth from which sprang armed soldiers; Penelope endlessly weaving; the three grey sisters who shared a single eye and tooth between them; Cerberus, the multi-headed dog guarding the underworld… I began to construct an amateur encyclopaedia of that haunting universe, unaware that it already existed, in other lands, other libraries.

* * *

From the East came *The Arabian Nights:* open sesame to genies in bottles, caves with cascading treasure, Sinbad the sailor on the wings of the roc, while the bleary-eyed Sultan lies awake, entranced by a tale. In a happy inspiration, my parents bought us a condensed *Ramayana* and *Mahabharata,* majestic Hindu epics which entered my bloodstream as I read and reread them, horrified as Yudhistra, man of honour, a hero of *The Mahabharata*, gambles against his cousins, the Kauravas of the loaded dice, and in a gambler's delirium, loses his thousand war elephants, money, jewels, slave girls, kingdom, and then gambles away his four brothers, his own freedom, and, finally, their best-loved "possession," their exquisite polyandrous wife, Draupadi. His victorious Kaurava cousin, Duryodhana, piling on humiliation, attempts to publicly strip Draupadi…but Krishna magically elongates her saree, the brutally yanked yards heaping up in front of the leering court. Finally, the two sides confront each other in an epic battle, a Hindu Ragnarok that, as in the *Morte D'Arthur,* destroys almost everything.

And in *The Ramayana*, Rama's stepmother Kaikei requests a boon--that King Dasaratha banish his son, Rama, an exemplar of a perfect human, and let her son, his stepbrother, Bharat, rule. Accompanied by his wife Sita and his loyal younger brother Lakshman, Rama uncomplainingly goes into exile--to the forests, from whence the Demon-King Ravana, in the guise of an ascetic *sadhu*, lures Sita out of a protective magic circle, and abducts her to his kingdom, Lanka. Hanuman, Monkey-God, overcomer of obstacles, leaps over the Palk Strait to rescue her, and when Ravana sets the monkey's tail on fire, clever Hanuman uses that fiery tail to set all Lanka ablaze. Finally, Rama's armies, aided by monkeys, bears, and eagles, face the demon hosts and rescue Sita. But, in a tragic twist, though Ravana has not touched Sita, though she endures a trial by fire (which turns to flowers), Rama banishes her. Sita had lived in the house of another man (or demon!) and people had talked–the Roman adage *"Caesar's wife must be above suspicion"* true here too! Sadly, righteous Rama privileged appearances and our national what-will-people-think obsession over the facts.

* * *

My father, who had always wanted to read the whole Bible himself, read chapters to me while I sat on his lap, absently, dreamily listening. Through reading in church, children's storybooks and my father, the Bible became part of the deep structure of my mind, a second language: The mysterious burning bush in the Sinai. *Take off your shoes, for the place where you stand is holy ground.* The Red Sea closing over the Pharaoh's horses and chariots...just in time. David given strategy to kill Goliath for the Lord was with him. Daniel's prayer subduing lions and the fiery furnace. *Mene, Mene, Thekel, Uparshim.* Angels singing: *And the whole earth is full of His glory.* And then: Jesus, magical man. Oh, that heady Biblical air, a miraculous world in which anything can happen.

Being Catholic, we also had a little pile of children's books about the saints—Joan of Arc, "The Little Flower," the saintly Genevieve, and the Belgian priest Damien de Veuster who volunteered at the leper colony at Molokai, knowing it would probably mean his death from leprosy, as it did. And incandescent Francis who hears an icon in the ruined church of San Damiano say, "Rebuild my church." And though a poetic saint, he takes the injunction literally. But you grow into vocations, and his was larger. It was to rebuild the entire Christian Church until it resembled its blazing founder. Who could not love him--Francis, who charmed the wolf of Gubbio; preached to the birds who sensed his gentleness, exulted in the Sun and Moon and all creation as his siblings—and experienced elusive perfect joy?

* * *

The Arthurian legends my father told me wove their ancient enchantments around me. The obscure boy wresting Excalibur from the rock; the Knights of the Round Table, in the gay morning of youth and idealism, bounding through the ancient kingdom, smiting dragons, aiding distressed damsels, questing for the Holy Grail, feasting, jousting, loving. *And every morning brought a noble chance/And every chance brought forth a noble knight.*

But there are serpents in Camelot: Arthur's envious half-sister Morgan le Fay, and the fact that his best friend, noble Sir Lancelot, adores Queen Guinevere--which Arthur, loving both, resolves not to notice until his treacherous nephew Mordred traps them all, and then, *All night long the noise of battle rolled.*

My father, who first encountered Arthur via the Tennyson he studied as a schoolboy, told me of Galahad, whose "strength was as the strength of ten because his heart was pure," of the holy grail floating in front of the dream-stuck knights, and "the hand in white samite, mystic, wonderful," drawing Excalibur into the lake. He broke off his reading to meditatively recite Arthur's last injunction as three mysterious women row him to Avalon, *"Pray for my soul. /For what are men better than sheep or goats/That nourish a blind life within the brain, /If, knowing God, they lift not hands of prayer/Both for themselves and those who call them friend."* It was his favourite passage.

The Belgian brothers who ran my father's boarding school, Montfort School at Yercaud, taught him Shakespeare and poetry in much the same way as the German nuns who ran my boarding school, St. Mary's Convent, Nainital taught me–by having us memorise the entire play or poem to be studied!

As a virtuous way of re-immersing himself in the magic of those plays, my father read me Shakespeare. We started with *Lamb's Tales from Shakespeare*, rich-languaged retellings by those eccentric childless siblings, a gateway drug into Shakespearean intoxication–starlight and fairy wings on midsummer nights, Bottom with his asses' head, his giant ears scratched by snooty be-witched Titania; Shylock, the unmerciful, unmercifully tricked, promised his pound of flesh, *and* death should he take one drop of blood or a single hair with it; Lear, deceived by glibness, disastrously misjudges his children, and Macbeth is tricked by the witches, for Birnam Woods do indeed march to Dunsinane, and Macduff was from his mother's womb untimely ripped. Tragedies of errors!

Eventually, my father read some of the great plays themselves aloud, almost to himself. I sat on his lap in the oversized green wicker armchair in the veranda as he read, he revelling in the intoxicating language, and I listening to cascades of blank verse, hypnotised by the words and rhythms like the waves of the sea, absorbing the music, lost in the dream, remembering snatches verbatim with my freak verbal memory, particularly sharp in childhood.

My father read *Hamlet* to me, more for his enjoyment than for mine, probably not expecting me to take it in, but I was haunted by the lunar gleam of the opening scene, the sorrowful and indignant enchained ghost stalking the dark earth seeking vengeance, fading at the crowing of the cock, his hints of a tale that would make "each hair stand on end, like quills upon the fretful por-pentine." That night, I woke to a luminosity, standing at the foot of my bed, a presence, very real, not evil, though it froze me.

I told the nuns at school that a ghost had visited us, like the ghost in *Hamlet*, and "I heard its chains clink," and parroting, said my hair stood on end like "quills on a porcupine," and my teacher told the Principal—"She's reading *Hamlet*, she's just six"—who proceeded to call me a genius and arrived at my First Standard classroom to instantly move me up to the Second Standard. I'd been given a "Double Promotion," the ultimate academic honour in Indian schools—thanks to *Hamlet*.

"Double, double toil and trouble, fire burn and cauldron bubble," my father glee-fully chanted. He invented Shakespeare games, inspired by his golden memories of watching Peggy Ashcroft, John Gielgud, Lawrence Olivier, Maggie Smith, Ralph Richardson, and Michael Redgrave perform from cheap seats in the Gods at the Old Vic as a student and then a Chartered Accountant in London in the forties and fifties. In the darkness, we played *Othello*, which he had seen in London with Laurence Olivier in the title role. I, as Desdemona, lay in fever-ish excitement on the bed in the darkened guestroom, waiting for him as Othello/Olivier to enter and strangle me. But first, he recited pure poetry:

> *Put out the light, and then put out the light:*
> *If I quench thee, thou flaming minister,*
> *I can again thy former light restore,*
> *Should I repent me: but once put out thy light,*
> *Thou cunning'st pattern of excelling nature,*
> *I know not where is that Promethean heat*
> *That can thy light relume.*

I shivered, waiting... And then he placed his fingers around my throat, squeezing, squeezing until I screamed in the darkness in delicious double bub-ble terror, especially when, as a special effect, he had first cupped his hands on the cave of ice that surrounded the meat section of our fridge and strangled me with ice-cold fingers. To his amusement, I'd beg, "Just *tell*, Pa. Don't *act*."

The words of Shakespeare had become part of my father, as they've become part of me. Perhaps thinking of things in his own life which had come to nothing, he quoted the dying speech of Wolsey,

> *Oh Cromwell, I charge thee,*
>
> *Fling away ambition.*
>
> *O Cromwell, Cromwell!*
>
> *Had I but served my God with half the zeal*
>
> *I served my king, he would not in mine age*
>
> *Have left me naked to mine enemies.*

From the time I was eleven, I'd sit in our large wicker armchair in the veranda with my father's massive, unwieldy navy blue *Complete Works of William Shakespeare,* brought back from England, reading the plays, memorising the speeches, intoxicated by the sound of the words even when I didn't understand their meaning, my mother ousting me before guests arrived, "Don't show off," she'd say, reluctant to have the attention of her guests diverted to me, though it was for the sensuous joy of it that I was reading and rereading until I knew "by heart" Mark Anthony's speech, *But yesterday, the word of Caesar might have stood out against the world, now lies he here, and none so poor to do him reverence,* or the perfect iambics of "To be or not to be" from *Hamlet.*

Ah, Shakespeare! The music of the words had a life, almost independent of their meaning. I shambled through the house, reciting to myself my father's favourite speeches from *Julius Caesar,* which I had memorised--Mark Anthony's flood of passionate heartbroken poetry awakening answering wells of sorrow in me.

> *O, pardon me, thou bleeding piece of earth,*
>
> *That I am meek and gentle with these butchers!*
>
> *Thou art the ruins of the noblest man*

> *That ever lived in the tide of times.*
>
> *Woe to the hand that shed this costly blood!*

I can still hear my father recite that!

At home from boarding school, I memorised, I memorised, escaping the present, walking through the house in a Shakespearean dream, mentally declaiming these speeches I learned by heart.

> *For who would bear the whips and scorns of time,*
>
> *Th' oppressor's wrong, the proud man's contumely,*
>
> *When he himself might his quietus make*
>
> *With a bare bodkin? Who would fardels bear…?*

Fardels, fardels, contumely, quietus; what did all those words mean? They didn't have to *mean* anything. They were music. They were magic. They were the undiscovered country towards which Shakespeare rowed me, a realm of cloud-capp'd towers, gorgeous palaces, solemn temples, in which all our upsets and boredom suffers a sea-change into something rich and strange.

* * *

Milton's majestic periodic music was indelibly imprinted on my father's neurons from his days at Montford School, Yercaud; once he started declaiming, it flowed, hypnotic honey, and when I finally read it for myself, there was a dreamlike sense of *déjà vu*.

> *Of man's first disobedience, and the fruit*
>
> *Of that forbidden tree, whose mortal taste*
>
> *Brought death into the world, and all our woe,*
>
> *With loss of Eden, till one greater man*
>
> *Restore us, and regain the blissful seat,*
>
> *Sing heavenly Muse...*

I grabbed his precious green cloth-bound *Paradise Lost*, brought back from England, and read those first sentences again and again, taking a deep breath and filling my lungs and spirit with that dimly comprehended strong magic.

* * *

As my father gleefully read me the favourite novels of his childhood, I listened, terrified, to *Treasure Island*–the tap, tap, tap of deadly Blind Seaman Pew's stick along the cobbled lanes; the ambivalently menacing one-legged Long John Silver; the lure of treasure turning men vicious, *Yo-ho-ho and a bottle of rum*. Meanwhile, back home in Scotland, David Balfour mounts a staircase to nowhere in *Kidnapped,* and the good Doctor Jekyll metronomically turns feral on the streets of Edinburgh. He loved too the perfect lines of *A Tale of Two Cities*: *It was the best of times, it was the worst of times… It is a far, far, better thing I do now than I have ever done. It is a far, far better rest that I go to than I have ever known.*

I read *The Three Musketeers* repeatedly after my father introduced me to it–*All for one and one for all*; the formidable Arthos, Porthos and Aramis and d'Artagan; Milady de Winter, ethereal and wicked, seducing her captors and enemies; Queen Anne ensnared in the affair of the diamonds by Cardinal Richlieu, who I discovered, shocked, was a politician, and not holy at all, as I assumed all *Cardinals* surely were, nor sweet and benevolent as our own Cardinal Picachy, who had been Bishop of Jamshedpur.

After my father, who enjoyed terrifying me with ghost stories, described the wailing ghost of Catherine Earnshaw tapping on the window in the snowstorm, calling for Heathcliff, I dashed to our copy of *Wuthering Heights* and plunged into the dark fascination of a world I somehow *knew*. That atmospheric brooding tale spoke to me at a visceral level–for have not most children experienced it all: joy, friendship, unreasoning love, fury at injustice, unfairness and favouritism, pure hatred? I identified with Heathcliff and his unquenchable but justified rage; reading it, I felt, like Catherine, that I *was* Heathcliff. And every time I read it, I cried over the early chapters of *Jane Eyre*, almost unreadable in their gratuitous sadness and cruelty, yet somehow speaking to generations of young readers who sip from the horrors and injustice of Brontë-world.

In the infinite—so it seemed--world and time of childhood, I read *Little Women* again and again, identifying, painfully, passionately, with harum-scarum tomboyish Jo, who shed fairy dust and possibility over being a writer for me as she has for generations of girls, and sobbed at each reading of the wrenching death of sweet Beth from scarlet fever. I, like Jo, wanted to shake Amy who, unfairly, not only got Jo's coveted trip to Europe but golden Laurie as well. Borrowing the sequels *Good Wives, Little Men* and *Jo's Boys* from the club library, I was relieved to discover that though-to my mind foolishly!-renouncing the androgynous Laurie (who was too like her for a grown-up marriage, though they would have had a delightful one), Jo married "Father Bear," solid, wise, loving, down-to-earth, her temperamental opposite, with whom, nonetheless, she was happy (in a way Louisa Alcott never was).

Books were mostly imported then, expensive, and not easy to acquire in Jamshedpur which had no bookstore, though Meghani's General Store stocked a few popular foreign novels and children's classics printed in Czechoslovakia in beautiful hardbound editions. So, I read and reread the classics I owned, given me as gifts by relatives and family friends, repeatedly exploring the secret kingdoms of childhood--*Peter Pan,* the wonderful boy, and sunny, funny *Winnie-the-Pooh.* And a little later, *Robin Hood, The Water Babies,* the illogical, terrifying, infuriating, magical childhood-mirroring world of *Alice in Wonderland; The Swiss Family Robinson,* a repeated reread, like sweet *Heidi* taming the grandfather— through which Switzerland and the Alps entered my bloodstream.

Very sadly, some of the new glossy or hardback books which generous Uncle Eric from Bombay gave us as presents–Grimm's *Fairy Tales,* Andersen's *Fairy Tales, Alice,* Stevenson's *Treasure Island* and *Kidnapped* which my father read to me well after I was easily able to read them myself–my mother irrationally locked in his grey steel Godrej cupboard, where I still can see them.

"You'll scribble in them; you'll dirty them; ask me for them when you want them," my mother said, but as an absent-minded, somewhat traumatised child, I rarely did so, except when I occasionally caught sight of them and indignantly demanded them. Some books like the Aesop in our living room, a beautiful hardback, I was never allowed to touch or read on my own, "You'll soil it," even though it was just one book among scores, and a bit of soiling would not have harmed her since she never touched it, but rereading Aesop would have given me great joy.

My mother valued appearances intensely, the glossy newness of books rather than the hours of life-changing pleasure and food for the imagination they contained; those books, locked-up to keep them nice, could have been a parachute, a magic carpet, an escape. I remember disconsolately asking in intense boredom, verging on despair, "What should I do?" but, perhaps judging me not worthy of their glossiness, she never ever offered the locked-up new paperback and hardbacks, rafts away from the tumult of my early childhood: my mother's nagging, blaming, and shaming; the strictures and chaos of school where I was always in trouble, and the meanness of some teachers. As I grew up, they were given away in a favour trade to her nephews or neighbourhood children; I do not now possess a single book of my childhood.

That food for a hungry and developing imagination, just locked up, in a town with few books. It's hard to see the redemptive possibilities in that, except that sometimes one loves, longs for and treasures what one lacked in childhood. Many careers, vocations, and ministries stem from childhood deprivation, and of course, my whole adult life has been books–reading them, writing them, and, professionally, publishing them.

My mother rarely bought me new books, even though books were what I loved best in life. (I remember the Christmas when I was six when I was given a workbasket with needles, thread, scissors, a measuring tape, and a thimble, none of which I knew how to use, for all I wanted to do was to read.) But books did appear in our house by osmosis–gifts, or borrowed, or outgrown by older friends. Whenever we visited Bombay, my grandparents, maternal aunts and uncles, and my mother's cousins, most of whom had studied English Literature at college, gave me their school and college Literature texts, books they had stored in boxes under beds or on the top of cupboards, relics of a school and college education saturated with British literature, and so, I returned with Jane Austen, the Brontë's, Scott's *Ivanhoe*, Hardy's *The Woodlanders*, and George Eliot's *Adam Bede*, classics in old blue cloth-bound covers, fading gold lettering on the spine.

On bored days, I repeatedly read an old cloth-bound anthology of *One Hundred Master Plots* which my grandparents had given us: summaries of perennial classics and old supplanted half-forgotten ones, images searing themselves on memory: the terrified Pip in *Great Expectations*, smuggling food to the convict who threatened to eat his heart and liver; hot-headed Maggie Tulliver of *The Mill on the Floss* (with whom I instantly identified), who weary of her aunts' criticism of her unruly hair, jaggedly shears the entire mop off, making matters worse, of course, of course. There was *Lavengro* (which mystified me) about English gypsies; Don Quixote and his comic, romantic delusions; *Lorna Doone* galloping on the moors and valleys of Exmoor; *Eugenie Grandet*, daughter of a compulsive miser, whose habitual deceptive appearance of poverty cheats her of marriage to the fortune-hunting cousin she adores, and *Madame Bovary* dead, black arsenic streaming from her lovely mouth.

I trotted through the ancient English Literature Readers of my maternal grandparents and uncles and aunts, for they were a family that rarely threw a book (or anything else!) away–reading short stories, essays, poetry, whatever came next, enjoying them all. When my father recited his favourite poems, the magic leapt across generations—*The tumult and the shouting dies/The Captains and Kings depart/Still stands thine ancient sacrifice/A humble and a contrite heart.* I memorised poems with a delicious, sensuous pleasure in the sound and rhythm, anthology favourites possessing me until I possessed them: "Tyger, Tyger burning bright," or Longfellow's, "How beautiful is the rain, after the dust and heat, in the broad and fiery street."

Our neighbour, Elsie Cherian, was, improbably, a blue-eyed Jewish woman from California–daughter of an eminent Berkeley scientist, Albert Krueger, who worked on germ warfare during the Second World War, she told us. She had fallen in love with a reserved Indian student at Berkeley, ten years older, whose major aberration from his quiet, conservative ways was marrying a voluble, outspoken, larger-than-life American woman, who had returned with him to Jamshedpur, where she became a traditional Indian housewife, and "went native," inexpertly draping her tall, lanky body in a saree, wearing *chappals*, flip-flops, coiling her hair, which she had grown out, into a bun, and cooking the traditional Malayali food from Kerala, India's southernmost state, that her husband loved.

While I do not recollect her American family visiting her or her five children, they sent love embodied in boxes of books through sea mail, which she passed on to us, so through the sixties, I read what my peers in America were reading (or not reading!): Little Golden Books, *Highlights* magazine, and, most memorably, *Charlotte's Web*, and each time I read of the death of the spider Charlotte, who saved Wilbur, the ingenuous runt pig, I wept. These American books gradually filled the floor-to-ceiling shelves in my room that I was so proud of: *Freckles, The Bobbsey Twins, Nancy Drew*, and *Zane Grey* riding the purple sage. (Years later, I coincidentally visited his birthplace in Zanesville, Ohio). I was enchanted by *In This House of Brede*, Rumer Godden's novel set in a

Benedictine Abbey at Stanbrook, which Mrs Cherian lent us. *"When you are in trouble," Abbess Catherine said, "Think of a bird caught under a net; the more it struggles and makes a flutter, the more it gets enmeshed; if it is still and looks about for a hole, keeping its strength, it has a chance of escape."*

I read omnivorously, indiscriminate as a whale, swallowing everything I could get my hands on, highbrow, lowbrow, no-brow: Rider Haggard's *King Solomon's Mines* or James Hilton's *Lost Horizon* with its mystical realm of Shangri-La. My life was in books. Hot oil splashed up and burnt my cheek while I deep-fried doughnuts on the high stove (which my mother uncharacteristically per-mitted me to do) while I stood on a stool, absently stirring with one hand, while, in my free hand, captivated, I gripped Rider Haggard's *She,* the tale of Ayesha, She-who-must-be-obeyed, a woman older than the sea. Less absorbingly, I read Catholic crisis-of-conscience novels lying around the house; a woman quotes "The Memorare" to the Virgin, "Never was it known that anyone who implored thy help was left unaided," concluding bitterly, "You left me unaided," for her beau refused to convert to Catholicism, and she rejected him.

Reading flowed into writing. In the plush, grey dairy I called "Darling Diary, my best friend," I copied poems I liked and composed some of my own, punctuated by *cri de coeurs* of boredom: "spent the afternoon longing for Pa to return from work." I published a story in the school magazine: A man confides a secret in the middle of a cornfield in the middle of the night; the next day, the entire town knows. Had his best friend betrayed him? No, the ears of corn had heard. I flicked through the magazine, "stumbling" on my name with a thrill: Anita Mathias. I loved the look of it. I had my name in print. I felt *famous.* I was delighted to discover my father's name in a history of the Lobos, his mother's family, and leafed through the book, thinking, "I know these men and women.

They have their names in a book. Are they famous?" How marvellous to have your name in a real book. I wanted mine in one.

Of course, I wasn't the only young reader in Jamshedpur. In that town, without television and with limited distractions, clever girls read. When adults talked to children, the interrogation followed a set format: "What is your name? How old are you? Which Standard are you in? What do you want to be when you grow up?" And a surprising number of us bookish girls said, "A writer," and a surprising number of us did publish. Two other girls from C Road, Anne next door, Sangeeta opposite, and Jane from church, all commercially published books, while Geralyn published in magazines.

And then we were asked, "What are your hobbies?" And "reading" was the most common reply (besides stamp collecting) and, then as now, in small-town India as in the rest of the world, the response was approbation.

Reading to me was chocolate, the brandy-and-water given me when I was feverish, the time-and-world forgetting lotus devoured by the dreamy island dwellers Odysseus stumbled on in the Tennyson poem my father read me. It was a way of losing myself, a way particularly sweet to those who long to be lost.

I Saw the Moon Rock: The Clubs

In 1969, astronauts walked on the moon--*in other worlds*--and, suddenly, everything seemed possible.

"Will we soon have picnics on the moon?" I asked.

My father considered the moon. "Yeeees," he said slowly. "I think so."

There it glowed, silent, luminous. It wasn't too far. Yes, he was probably right.

* * *

In 1970, a travelling exhibition of Apollo 11 souvenirs came to the United Club.

In a glass case lay a maroon-black rock, one of the fifty brought back from the moon. It looked like … well, a rock.

As we left, we were each given a fluorescent yellow and orange sticker: *"I saw the moon rock."*

I stuck it onto my vanity case when I left, the next March, to boarding school, right across India, to Nainital in the Himalayas–where I showed it off. I was the only girl who had ever seen *a moon rock*, something from *another world*!

* * *

Community life in Jamshedpur revolved around the two private clubs we belonged to--the egalitarian United Club, walking distance from my house, and the more expensive and exclusive Beldih Club (formerly the European Club to which the Durrells of Corfu once belonged), which required recommendations from members to join.

Once a year, for ten nights in a row, there was an open-air One-Act Play Competition, open to teams from schools, colleges, and hastily improvised theatre troupes. I remember sitting enchanted, under the stars, lost in a long-dead writer's imagination–*The Monkey's Paw, Mutatis Mutandis, The Elephant Man*, and *The Bishop's Candlesticks* (a dramatisation of a scene from *Les Miserables*). I particularly enjoyed the plays directed by Perin Mehta (whose claim to fame was that she was the sister-in-law of the German-Jewish Ruth Prawer Jhabvala, who dwelt in the Elysian realms of real art and real fame--Booker Prize winner, and the screenwriter of the Merchant Ivory triumvirate).

And suddenly, quiz competitions became the rage--inter-school, inter-family, couple, mother/daughter and, at the local business school, Xavier Labour Relations Institute, XLRI, where my father taught post-retirement, faculty/student. The secret of success was, partly, getting hold of the books the quizmaster used: BBC Mastermind or Quizmaster. My mother and sister prepared feverishly, almost memorising the book—all our family have excellent memories—and usually won.

What was Woody Allen's real name? *Allen Konigsberg.* What was the world tree in Norse mythology which ran through the nine worlds? *Yggdrasil.* Whose epitaph was *Home is the sailor, home from the sea, | And the hunter home from the hill?* Robert Louis Stevenson. Where is Timbuktu? *Mali.*

Since the quizmaster played snatches of Handel's *Water Music* or *The Ode to Joy* or projected slides of Botticelli's *The Birth of Venus*, Monet's *Water Lilies* or the Parthenon, our ambitious quiz preparation involved listening to my father's magisterial collection of classical music, brought back from England, and leafing through his art and architecture books. We memorised too the images on the calendars my grandmother sent us of the famous buildings of the world (used to cover our favourite books), which have become part of my visual memory, the *Arc de Triomphe*, *Sagrada Familia*, and the Parthenon.

"So-and-so called Ma a Mastermind," my father said, flatteringly, always a bit paternal towards my mother, who was fourteen years younger. However, when he saw me read quiz books, he scoffed at this scattershot knowledge. "Oh no, that's not real knowledge, Anita," he said. "Absorb knowledge in context by reading widely, *books*—not *quiz books*."

* * *

The Clubs fizzed and whirred. Charminar, a cigarette company, sponsored "Made for Each Other" dance competitions at the Beldih Club with prizes for "the most charming couple." There were classes for housewives: Ikebana, Batik, Tie and Dye, and oil painting, all of which my mother took; billiard tables, golf courses, basketball courts, outdoor swimming pools, open year-round, and Bharat Natyam Indian dance classes, which my sister took, but my mother refused to let me take. "There'll be more complaints; you won't behave," she said with a little smirk.

Every summer, my mother entered our garden's best flowers, fruit, and vegetables, and her dreamy ikebana arrangements to the United Club's Annual Fruit, Flower and Vegetable Show, winning prizes each year, though–shades of Downton Abbey sycophancy–not as many as Lady Ghandy, widow of a Company Director, who had a larger garden, and more gardeners. Our flowers were over-bred to magnificence: outsized dahlias; chrysanthemums with twirled petals; gerberas, asters, and exquisite roses, grafted with rags until they were indigo, purple, or magenta, most unroselike colours, and eventually–oh perversity of experimenting gardeners! –a pitch and velvety black.

Shalini and I, passionate stamp collectors, drank in the philatelic exhibitions at the United Club, the world under glass–bright, brilliant stamps, triangular, circular, or snazzy 3-D, acquisitiveness and longing bubbling up within us. Countries that no longer existed, Aden, Zanzibar, Tanganyika,

Malaya, or those that had recently begun to, Zambia, Gambia, Tanzania, were there, represented by their stamps, and the smaller and more obscure the country--Brunei, North Korea, Bhutan, Trinidad and Tobago--the bigger, more eye-catching the stamps, the more unusual their shape.

A visiting magician asked for a volunteer to lie in a coffin and calmly sawed her in two; we screamed. To our astonishment, he "saw" the hand of cards we held close to our chests. Iridescent scarves swished from his sleeves, and from his hat, pigeons flapped. A terrified rabbit materialised and blinked sadly at us while held up by its ears. *"How did he do it? How did he do it?"* whispers coursed through the hall.

A travelling hypnotist announced: Those who dismiss hypnosis most vigorously succumb most easily.

"Who doesn't believe in hypnosis?" he asked.

Brash young company workers waved their hands. "There's no way *you* can hypnotise *me*," a young man shouted.

And then, astonished, we saw those very men raise their hands in the air at a command and leave them there until the hypnotist gave the word. He fed them raw potatoes and told them that they were apples; they pronounced them delicious. However, as the hypnotist broke the trance, they spat them out in disgust.

I was enthralled by a guest ventriloquist. I looked around, amazed, as his voice bounced from every nook of the hall. Determined to master ventriloquism, I assiduously practised at home, projecting mews, barks, hoots, and howls with a deadpan expression while barely moving my lips. I later disrupted hated physics and singing lessons at boarding school with these meows, woofs, wolf-howls, and tu-whit tu-whoos, and while the nuns thought it *had* to be me, they couldn't accuse me, for my innocent, expressionless eyes gazed gravely at them.

* * *

In 1972, the United Club hosted Dr Bolar, a naturopath who offered "a nature cure" to reverse myopia and, overnight, made eye health an obsession. At his recommendation, everyone read Aldous Huxley's *The Art of Seeing,* looked at green at every opportunity, splashed water into their eyes in the mornings, "palmed" their eyes after half an hour of reading, ate bowls of grated carrots, and drank carrot juice at every meal.

Dr Bolar and his wife, an ill-educated, crude, always-smiling couple, became the Rasputin-saviours to every family whose children had weak eyesight, and there were many in that intense, upwardly mobile town, dominated by Zoroastrians, Parsees, an inbred community. In Jamshedpur, education was the pathway to worldly success, but too much study strained eyesight. The Bolars were feted, invited to dinner everywhere.

My parents, too, placed their faith in Dr Bolar. My father was worried about his own eyesight, but particularly about Shalini's, since she'd had eye surgery aged ten and had worn contact lenses ever since. Dr Bolar entered the living room of our house, originally built for British executives, observed the souvenirs from my father's eight years in England and his travels on work in Europe, Japan and America; settled deep into the sofa, and sighed, saying, "Oh, this is just like an English house"–endearing himself to my mother with this remark that lingered in her memory, even though…

Dr Bolar checked everyone's eyesight at the start of the course, prescribed eye exercises, and followed up with weekly checks, pronouncing remarkable improvement. Mrs Surti triumphantly took her children to their regular optician. The original readings had indeed been correct; the rest were fiction. The "doctor" had typed out eye exercises, and dietary recommendations from Bates' *Better Eyesight without Glasses*—"Light should fall over the shoulder and onto the book"—and was no more a doctor and knew no more or less than anyone else who had read that book. She threatened to sue unless he refunded, and, astonishingly, he did indeed return everyone's money and slunk back into the outer darkness of Bombay, from whence he came.

Every Christmas, the Clubs had a party. One of my earliest memories: my grandmother Molly picked me up from one of these, aged three, and I handed her my *laddoo*, a golden-orange ball of chickpea flour, butter, and sugar, studded with raisins and nuts, that I'd saved in my napkin for her, my favourite sweet. "See, she's a generous girl," she told my father, who had waited in the car. Then we went to the hospital and found my mother nursing a baby, which I had not been told was coming. I reached out to touch my mother's breast, and she slapped me.

At these parties, after children gorged on iced cupcakes and buns, Santa appeared, all dressed in red. *Ho-ho-ho.* At the Beldih Club, Santa impartially gave every girl and boy between the ages of one and twelve an age-appropriate gift, wrapping all of them in the same paper. The winter I turned twelve, the end of childhood in India, the twelve-year-old girls got a make-up set, a coveted palette: gooey eyeshadow, eyeliner, mascara, lipstick, and "blush-on." However, my mother had, perhaps Freudianly, recorded my age as two, and while the toddlers processed up in their frilly, gauzy dresses, I heard my name on the loudspeaker and got a *teddy bear*—to my tears and mortification.

In the United Club, however, the more egalitarian dues did not cover children's Christmas presents. Parents bought their own presents, wrapped them, and secretly delivered them to the Club office before the party. The poorer children got cheap rip-off Monopoly, Ludo, or plastic badminton sets; the nouveau riche got bikes, bedecked in tinsel, bows and ribbons; the more sophisticated got hardbound editions of The Children's Classics or Illustrated Encyclopaedias.

I looked around. Why would Santa give rich children rich presents and poor children poor presents? It just wasn't fair. An outrageous thought: Was the Santa Claus of song and story, who knew if we'd been good or bad, and sleighed in from the North Pole, hauled by Rudolf, the red-nosed reindeer, the Santa Claus whom Enid Blyton and my father told us about—was he, incredibly, incredibly–an enormous invention, a conspiracy by the entire adult world to deceive children, a secret even the meanest adult managed to keep?

"There is no Santa Claus?" I asked my father.

"Oh really? Why do you say that? I think there is," he said lamely.

Huh!

"There is no Santa Claus," I informed my sister. "Of course, there is," she said passionately. "As if Ma and Pa and the nuns would lie to us!"

"There is no Santa Claus," I told my classmates. "It's our parents."

"Of course, there is," said those who got good presents at the Club. The rest were silent.

Reason prevailed. Santa died, and I turned seven.

* * *

The Beldih Club screened three English language or European films a week, with a children's film every Friday evening, while the United Club's three films included Hindi movies, which our friends never admitted to liking or even seeing--though, of course, every seat was taken. The clubs staggered days, so you could drive to a movie seven days a week, and we often did!If one thing united India, if there was a lowest common denominator shared by both the rickshaw-puller in the streets, and the people they transported, a passion shared by rich and poor, Hindu, Muslim and Christian, it was love of film, especially Hindi movies from Bombay, Bollywood, our field of dreams. Teenagers passed around their copies of *Filmfare* and *Stardust*, gossip magazines about Bollywood stars, who were known by their first names, Dimple, Jaya, Amitabh, Rishi,

Shashi, Rajesh; their families, marriages, affairs and divorces, all public knowledge.

Movies were either A, Adult, or U, universal. If our parents allowed us to accompany them to an Adult movie, we wore sarees and slathered on make-up. Mr Bhardwaj, the kindly membership secretary, stood at the entrance, monitoring, letting me through when I was below sixteen, but, sometimes, mystifyingly, challenging me when I was older, leaving me both flattered and offended. We owned no ID; the clubs hoped that we, or our parents, wouldn't bluff in full view of the community who had a shrewd idea of our ages.

The movies were shown outdoors on a massive screen the height of a house, with a covered balcony for the old and cold. Children sat together in the front rows outside, in bright starlight, amid the night chorus of crickets, a communal immersion in a shared dream.

The triumphant crow of Woody Woodpecker: cartoons came first. Bugs Bunny hung from a ledge while his arms elongated; Wile E. Coyote was flattened by cars, only to pop up again; heart-pounding chases, ever-present pain and danger, while the audience callously laughed. Donald Duck and Micky Mouse, Yogi Bear, and The Flintstones: I soon felt too old for them.

Insects flittered in the golden beams of projected light. And then Disney's Magic Kingdom faded. The MGM lion tossed its mane and roared, or Paramount's Everest or Columbia's Roman virgin transported us to the African veldt, uptown Manhattan, or Scandinavia.

Children's films were screened again and again. We knew them thoroughly, especially *The Sound of Music, the* English language film for our generation, whose songs we knew by heart: "My favourite things," "A lonely goatherd," and "Edelweiss." Other favourites: *Mary Poppins:* "Chim Chim Cheree" and *"Supercalifragilitsticexpialidocious".* (When my friend Dany visited, we'd hold umbrellas and jump down from my dresser, hoping we'd one day be able to fly. Tiring of that, we sharpened our nails and chased my sister, pretending to be tigers.) *My Fair Lady:* "Wouldn't it be lover-ly." *Willy Wonka and the Chocolate Factory, To Sir with Love:* "Those schoolgirl days of telling tales and biting nails." *The Man Who Knew Too Much* was my favourite, the Hitchcock thriller, in which Hank, the precocious little boy who can spell "haemoglobin" but not cat, is kidnapped, and his mother, Doris Day, my favourite actress then, finds him by passionately banging out their family song "*Que Sera, Sera,* whatever will be, will be," on the piano, while hidden Hank hums along.

The clubs screened a slew of films about the Second World War and the Holocaust, the gratuitous cruelty so scarring me that I may never watch another Holocaust film. There were Westerns which I disliked and found boring, and thrillers which I found (and find) unbearably stressful, Hitchcock being a Club favourite. I often fled to the sanctuary of the library, then as now, unable to watch films which involve torture or gratuitous violence. I sobbed bitterly through so many films about suffering animals that I still refuse to watch such films. "Do you love animals more than humans?" my father asked reproachfully. I certainly feel the greatest, most painful empathy with the suffering of the innocent and defenceless—both animals and children.

Kramer vs. Kramer, Hannah and Her Sisters, Annie Hall, Woody Allen, Truffaut, and Bergman: the films were eclectic. We watched Scandinavian brilliance, French New Wave, and New York auteurs too young, often just absorbing the flavour, not the artistry or even the intricacies of the plot. *The Story of Adele H., Gone with the Wind, A Man for all Seasons…* long past our bedtime, we watched Shakespeare beneath the stars; Anne Boleyn laid her lovely head on the block; Mammy made Scarlett O'Hara's waist seventeen inches; prized sewing machines were wrecked during a Russian pogrom, and Elsa the Lioness who was *Born Free* roared.

INTERVAL: giant yellow words flashed across the screen. We snapped out of enchantment and rushed with the throngs to the tables on the lawn on which little carbon-leaved order pads lay scattered. You scribbled your order in a frenzy, signed it, ripped the chit, handed it to the servers behind the counter, "the bearers," and got a brown paper bag of hot fresh-cooked *bondas,* soft, spicy, mashed potato, deep-fried in chickpea batter. At the end of the month, the bookkeeper collected the chits and mailed out the bill.

* * *

The white-uniformed bearers in their paper-bag-shaped white hats were mobbed. Everyone brandished their chits over other people's heads, shouting orders for *pakoras*, slivers of vegetables deep-fried in chickpea batter, or soft dinner rolls stuffed with "Beldih Spread:" a savoury chicken spread.

Most often, we hollered for the golden, paper-thin, crisp, freshly fried salty potato "chips," as they are universally called in Indian English. The management of the Beldih Club, however, craftily decided to dub these chips (or crisps!) which sold for one rupee "potato wafers," and christen the thick wedges of potato, or "French fries" which sold for three rupees "potato chips," in the British style. Through force of habit, however, both we children and our father signed chits for "potato chips;" the bearers, understanding what we meant, gave us the crisp, salty "potato wafers," and we were eventually billed three rupees for the French fries or "potato chips," in the Beldih Club's official parlance, to the irritation and scoldings of my mother.

I suddenly noticed that the semi-illiterate, harried bearers never looked at what we'd written but just gave us what we shouted for. Besides, they had no way to check our signatures.

Ah-ha! Using the think-differently gifts with which we later both founded (legitimate) businesses, my sister and I realised that we could get as

many treats as we liked if we signed as someone else. So we ordered wildly–
though our cleverness did not extend to inventing a name; instead, we tidily
wrote our neighbour's name, Mrs Cherian, not realising that she would have
written Elsie Cherian.

"Are you *sure* we won't get caught?" my sister, more cautious, occasionally asked. "How could we?" I retorted. "How could anyone know it was us?"

We sipped ice-cold Fanta, had fresh potato wafers *and* potato chips. "Mrs
Cherian" signed for them.

* * *

"Cel-een," at the end of the month, an irate cry resounded from the
opening in the hedge which separated our house from our neighbour's. A very
annoyed Elsie Cherian, six feet tall, stood at the hedge between our homes. She
held out a wad of chits.

At the end of our bloated month, Mrs Cherian opened her bill to discover that all month, apparently, *she* had gorged on pakoras, potato wafers *and*
potato chips, Coca-Cola and Fanta, all signed for in childish handwriting, MRS
CHERIAN.

"Oh, I just wanted the earth to open up and swallow me," my mother
groped for metaphors.

Mrs Cherian paid the bill; my parents repaid her.

After this, we ordered more abstemiously, signing in with our real names,
and lost ourselves in the movies, sipping ice-cold bubbly Fanta, then the ambrosial taste of heaven, mindlessly munching fresh-fried salty crisp "potato
wafers," while late into the night, elegant ladies in long gowns fled the French
Revolution, and the Scarlet Pimpernel kissed the earth where his disdainful wife
had walked. In the car on the way home, the sun, which had been a blazing
orange ball floating beneath the horizon when we left for the Club, was replaced
by glowing stars, at which I gazed, in a post-movie haze, until the towering *neem*

and eucalyptus trees and jasmine bushes outside blurred with the moon and the after-glow of images. I drifted into dreamy sleep in the back seat as Hera and Zeus settled the Trojan War in a game of chess, and Christ—in one of the frequent Bible movies eclectically screened—stretched his arms across the screen: *Lo, I will be with you always to the end of the age.*

* * *

A few times a week, the *ayah,* our live-in help, walked my sister and me to the poky little library in the United Club to borrow books. The books I owned formed the emotional and imaginative centre of my life, but these were soon read multiple times, and the library was a heart-beating faster excitement. Jamshedpur felt safe, so my parents left us in the club library while they watched "A movies," adults only. We joined other children in the billiard room, shooting bright balls across the green baise table, or congregated around the low tables with children's magazines: figuring out what was awry in images, spotting the difference, cracking mazes, and connecting dots, puzzles I loved for their easy, proud sense of achievement.

Comics covered tables, Turkish-delight enchantment, Richie Rich and his boundless wealth, every whim gratified, the American dream never metastasising to nightmare—though we laughed at the poor little rich boy, sour grapes on our tongues. Dennis the Menace asks the preacher, "What if I love my neighbour and he don't love me back?" while Mr Wilson scowls. We pored over those tattered missals: Archie, Veronica, and Betty, and the silly sexualised world of American teens. There was "Bringing up Father;" "The Moomins," a rare Scandinavian comic, and lashings of the supernatural: Caspar, the friendly ghost; Wendy, the good witch; Hot Stuff, the naughty devil; Spooky and the Three Boos, besides "Phantom, the Ghost who Walks," Batman, Spiderman, and Clark Kent, who morphed to Superman with whom we unconsciously identified, for didn't we too have secret dreams and ambitions-and powers-unguessed at by the adult world.

* * *

The barrister bookshelves in the clubs had rows of the novels of Enid Blyton, the most popular children's author in English-speaking India, who wrote books in addictive series, begged and borrowed by both boys and girls, whether intellectually aspirational or not. My father showed me her obituary in *The Statesman* when I was six, and I cried, realising there would be no more Enid Blyton books ever again, no more *Malory Towers*, no more *St. Clare's.*

Enid Blyton, incredibly, wrote seven hundred books, a book a week at the height of her powers in her fifties, books which accompanied us from infancy to adolescence. She wooed us young with Jack Frost painting the nursery windows with crystals, and her fairy tale world of elves, goblins, pixies and brownies in *The Enchanted Wood, The Faraway Tree*, and little Noddy zipping around Toyland in his cheerful yellow car, protected by the Gnome, Big Ears from bad teddy bears, goblins, and "golliwogs."

After that magic moment, aged six, when Enid Blyton helped me leap from only reading picture books by myself to reading a hundred-page book with just text and not finding it boring at all, I read every Enid Blyton novel I could find, those enviable adventures: The Famous Five (and Timmy the Dog), The Secret Seven, The Adventurous Four, and The Five Find-Outers, children solving what adults could not, living in a whirl of never-ending excitement—just the way *I* wanted to live.

Blyton introduced girls not just as enthralled readers but as heroines to adventure stories as thrilling as *Treasure Island* or *The Three Musketeers,* which had hitherto been the province of boys. A wondrous world--of freedom, adventure and camaraderie, in which children cycle around the idyllic English countryside for hours, without adults, but with picnic hampers of cold chicken, devilled eggs, scones and, of course, chocolate. They forage for berries when hungry; sleep on beds of heather; cook over bonfires lit with magnifying glasses; keep cheese and clotted cream cool in nooks by springs, and have midnight feasts of pork pies and condensed milk.

What a world! Disused lighthouses, buried treasure in secret trails, ruined cottages, treacherous misty moors, gold ingots, camping, magical islands, the sea, the sea! A shipwreck, a concealed map sought by villains, thousands of pounds in counterfeit money. The children find stolen pearls and dogs and war medals, are kidnapped and held at gunpoint until rescued by their "chums." They outwit smugglers, thieves, spies, and blundering Bobbies, for are they not smarter than most adults around them as, in essential things, children are. We loved them. How could we not?

And the food! Gargantuan picnics. Crusty loaves of fresh homemade bread, large hams and tongue, enormous cheeses. Cucumber sandwiches, ginger cake, and apple pie. Ginger beer and lashings of lemonade. Humbugs and toffees. Foods for childhood's hearty appetite and, to us, storybook foods. What on earth were devilled eggs?

Paradoxically, every girl I knew identified with the tomboy Jo of *Little Women* or Blyton's Georgina, George, the girl-who-was-as-good-as-a-boy, who could out-swim, out-climb, and outwit anyone. Anne, the other girl in the Famous Five, could magic a cosy nest and aromatic meals out of nothing, in the middle of nowhere, but I wanted to be George. Didn't everyone? George who wanted to be *one* of the boys, not cater to them; George in comfortable boyish clothes, with her best friend, Timmy the dog, "short-haired, freckled, sturdy, and snub-nosed," "bold and daring, hot-tempered and loyal," based on Blyton herself.

Blyton was, apparently, not a nurturing mother (like many children's writers, she remained a child imaginatively and emotionally–which perhaps explains their success); however, she wrote accurately of school-world, the traitorous and the true, the smarmy, the fake, and the straight arrows. *Malory*

Towers and *St. Clare's,* her most popular boarding school novels, portrayed *The Lord of The Flies* world of boarding schools—kindness and malice, deep bonds and deceit, excitement and anguish, politics and joyous friendship. When I went to boarding school, aged nine, I discovered that those stories, universally beloved in India, scripted the things we did there, life imitating art: midnight feasts, snowball fights, and sending people "to Coventry"–the whole class agreeing not to talk to a girl, a psychic strain which led two girls to attempt suicide and others to try to run away. I also loved *The Naughtiest Girl in School,* a moniker I acquired in both my schools, and a kind of redemption story, for eventually Elizabeth Allen, *The Naughtiest Girl Becomes a Monitor,* which one year I did.

I read all the libraries' boarding school stories, a version of the orphan story beloved by children–*A Little Princess*, rife with petty cruelties over which I wept each time; Angela Brazil's secret world of foreign boarding schools; *What Katy Did at School, The Chalet School, Just William,* Nancy Drew, and set in England, the fat bespectacled Billy Bunter, a direct ancestor of Harry Potter.

* * *

Sometimes, our whole family read the same books: James Herriot's *All Creatures Great and Small*, about his adventures as a vet in the Yorkshire Dales; the amusing vivid adventures of the naturalist Gerard Durrell who, like me, was born in Jamshedpur; and volume after volume of the understated, pitch-perfect, quintessentially English humour of P. G. Wodehouse, whom my father called the blind pig, and I loved!

I read every Agatha Christie mystery I could find when I was eleven, falling under the spell of clever Hercule Poirot, the Belgian detective of the magnificent moustache and a head exactly the shape of an egg, and the genteel, fussy, elderly spinster, Miss Marple, reading rapt, determined to guess the murderer.

At the age of twelve, sadly, I went through a phase of reading romances, inexplicably deciding to read *every* Mills and Boon ever written, keeping a list of each title I read and the number on their spine, but, fortunately, losing interest after having read one hundred and two Mills and Boons. I devoured too Ruby M. Ayres, Denise Robbins, and Barbara Cartland's historical romances; my favourite writer, aged thirteen, was Georgette Heyer, who recreated a meticulously detailed gracious Regency world. I read each novel of hers that I could find and thought them elegant, particularly those which traced the fortunes of an aristocratic family through four generations–William Faulkner's Yoknapatawapha County for everywoman. By the time I turned thirteen, I decided to give up romances, and for life! Phew!

And next: Taylor Caldwell's rags to riches stories, set in nineteenth-century America; the brooding Gothic romances of Daphne Du Maurier and Victoria Holt, and the historical novels of Jean Plaidy (also known as Philippa Carr, one of the eight pseudonyms of Eleanor Hibbert who wrote two hundred books, many of which were in our boarding school library). In my historical novel phase, I devoured each one I could lay my hands on: *Quo Vadis?*, set in the time of Nero; *Ben Hur, Desiree,* about Napoleon's true love; *The Last Days of Pompeii; The Hunchback of Notre Dame,* Arthurian romances like Mary Stewart's *The Merlin Chronicles,* and frothy Restoration novels, Like my father, I devoured the Scarlet Pimpernel novels, the tale of Sir Percy Blakeney, English aristocrat and daring cross-Channel rescuer of threatened aristocrats during the French Revolution, who poses as a lethargic fop. The Second World War, the Nazis, and concentration camps were live literary and cinematic subjects then, Second World War novels flooding the clubs' libraries. I felt emotionally and psychically branded by second-hand Holocaust horrors: yellow stars and hidden attics, windowless cattle trucks, the punitive shooting of every tenth person, the hunger, exhaustion, humiliations, and cruelties of the Camps. I read *The Diary of Anne Frank,* of course; Corrie Ten Boom's *The Hiding Place,* and the novels of Leon

Uris: most memorably *Exodus*, the gripping story of the birth of Israel; *Mila 18* about the Warsaw Ghetto Uprising, and *QB VII*, a gruesome novel about medical experimentation on Jewish prisoners. They so scarred me that I might never read another Holocaust novel.

And then, thrillers—a mindless gulping of Frederick Forsythe, Arthur Hailey, Peter Benchley, Helen MacInnes, Edgar Wallace, and Nevil Shute. My father was outraged when he saw me read the too-graphic novels of James Hadley Chase and Harold Robbins, snatching them away, red-faced, scaring me. After this mid-teen phase of thrillers, I gave them up for life—devouring and discarding entire genres in the United and Beldih Club in my teens: boarding-school stories, adventure stories, mysteries, romances, thrillers, Holocaust, and war stories.

I read the few and random "Christian" novels in the club libraries in that Hindu and Parsee town to catch rare reflections of my Roman Catholic identity in the pages of a book. Along with my parents, I read all the novels of A. J. Cronin and remember getting deeply upset and tearful, my blood boiling at *The Keys of the Kingdom,* the life of unlucky, sweet, naïve, unpolitical Father Francis Chisholm. I remember *God's Smuggler*, the outrageous exploits of Brother Andrew, who believing in the dynamite of the Bible smuggled them behind the iron and bamboo curtains; Taylor Caldwell's fictional biographies of the Gospel writer Luke, *Dear and Glorious Physician*, and of the Apostle Paul, *Great Lion of God*; Catherine Marshall's *Christy* about her young mother's volunteering in Appalachia, and Margaret Craven's haunting and very beautiful *I Heard the Owl Call my Name,* set among the First Nations of British Columbia.

I ravenously swallowed whatever looked remotely interesting—nonfiction about Indian and sub-continental history: *Freedom at Midnight,* which I read and reread; Gandhi's moving and inspiring autobiography, *The Story of my Experiments with Truth; The Judgement* about the striking time when the courts sentenced Prime Minister Indira Gandhi to a jail term for electoral fraud;

biographies of Nicholas and Alexandra; the Rothschilds, Queen Victoria, Napoleon; genius and dross, *Tarzan of the Apes*, *The Leopard* by Lampedusa, and Arthur Koestler's *Darkness at Noon* of which I absorbed little more than the atmosphere. I read *Animal Farm: A Fairy Tale* when I was ten, disgusted to discover it was not a fairy tale or even a happy animal story.

My father was sceptical of my reading projects. "You'll never finish that," he said, as he eyed me with Dicken's thousand-page, hard-luck tales--*Dombey and Son* or *Nicholas Nickleby,* but I did, gulping them down in massive windsprints, as much through determination as enjoyment. I borrowed Plato's *Republic* at ten because the jacket said it was one of the greatest books ever written. "You might understand the words, but not the meaning," my father said, which seemed like *Alice in Wonderland* nonsense, and so I ploughed through it, indeed understanding most words, but suffering, deeply bored! I have never read it again.

"You are reading too fast; you won't remember what you are reading," my father said, quizzing me on what I'd read; however, my retentive memory was particularly sharp in childhood, and I passed!

* * *

Having read through the children's bookcases in both clubs, I started working through the adult cases, the good, the bad, the indifferent, "because they were there."

The libraries were run on the card system. You took the borrowers' card out of the little envelope pasted onto the inner front cover, examined who read it before you, wrote your name, handed in the card, took the book. "Are you sure you should be reading these?" the librarian asked doubtfully, seeing me check out adult books, but he accepted my glib assurances.

I checked out the risqué Angelique novels because they appeared to be historical novels, which I then adored. They were written by "Sergeann Golon," the composite name of a husband-wife team, Serge Golub, a Russian aristocrat who fled the Revolution, and his French wife, Anne Golon.

The novels detailed Angelique's sexual adventures in *ancien régime* France; she improbably gets kidnapped by pirates; is enslaved in the harem of the Sultan of Morocco; becomes a countess; stabs King Louis XIV, the Sun King, when he tries to rape her. Mild erotica: brutal but apparently thrilling sex (the first such books I'd ever read) redeemed by the historical setting and personae and the elegant clothes.

* * *

My parents had let me choose my own books ever since I was old enough to read by myself, and so I did, reading five of the Angelique novels at home, unremarked on. On my fourteenth birthday, Mrs Cherian hollered for my mother at the gap in our hedge. "Tell her I'll talk later," my mother said, putting the finishing touches on the cake. I relayed the message, my thumb as a bookmark in *Angelique.*

But Mrs Cherian could not wait.

She was back in minutes. "Celine, Celine, Celine," she hollered urgently.

My mother came running.

"Celine, do you know what *she* is reading?"

"No. What?" Two lawns away, where I sat reading, I heard Mrs Cherian's voice in a dramatic hush, *"Angelique."*

"What's *Angelique*?" my mother squawked.

"*Angelique* is a dirty, filthy book," Mrs Cherian exclaimed.

* * *

"Noel," my mother shrieked the moment my father came home.

Shouting, screaming, tears, "Your books will take you to hell," and *Angelique* banned forever, though I bought one on a railway platform on my way up to boarding school, where the good nuns were deceived by the gowns, the bustles, and the ambience of historicity, and I was allowed to keep it.

A rather confused and bewildered Anita with a newborn Shalini and our grandmother, Molly Coelho

Symphony in Steel:
Jamshedpur, "The Steel City"

"Symphony in Steel:" a tall silver gyre, dazzling, twisted ribbons of steel which joined at the heart, then swirled and spiralled upwards in the sunshine, soared at the town's centre, the market district of Bistapur.

Symphony in steel, symphony in steel, I murmured, savouring the words each time we entered the raucous streets of Jamshedpur.

My vocabulary had evolved from my first word, *"Ijit,"* which I said whenever my father slammed the brakes…and just before, he too, predictably, muttered: *Idiot!* Perhaps a cow had shambled across the road, chewing banana stalks, or pedestrians had sauntered in front of us, chatting, animated, oblivious. My father terrified us with stories of his earliest driving days in Jamshedpur: the sacred cow whose leg he'd crushed, the killed golden goose, the Billy Goat Gruff who… until we shrieked, begging him to stop. He did. Temporarily. But the next accounts were even gorier.

Iron and steel: magnets which drew us to Jamshedpur via The Tata Iron and Steel Company, one of the world's oldest, largest steel companies, at which my father worked for twenty-four years. Jamshedpur was developed in 1907 after Jamshedji Nusserwanjee Tata, a Parsee industrialist, discovered that the laterite-red soil was rich with iron ore. Jamshedji's birthday, the third of March, was lavishly celebrated each year as Founder's Day, with parades, and free boxes of Indian sweets, though the "Red Letter Day" acquired a dark tinge after fifty people died in a fire in the VIP's *shamiana,* marquee, while watching a marching band.

Tata Iron and Steel used to be the largest steel company in the British Empire, which meant something in the days when the sun never set on it. I have seen iron plates covering storm drains in Central Park in New York, in Williamsburg, Virginia, where I once lived, and in Oxford, England, where I now live, with the legend, "Made in India," and smiled, for I knew they came from my hometown, Jamshedpur.

The Company was proud of the jagged industrial skyline it impressed on the city, a tableau of cooling towers and mighty blast furnaces which huffed blackness into the skies, a skyline which echoed from the Company's ubiquitous goodwill calendars and diaries. The coal mines at Dhanbad; and the Works at Tata Iron and Steel, where, night and day, the great blast furnaces roared: this was the industrial backdrop of my childhood. Feeling immensely grown-up, we showed our houseguests around them, for our father, ignoring company rules which banned children from the Works, took us to the factory floor, murmuring an open sesame phrase to the *chowkidars,* guards: "my children." He did, however, ensure that we swallowed the compulsory salt tablets–Communion demanded by the God of Steel–before we entered the Works, lest the dehydration, and electrolytes lost in drenching streams of sweat led us to faint and tumble into great glowing rivers of orange molten iron, hypnotic and terrible, which flowed from the furnaces into which shirtless, sweat soaked men pitched coal.

* * *

Jamshedpur, proudly called "The Steel City" (and fondly called Jampot), was India's first planned industrial city, laid out by Julian Kennedy of Pittsburgh, America's steel city, with twenty-six parallel streets, unimaginatively named from A to Z, East and West. The address of our company house was 6 C Road East, walking distance from the Company's offices, close to a tiny, lush oasis of a park with bougainvillaea, canna, and a jungle gym, one of the many little parks created by enlightened urban planning. Further down the road were the Director's bungalows, buffered from the street by large, high-walled gardens with bored guards at the gates, and magnificent Alsatian watchdogs, whom we befriended, charmed, and betrayed into bounding up to the gates with unprofessional joy as we called their names.

Jamshedpur is the world's oldest and largest "company town" still in existence. It did not have a municipal corporation; TISCO provided electricity, sanitation, free health care and a free telephone service for its forty thousand employees. All employees received free housing, the size, location, and luxuriousness varying according to the employee's position. The large houses of TISCO executives faced each other across broad tree-lined streets, swept daily, shaded with mature trees, and lit by company streetlights. At the back of each house were the servants' quarters which also faced each other across dirt alleys. Each servant family was given a room, though no toilets or bathrooms. They squatted in the back alleys.

* * *

My father watched three waves of international influence on TISCO. After Independence, the British managers were followed by Americans, such as J. L. Keenan, the General Manager of TISCO—remembered in the eponymous Keenan Stadium, site of enthusiastic cricket, watched by everyone from company executives to domestic workers. However, in the seventies, India gravitated towards Russia and Pakistan towards America (though both nations were technically "non-aligned"). So, Russians appeared in Jamshedpur with technical expertise–giant men, blue-eyed and blonde, passionate about basketball, to which they challenged the town. The community gathered in the evening at the United Club to watch their sleight of hand and wizardry and cheered, even when, inevitably, the Russians won. "It's because they are seven feet tall," we said, though our dazzled eyes probably added some inches.

Jamshedpur, a small Indian town, did offer a sprinkling of diversity. Appropriately for those Cold War years, we had resident Americans to balance the Russians–Jesuits from the Baltimore Province who ran both Loyola, the local boys' school, and a prestigious Business School: XLRI, while The Sisters of Mercy of Philadelphia ran the TB hospital. Besides, The Tata Iron and Steel Company, a major Indian company with generous perks and benefits, drew ambitious executives from every part of India. Indeed, almost everyone was from somewhere else, from Tamil Nadu or Kerala in the deep South to Uttar Pradesh and Kashmir in the north, and because of the influence of meritocratic, technocratic professionals, who had risen by brains and diligence, both culture and education were intensely valued in our small town.

By the early seventies, a reverse movement, the much-bemoaned "brain drain," began. Executives took early retirement from TISCO and worked in developing countries-Peru, Iran, Iraq, and Dubai, often through United

Nations agencies and programmes, and, uncannily, several died of heart attacks or stress-induced ailments while working overseas. Many professional Catholic families from Jamshedpur also began to emigrate in the early seventies to Canada, Australia, America, and Britain. Always eager for adventure and a bigger world, I begged my father to emigrate to the West, but he flatly refused. The sudden deaths spooked him, and, besides, he had been an immigrant in London in his twenties and thirties, a mixed experience; there was no way he was going through emigration in his fifties, and there was no budging him.

In Jamshedpur, my father said, you *were* your job. People universally bowed and scraped to became *persona non grata*, cold-shouldered, and ignored once they retired. He vowed to leave town the instant he retired, as he did–after his second retirement at sixty-eight, from being the Financial Controller and a Professor at the excellent local American Jesuit-run business school, Xavier Labour Relations Institute.

* * *

The economic and cultural life of Jamshedpur was dominated by Zoroastrians, Parsees, followers of the Prophet Zoroaster who had fled to West India in the tenth century, fleeing Islamic persecution in Iran. The Parsees were an educated, Westernized, relatively affluent minority, and Zoroastrianism was a unique race-based faith. One could not convert to this patrilineal faith, and the children of women who married out of the faith were no longer considered Parsees. This, in addition, to late marriage and relatively low marriage and birth rates, means the community is facing extinction, with deaths each year outnumbering births.

On a quiet side street lay their mysterious fire temple, the *Agiary*, in which a perpetual flame burned, fire which they worshipped, my father said. Non-Parsees could not enter this Agiary, as mysterious to us as the local Freemason Lodge, which felt esoteric and fascinating because my father refused to tell me about it, perhaps because he did not know much, or perhaps because membership was forbidden by the Catholic Church. As we passed the Agiary, my father told me of the Towers of Silence in Bombay, on which dead bodies were exposed to be devoured by the vultures which circled and swooped around them, in a chilling and ecologically sound recycling, though one as sanitary as the Hindus who burnt their dead at the *ghats* and scattered the ashes into Riversmeet in Jamshedpur, the sacred confluence of the Ganges and the Subarnarekha.

* * *

Russi Modi, the Managing Director, a character, educated at Harrow and Christ Church, Oxford, had extraordinary people skills and prided himself on knowing the names of every TISCO employee from management to the stenotypists, punch operators, peons and the workers manning the blast furnaces,

TISCO's benevolent management practices were perhaps influenced by American Jesuit-run Business School, XLRI; many company executives attended evening and weekend classes there, some of which my father taught. The Company sent my father to study the technology and management styles at steel companies in the US (Pittsburgh!), Britain, Europe, and Japan, with TISCO adapting what was practicable and sometimes going even further.

The Company ran a state-of-the-art hospital, Tata Main Hospital, at which I was born, which provided free medical treatment to all employees and their families, and free medical treatment for life to anyone who had worked for the Company for twenty-five years, a valuable perk. Retirees frequently returned to Jamshedpur for surgery or chemotherapy.

The TISCO cafeteria sold tasty food at radically subsidised prices so that every employee could have inexpensive meals at work and take food home if they wanted, and no employee family would go hungry, despite dire money management or circumstances. We tried to wheedle my father into bringing these delicious fresh-cooked snacks home for tea, but he generally refused, being too proud and snobbish to contemplate queuing with TISCO clerks, sweepers, and factory workers. No senior management went, he said. Appearances mattered in our shame-based society, and being suspected of struggling financially or of stinginess was as feared as the fact of it.

On rare occasions, however, we prevailed. Setting pride aside, my father sent his peon to pick up snacks from the canteen and returned home for tea, frowning and grumpy-faced, with heavily subsidised banyan-leaved, twig-threaded containers of hot *jalebis*, orange Catherine wheels, their crisp concentric circles bursting with warm, flavourful syrup; the bright orange globe of *laddoos, pakoras, samosas,* or *bondas,* a mouthful of soft, spicy, mashed potato, deep-fried in crisp chickpea batter, India's heavenly snack foods, on which we pounced with jubilation.

* * *

Once a year, the Company whisked its entire management and families on a picnic to a "beauty spot," like Dalma Hill or Dimna Dam. Lunch was cooked out-of-doors, a major undertaking—on plates of banyan leaves, threaded together with twigs, we ate chicken *biriyani, parathas,* and freshly cooked melt-in-the-mouth burnt sienna *gulab jamuns*: balls of wheat, sugar, and milk, floating in a thick, ultra-sweet rosewater syrup flavoured by cloves and cardamom.

Those of whom we had overheard in snatches of drawing-room gossip we now saw: all my father's colleagues and subordinates; the company doctors; all our school friends' fathers, with their wives and children. The management was almost entirely male; the female employees were secretaries, stenotypists, punch-operators, or telephone operators. (My father once had a female managerial subordinate and, to her shock, superseded her. He imitated how she burst into his office, sobbing, "*You superseded me,*" for she had believed he lacked the misogyny of the culture. Looking back, I think his mockery concealed guilt.) My father snorted when I said I would definitely "work" when I grew up. "Not in business!" he said. "Besides, why spend your life making a rich company richer?" Why indeed!

* * *

We used to visit our fellow Catholic parishioners, the Andrades, who had a tiny, clay-walled, dark house on the outskirts of town, and listen to Mr Andrade, an elderly, uneducated Goan man, a manual worker at the steel factory, boast that the Managing Director Russi Modi knew him by name, and they advised and scolded each other about their respective health, a subject on which all Indians had, or feigned, a paternalistic interest, dispensing unsolicited advice.

Both Mr Andrade's sons were entirely devoted to the Catholic Church. In their late teens and twenties, they had cycled around to our house to collect the monthly contributions the Catholic Church expected every parishioner to make, with the amounts published in the weekly bulletin in descending order, a visible marker of financial success and social position. I urged my parents to donate more to have our names right at the top, but, fortunately for our family's finances, they resisted both ecclesiastical and filial pressure, leaving that position to local hoteliers and private nursery school owners.

As Vince and Mart rose up the company ranks, they no longer cycled to see us, but zipped around on a new scooter, then on a new motorcycle, and, finally, in a new car. And though their father was a manual worker at the factory, the Works, the boys went to Loyola School, along with the town's middle class, and received the same education. They worked hard at TISCO, volunteered hard at church, and steadily rose through the ranks of both Company and church.

When we travelled, my parents locked the house and got Vince and Mart to sleep on the floor on the verandah as a safeguard against thieves. Eventually, Vince reached a senior position in the Company and moved from the tiny clay-walled house on the grubby outskirts of town to our sprawling twelve-roomed colonial house with the one-acre garden, outdoor kitchen and garage, and quarters for two servants at the back of the garden, the house he had as a young man wistfully visited on his bike–in a classic arc of upward mobility which must have been sweet.

Social mobility through education and hard work! This surely pleased the American Jesuits who ran the school and Parish and the liberal Parsees who ran the Company: The Jamshedpur Dream.

Everyone on our street was a Tata employee, for most houses in town belonged to the Company. The Cherians, our neighbours to the left, atypically, were an Orthodox Syrian Christian man from Kerala married to an American Jewish woman; the neighbours to the right, the Vazifdars, were Parsees, while the rest of the street was populated by Hindu families from all over India. I went to boarding school in Nainital, in the foothills of the Himalayas, a forty-eight-hour journey by train and mountain bus, because Marcheta and Benita Fernandez on D Road went there, and Sangeeta, who lived opposite us, eventually followed in my steps. Every winter, the population of the street and the town increased with the return of teachers from hill station boarding schools, Kalimpong, Panchgani, Darjeeling, Kodaikanal, Mt. Abu, and Ooty, for the three-month winter vacation–single women who lived with their fathers or brothers, and whom I loved meeting because they loaned me good books and represented a familiar world.

And in the background, the caste system. Though being Christians, we were out of it, beyond or above the pale, we knew everyone's caste, often embedded in the surname, though some conservative Hindus had caste marks in sandalwood paste on their foreheads. And rumours of horrors rippled. Upper-caste Hindus who had economic and political power lay in wait for the tribal people, known as Adivasis (or The Scheduled Tribes, after the schedule in the Indian constitution which guaranteed them affirmative action or "reservation" of jobs and university places). They ambushed these Adivasis on their way to the market, their carts full of vegetables, the fruit of months of toil. These the upper-caste bullies commandeered, saying, "On your way. On your way." If the tribal people protested, the *goondas*, goons at the disposal of the upper castes, beat them up, or they were reported on trumped-up charges to the police, who sided with the upper-caste complainants. In a horrifying incident, the police took the side of landlords against men from the lowest Hindu caste, the Sudras, who had asserted their rights in a land dispute, jailed those men (called Harijans by Mahatma Gandhi, which means "children of God," but then generally called as the "Untouchables," their touch or shadow meant to pollute). They arrested these Dalit men, gouged out their eyes with large needles and poured acid in the sockets. I remember those scarred, blinded eyes on the front cover of the crusading magazine *India Today*, through which this atrocity, known as "The Bhagalpur Blindings," came to light. Others did not.

With my father, grandmother and Shalini at Dimna Dam

At Dimna Lake

At Riversmeet

Anita, 8, and Shalini, 5, with Uncle Ronny at Riversmeet

The Food of Love

Meals were the scaffolding of our day, its liturgy of hours. They were served "on the dot", dots determined by both the servants' sacrosanct schedule of work, punctuated by breaks, starting early in the morning, and ending after they washed the dinner dishes, and by my father's punctiliously observed work schedule.

Breakfast, elevenses, lunch, tea, dinner–and, if we claimed hunger, a bed-time snack–were the day's chorus, the glue that made us a family, with my mother spending the inter-meal limbo in supervising the cook's interminable chopping of vegetables and grinding of spices, and the *ayah*'s twice-daily Sisy-phean task of sweeping, mopping and dusting the house, and handwashing, hanging out, retrieving, ironing, and folding clothes. When not at school, I grabbed a book and sat in a garden chair reading, almost motionlessly, all day, until summoned for the next meal.

My parents woke at five in the morning to South Indian ground coffee, percolated or boiled in a pan, grainy and too weak; I despised it. What I did love was instant coffee, Nescafe´, with creamy milk and sugar, a bit of a treat since, being part-owned and marketed by a multinational, it was more expensive than Indian ground coffee, advertising and foreignness bestowing glitter.

Every morning, just before seven, my father appeared at the foot of my bed, persistently whispering my name until I tumbled out half-awake—I had surreptitiously read as late into the night as I could without my mother discov-ering and desperately pleading with me to go to sleep; any activity which she was not tightly controlling made her feel extremely stressed. "Go to sleep for my sake," she'd plead.

We had to appear at seven for breakfast because that's when the cook Durga, who reported to work at six-thirty, served it. My parents never let us sleep in since that would throw off Durga's fine-tuned schedule: he had to clear and handwash the dishes, marinate the meat, and soak rice or *dal,* red lentils, for lunch before he left for his mid-morning break from which he returned at ten-thirty to start lunch. My mother ring-fenced his breaks, which kept him unfailingly cheerful though he spent six and a half days a week preparing break-fast, elevenses, lunch, tea, and dinner for us.

Our favourite breakfasts involved bacon, sausages, ham, salami or "luncheon meat," which we considered delicacies since they were relative rari-ties, substantially more expensive than fresh lamb, beef, or chicken, and only available from the town's sole "cold storage," a large, refrigerated room at the Beldih Club. They were served, most often, with eggs scrambled with ghee, and browned onions, speckled with mint and coriander. I secretly liked the cook's omelettes made with onions and mint, thin and massive, covering the entire plate, but which were, according to my father, lower-class omelettes, railway station horrors, served—oh abomination! he said—with ketchup! On the cook's half-day off, my father demonstrated *the perfect* omelette, pounding his eggbeater (which they'd bought in Harrods in London, my mother said) in a plastic tum-bler until the egg was stiff froth and then—showing off! —upending the tumbler while the egg stayed put, upon which he sent my mother to make a fat, fluffy omelette. *An upper-class omelette*, he said, delighted.

Other breakfasts: sandwiches bursting with butter, lettuce, mustard and "corned beef," as we termed our home-salted beef, or with slices of rosy home-cured pork or tongue, which the cook cured by pressing it beneath kilo weights in frequently changed brine. Closed or open-face garden vegetable sandwiches–

thick butter, homemade mayonnaise, Colman's mustard, lettuce, and slices of tomato, cucumber, radishes, and peppers. Or buttery cheese sandwiches with garden lettuce and Amul Cheese, a mild processed cheese whose taste I then loved, sold in tins, or, sometimes, its upstart cheaper competitor, Teg's, also tinned. Amul Cheese, the main commercially manufactured cheese in India then, enjoyed a near-monopoly; "Cadbury's" and "Amul" were synonymous with chocolate or cheese.

Eccentrically, we sometimes had rich date cake for breakfast, or "Midnight Chocolate Cake" made with double the cocoa, eaten according to a formula my mother devised to mitigate the decadence of *cake* for breakfast: "a small bite of cake; a big bite of bread." Similarly, she instructed me to eat a small bite of meat, fried fish, cheese, or "cutlet" (homemade beef or fish burgers) and a big bite of bread or rice to stretch out the pricier food, and I ate that way for decades--the power of early imprinting (though I now skip wheat, rice, and potatoes altogether). Another ancestral habit: meat, fish, and cheese were *always* eaten with rice, bread, potatoes, or parathas, it being extravagant to eat them "plain."

Traditional Indian breakfasts, whipped up by the cook, included *upma*, a spicy dish of fried semolina, split lentils, tomatoes, and peas, fried with mustard seeds, onion, and turmeric. However, the default breakfast, like the default high tea, was sliced white buttered bread, delivered daily, eaten with homemade jam from garden produce—mulberries, gooseberries, roselle, marmalade, and "tomalade" tomatoes and lemon, though, again, we irrationally preferred the more expensive bought jams, especially strawberry jam.

Our cooks in early childhood were Muslims from the villages around Jamshedpur, Naseem, very dark, quiet, and soft-spoken, and Ataullah, who made me feel nervous, his name and villainous cast of countenance recalling rogues from *The Arabian Nights*. I once woke at dawn and saw the limp ghostly shape of the chicken Ataullah had ritually slaughtered for our lunch, hanging upside down from the guava tree behind our house, blood dripping out of it, drop by drop, pooling in the mud. And I screamed. Unmoved by my tears, the cook claimed that *halal* was the most humane method of animal slaughter and that the hen did not feel anything. How did *he* know? My father refused to intervene. "He's saying the Koran tells him to kill chickens that way. How can I tell him to disobey the Koran? How would you like it if *he* tells *us to* disobey the Bible?"

For most of the year, Naseem and Ataullah, both illiterate, cooked Mangalorean food from the recipes my mother described. However, on their feasts: *Bakri-Id*—celebrating the slaughter of a *bakri*, a ram instead of Ishmael (not Isaac, as Christians believe); and Muharram, or *Eid ul-Fitr*, the ecstatic feasting that terminated the fasting month of Ramadan, they bought ingredients from their own small salaries and cooked us Aladdin feasts of Indo-Muslim food— yellow biriyanis with chunks of tender lamb and favoured with saffron; fragrant chicken pullaos bright with saffron; or orange and pink sweet rice with a side dish of spicy chicken *kaleji,* liver. Breakfast was *suji halwa*, rich, dessert-sweet, pink, orange, or green semolina, fried with nuts and raisins. I loved Mughlai cuisine and would gladly have eaten it every day, but my parents preferred their customary blander Mangalorean or Anglo-Indian food.

After a respite, during which I read, we had "Elevenses." My mother had her Phosfomin, a green nerve tonic with phosphorus; her nerves were *shattered* because of the strain of dealing with me, she said; she needed to build up her strength. Believing cream provided strength and energy, she heaped a savourless biscuit, a "cream cracker," with cream skimmed off daily from the unpasteurised fresh milk that the cowherd, the *dudhwallah*, delivered, still warm, which was precautionarily boiled. I asked for a taste once and was so appalled by the tasteless cream that I never asked again. My mother ate bowls of cream when pregnant, to which she attributed her ten-pound babies. She was blessed with both a good appetite–loading her plate with astonishing quantities of white rice–and a good metabolism; she was immensely proud of her figure. We children, meanwhile, had biscuits, on which were imprinted an English cottage beside a mill, the water always churning, always frozen into tranquillity, the birds static in their perpetual flight. And beneath this idyllic template–sweet creamy goo. Elevenses were starchy: a sweet potato drizzled with sugar or honey; a boiled potato lavished with butter and sprinkled with salt and pepper; a cup of freshly cooked chickpeas with lemon juice, chilli powder, and salt; or *bhutta*, buttered corn on the cob. Simple pleasures!

Lunch was served moments after my father, who left his office promptly at twelve-thirty and drove or walked home, entered the house; we always lived within a mile from his office. Following the custom of Anglicised India, we had light "English" or Westernized food for dinner, and Indian food for lunch-- rice, dal, *chapatis* or *parathas*; a curry of either meat, fish, crab, shrimp, or mutton "brains;" one or two overcooked curried vegetables I detested, and a sweet for dessert.

My father had a half-hour nap after lunch, lying flat on his back, in the yogic position of deep rest, *shavasana*, corpse pose, placing a handkerchief over his eyes, and drifting off within minutes-as I do too-then waking in exactly half an hour, without an alarm, and completely refreshed (as I do). Going home for lunch–and a nap was customary in small-town India, naps providing two days for the price of one. Sleeping in, anyway, was impossible for my parents, who woke at five when the sun blazed through the windows; they never considered replacing their cotton pink patterned window curtains, grown sheer over years of washing.

I read myself to sleep after lunch, from which I'd be woken, sleep-drunk and heavy-limbed, at three-thirty, for tea, often a cooked snack like *pakoras*: slivers of cauliflower, potatoes, onions, and fantastical whirls of spinach, deep-fried in a chickpea batter. Or panpale, thin crêpes with a filling of grated coconut, and jaggery (unrefined sugar). There was bread slathered with Ferradol, an iron-rich syrup, or Ovomaltine, a chocolate spread with much-vaunted but dubious health benefits, or sometimes, just thickly buttered and sprinkled with sugar, the way we liked it! And, always, much-detested milk, considered indispensable nutrition, served with a spoonful of bribery: Bournvita or Ovaltine, made of cocoa, sugar and malt extracts, or Horlicks–wheat, malt, and sugar, beverages extensively marketed to the developing world, advertised as healthy drinks, good for "building you up"–a marketing scam! Then there was homemade cake and *halwas* from garden produce like beetroots, carrots, and guavas, which we ate in the most minuscule bites to maximise pleasure. Food was shorthand for and an incarnation of love in butter and sugar, fudge, and condensed milk toffee. (Vegetables were never the food of love!) On torpid summer afternoons, we had creamy iced *fools* for tea—gooseberry or mangoes blended with milk and sugar.

As five o'clock neared, when my father punctually left the office, we kept asking, with increasing restlessness, "When is Pa coming home?" He never worked a minute beyond his nine to five on weekdays and a half-day on Saturday, but being proud, punctilious, and duty-driven, appalled at the thought of failure or criticism, he never ever took his whole four-week vacation or his sick leave, much to my annoyance, for I wanted him to stay home and play with us.

We ate at seven, a lighter, more Western meal--dinner rolls with "Beldih Spread," shredded chicken fried with onion, garlic and coriander in a mustard, mayonnaise, and tomato sauce (a bit like Coronation Chicken, a recipe my mother cajoled out of the chef to the envy of her circle). Or we had aubergines, tomatoes, or peppers stuffed with mince, and then baked golden with egg and breadcrumbs; brain, beef, or fish "cutlets," or croquettes. Our favourites were "potato chops," or "pan rolls," pan-fried crepes with a spicy oniony ground beef filling, fried golden with bread crumb bristles, an East-West fusion for our mildly Westernised palates. Dessert was Britishy--blancmange from a sachet and, less liked, custards, semolina pudding, bread pudding or rice pudding.

* * *

My mother, each morning, pored over her handwritten, much-tweaked recipe books assembled through trial and error: recipes that worked. She measured out a cup of rice and one of lentils, weighed out the meat or fish and vegetables, and handed Durga a round stainless-steel tray with spices arranged in colourful still life--an orange pod of turmeric, faithful mustard seeds, grains of cumin, pods of cardamom, spiky cloves, a few red chillis and a pile of fresh herbs. The cook ground these using his black phallic rolling-pin-like handstone on a round quern-stone or a ridged stone slab, creating a little wet orange cake of ground ginger, garlic, and turmeric, and a green one of mint, coriander, green chillis and onions. I half-consciously overheard my mother intone the litany of recipes so often that the only time I think in Hindi is when I invent or recall recipes, the incantation *adrak, losan, dhania, pudeena, jeera, haldi, elaichi, sursu,* ginger, garlic, coriander, mint, cumin, turmeric, cardamom, mustard surfacing from the mists of lost time. Scrambled eggs, of course, must have *pudeena*, mint, *dhaniapatta*, coriander, and *pyaaz*, onion. The first stage of any sensible recipe, to my mind, begins with fry *adrak* and *losan*, ginger and garlic, with onions, *pyaaz*, and mustard seeds, *sursu,* perhaps adding a pinch of *haldi*, turmeric, and some *currypata*, curry leaves.

Durga, though illiterate, was obviously intelligent with an infallible sequential memory; my mother could describe the steps in a complex recipe, hand him the ingredients, and he'd produce a perfect, standardised dish without supervision. Since my mother requested the recipe of any spectacular dish served

to her, the delectable foods of North India gradually appeared at our table--
kulchas, chola bhaturas, alu parathas, tandoori chicken, and *Shrimp Pundra Numbur,*
Shrimp Number Fifteen, named after a succulent dish of fried shrimp, tomatoes, onion, and potatoes in a spicy tomato sauce, served us by Mrs Mangrulker,
who lived across the road at 15 C Road East. Though my mother rarely cooked
when we had Durga, she prized her reputation as a brilliant cook, which had
reached those who had never met her. When relatives in Mangalore, which she
never visited, said, "Oh, I hear your mother is an excellent cook," I, loving truth
and precision, would clarify, to her intense annoyance, "Actually, she doesn't
know how to cook; Durga does all the cooking."

On Sundays, Durga prepared Sunday lunch while we were at church–
roast chicken, stuffed with fried bread, raisins, garlic, onions, herbs, and its own
chopped-up liver, kidneys, heart, and gizzard, served, washed up, and then took
his treasured half-day off to hang out with his friends who guarded houses, to
visit his mother, or to get drunk. And then, for the last two meals of the week—
a Sunday tea of homemade mango, coffee, chocolate, or *kulfi,* almond ice cream,
and a light dinner, we were on our own.

Having a full-time cook and *ayah* tripled the time available for domesticity, making it more important to do things economically rather than efficiently,
to save money rather than time. So my mother hid the imported electrical appliances, the mixer, blender, food processer and electric grill from the cook lest
he use and perhaps ruin them; they appeared only when she cooked Sunday's
supper—delicate morsels of marinated chicken and shrimp on the grill, or
creamy spinach or tomato soup whisked in the old red blender, brought back
from England.

When left to fend for ourselves, we also brought out gifts of packaged
or canned food, then exotic to us, smuggled into the country by people

returning from trips to England or America, or even Sri Lanka, Singapore, and the Gulf States--countries which had open markets unlike India's strict protectionist economy, which at that time only allowed capital goods to be purchased with the nation's precious foreign exchange, and certainly not consumer luxuries or foodstuffs (a reaction to the decade after independence when India imported even ketchup and jam from England while we built our own factories). Expatriates and business travellers returned from trips with quantities of foreign foodstuffs, their scarcity adding value: it was not uncommon to be presented these by people whose *relatives* had been overseas— "Oh, my brother brought these Maggi noodle soup packets, and Maggi soup cubes from Malaysia," which we used with onions and tomatoes as a base for the homemade vegetable soup our family drunk in mugs on cookless winter Sunday evenings. My mother's locked cupboard had stockpiles of imported foods people brought back for her as gifts from overseas trips, their foreignness adding cachet: tins of Spam or Kraft cheese, red wax-wrapped Baby Bell, round boxes of creamy Laughing Cow cheese, Mars Bars, and packets of Jell-O.

When my Uncle Eustace was based in England, he brought us whole suitcases of Toblerone and Quality Street; tins of sardines, mackerel, pilchard, oysters, caviar, Danish Ham; bottles of my father's favourite Colman's Mustard for our salt beef sandwiches, and packets of the instant bachelor food he ate in London. We added boiling water to sachets of desiccated potato or powdered soups and ate them savouringly, because they were foreign, when, ironically, we could easily have had the cook prepare fresh, organic, tasty mashed potatoes, and soups. People considered canned meat and fish delicacies just because they were either imported or grossly over-priced, preferring even the Indian canned sausage and luncheon meat that began appearing on the market to freely available fresh meat and fish or driving to the "cold storage" for ham or sausages. A local Anglo-Indian, on returning from her trip to England, repeatedly said dreamily, "Oh the *tins* we had," a statement which my father mocked, along with her other pronouncements, "Oh, mangoes are *so* messy," a post-England epiphany, and her answer to her children's dilemma of what to be when they grew up, "Baby, the money is there; the choice is yours."

Serving delicious food was my mother's way of showing care and affection, almost her only way (as later giving jewellery and money were). Thus food—especially sugary, salty, and high-carb snacks—became associated with love, with reward, with caring and uncaring, for nobody, then or now, believed that sugar was a blessing to the human body. My mother produced a constellation of homemade sweets, deep-fried snacks, and buttery melt-in-the-mouth *nankati* sugar cookies while mocking me for "my thighs like the rocks of Gibraltar," though I only weighed a hundred and nineteen pounds when I left school at almost seventeen, definitely a healthy weight. However, because of her lamentations, I believed I was grossly overweight and fatalistically gave up trying to be slender, sowing the seeds of a problem with weight which took decades to begin to reverse, a continuing process.

Once we moved to faculty housing at XLRI, we no longer did anything as a family except eat together. Visits to parks, walks, family games, visits to or from friends, hosting or going to parties all stopped; my mother was probably depressed in the smaller, gardenless flat. I ate breakfast, read; ate lunch, read; had high tea, read; had dinner, read…a novel a day, Jane Austen, Hardy, Aldous Huxley, George Orwell, intellectual energy I am trying to recapture. So, food was our only human interaction, the only break from my self-imposed intellectual intensity, except for the Family Rosary my mother insisted on, a noisy repetition which I found intensely irritating and passionately detested.

"You are too happy," my father said, for I am naturally sanguine and bubbly. "You should develop a worry; that would help you lose weight."

"But what should I worry about, Pa?" I asked.

He thought, and then "Worry about your weight!" he said.

Once I left home, I dealt with stress, busyness, nervousness, boredom, sadness, intensity, and even joy and elation with food—bags of chocolate, potato crisps, and cookies, spicy snacks, or restaurant meals, gaining more than a hundred pounds until I steadily began to reverse that. It is never too late to treat yourself gently. Food is only love when it loves you back, its molecules building mental, emotional, spiritual, intellectual, and physical health. I rarely eat things which cause ill-health anymore–sugar or chocolate or savoury snacks or even bread, rice, or potatoes, in big bites or small. Instead, I fill the treasure box of my heart with other things—reading, running, gardening, meditation, yoga, friendships, travel, gazing at art, hanging out with family, and, always present, the love of God. And writing, always writing.

The Goblin Market

In the unvarying rhythm of childhood, Wednesday was shopping day. All Tuesday evening, my mother pored over her cookery scrapbooks, crammed with recipes clipped from magazines or cajoled from friends, and, sometimes, brought out her classic cookbooks: Premila Lal for North Indian food, Isidore Coelho for Mangalorean food, or, excitingly, *Mrs Beeton's Cookery and Household Management*, a fragile yellowing volume my parents bought on their trip to England in the fifties, during their storied seven years of married life before we existed–of which my mother often spoke, wistfully. And we'd hopefully suggest the foods we'd read of in Enid Blyton, and the English children's books which were the meat-and-boiled-potatoes of our childhood, and thus my mother, with coriander, mint, and chilli powder to enliven the blandness, occasionally made steak-and-kidney pie, Welsh rarebit, and devilled kidneys on toast.

After almost two centuries of British rule, a Sabbath felt like an inalienable right (though no religion except the monotheistic three, Judaism, Christianity, and Islam, observed one). Sunday, the day all schools and offices closed, was too lucrative a day to even consider closing the market on. So the day off in Jamshedpur became a moveable feast, requiring mental agility to remember when the dry cleaners might be closed, the petrol station, or your favourite restaurant.

We shopped on Wednesday since my father flatly refused to be seen food shopping in the market by his clerks, punch operators, and stenotypists on Sunday, when the market was crowded as working men thronged in with their woven plastic or jute bags to shop intently, intensely. Women shopped with more flair and drama. "Oh, come on, twelve rupees for that? Don't try that on *me*!" they'd say, jocular, joshing. And then, suddenly turning shrill, "He wants *twelve rupees* for that old goat he's calling lamb," a woman called to a fellow shopper, "Can you imagine *the cheek*?" And then, after deriding the butcher for trying such a stunt on her, his *best* customer, she'd buy it for eleven. Later, the same aggrieved housewife, bumping into her neighbours, boasted of the amazing deal the butcher had given her, his *special, favourite* customer. "Use my name to him whenever you want a good price," she'd say. *"The buyer says, 'No good, no good', then goes off and boasts of his purchase:"* The Book of Proverbs.

The open-air market closed on Tuesday and resurrected on Wednesday, when the cook accompanied us, carrying our shopping bags. In a world in which pennies counted, vendors did not hand over plastic bags gratis, or at all. Instead, housewives saved plastic bags beneath their mattresses or accepted their fruit in homemade paper bags vendors bought from the paper man who went door to door buying scrap paper which he glued into paper bags. Almost nothing was wasted.

We drove into Bistapur, the shopping district, past "Symphony in Steel," the silvery gyre, past the town's best hotel, the Boulevard, owned by the D'Costas, Goan brothers, and past the Soda Fountain, where my father secretly took me on Saturdays to eat Tutti Frutti ice cream. And past Meghani's, the little general store, from which most gifts given in Jamshedpur were bought and whose shelves were crammed with *everything*--ceramic bowls, vases, lipstick, Scrabble, or The Illustrated Classics, handsome hardbacks.

Behind the little crammed, cramped stores, the open-air market sprawled. We entered through a narrow lane, its drains clogged with rotting banana stalks and overripe crushed custard apples, around which iridescent flies buzzed, attracted by the scent of sweet decay. Lepers sat on makeshift sledges, features paled and blunted by the disease, begging cans balanced on their stumps, wearing an expression of patient despair, dreaded though tolerated. A light-skinned woman with a soft, gentle face shuffled up to us if she saw my father. "Raja Sahib," she said simply, holding out her hand. My father always gave her a rupee because she reminded him of his mother. My mother never did, for probably the same reason.

As we approached, raggle-taggle children stopped playing with stones and tin cans, switched expressions to winsome misery, though with hints of mischief still in their eyes, and extended their palms. To give even one paisa to even one was to become the Pied Piper, people said. You would be mobbed. I experienced this when, with a jumble of guilt and empathy, I gave a child with particularly sad eyes some of the pocket money I'd earned translating a story in English into Hindi for practice—and had saved to buy little sugar-sprinkled colourful chewy jujubes, or boiled sweets shaped into variegated striped marbles, or the segments of an orange, a paisa a piece. The market had the eyes of Argus, and a crowd of plaintive, insistent children suddenly appeared, who refusing to believe that I had no more money followed me, shrilly calling "Ma, Ma, Ma," half-playfully but with sticky hope.

If we did not have the cook with us to carry our haul, my mother hired one of the bare-footed *rejas,* female porters, who squatted at the entrance to the market. They coiled a rag, placed it on their heads, positioned a round bamboo basket on it, and leapt into action, shepherding their shopper to the best buys (or to their own friends), snapping *bakvas,* "Nonsense," when too exorbitant a price was demanded at the outset of the bargaining which prefaced the purchase of a bunch of coriander or a kilo of beef. Even the richest haggled, even with the poorest. Bargaining was a way of life. (My father, almost alone among the shoppers, never bargained. If the price seemed right, he bought; if not, he quietly went on, a strategy I imitate, though I often lazily succumb.) However, my habit of buying something without first asking the price, a habit I haven't quite shaken, infuriated him. "They take one look at your face and say, 'Here's a *buddhu*, a fool, coming,' and then raise the price," he claimed.

At dawn after rainy nights, my mother and the cook went early to the market to snap up wild long-stalked mushrooms, joining the jostling throngs of early shoppers from the Tata Iron and Steel Company, who rapidly stuffed their shopping bags with the freshest fruit and vegetables and the best cuts of meat. Large mushrooms sprouted overnight in the dense green forests around Jamshedpur after heavy rain–mysterious, succulent wonders, beloved by the Adivasi tribal people who gathered them at the first brightening of day and trudged into the city to squat in the market, spreading their precious pickings on an old saree.

Mushrooms, not commercially grown in India then, were coveted by Jamshedpurians on opposite spectrums of society: the more affluent and westernised Indians with Western recipe books, and the Adivasis, the very dark-skinned, aboriginal Indians, who had distinctive tattoos on their foreheads which proclaimed their tribe, Oraon, Kharia, Munda, or Ho. They had lived off the land long before the waves of Aryan migrants, and for them, since childhood, mushrooms had been a secret, unpredictable gift of the Gods. Some Adivasi manual workers, *rejas,* self-exiled from their dense green forests, who, all day, carted away still-hot slag in bamboo baskets on their heads from the blast furnace, sifting it for refinable bits of iron before then taking it to the dump, whose homesickness was compounded by their hot, monotonous work at the steel factory in our industrial city whose skyline belched soot, appeared. They crowded around the expensive, broad-gilled mushrooms, competing with us to snap up a few, then knotting their mushrooms in the corner of their sarees for an after-work treat, went to the steel factory while we returned home and waited for the cook to fry ours with butter, onion, garlic, coriander, and mint and serve them on hot buttered toast, a favourite meal.

We despised vegetables on principle in the immemorial way of children—limp, tasteless, dull, and *so good* for us, whereas sweets, chocolate, and fresh-fried potato crisps, everything we loved, were pronounced *bad* for us. We tried to drag our mother past the vegetable stalls: the glutinous *bhindi*, okra or "lady's fingers;" the deep purple *brinjals*, as they were called in Indian English (aubergines in British English); past *capsicums*, my parents' word for bell peppers; and *karela*, or bitter gourd.

The vendors, village women, often had just a pile of a one vegetable to sell, bounty from a little patch of ground; they sat behind burlap sacking spread with emerald piles of *methi,* fenugreek, or *baaji*, Indian spinach, delicious when fried with onions, finely chopped potatoes, and cumin. In the season of glut, tomatoes were sold so cheaply that my mother felt sorry for the farmers, finding it hard to imagine how they could possibly make any profit.

The fruit market blazed, the air heady with the scent of ripe fruit. I had memorised Christina Rossetti's "The Goblin Market," as a child. Its rhythms and images rainbowed our fruit market.

> *Come, buy, come, buy.*
> *Plump unpecked cherries,*
> *Melons and raspberries,*
> *Swart-headed mulberries,*
> *Pineapples, blackberries,*
> *Pomegranates, full and fine,*
> *Sweet to tongue and sound to eye,*
> *Come buy, come buy.*

The fruit man, *phulwallah,* cross-legged on a plywood platform covered with plastic sheeting, presided over pyramids of edible jewels—maroon cherry-like *jamuns*; *lychees*, the strawberry-red rind concealing translucent ambrosial flesh; pomegranates. Jackfruit of prickly exterior and yellow honey-sweet flesh. The orange, black-toothed grin of sliced papayas. Custard apples, a swiftly melting mouthful of sweetness, shiny black seeds cloaked with sweet, creamy whiteness. Pink-centred guavas. Gooseberries, mulberries, *chickoos* or sapodilla, and roselle, *hibiscus sabdariffa,* tart edible flowers, from which we made jam. Plump orange mangoes-the archetypal and most beloved Indian fruit, occasionally even Alfonso mangoes, "the King of Mangoes," expensive, for the best were exported to the Gulf States where expatriate Indians gladly paid for that nostalgic sweetness, for a taste of India.

We cherry-picked fruit, which the fruitwallah weighed on "cheating scales," my father said wryly as just a few mangoes incredibly swayed still against a rusty kilo weight. If the fruit we had painstakingly picked came up short, the fruit man, at the speed of light, tossed in grapes or *lychees* stacked at the sides of the pyramid closest to him, invariably crushed or rotten, people said–sadly true, unlike other childhood bogies: that a tree would grow in your stomach if you swallowed an apple seed, the branches emerging from your ears, as a classmate said; or that your stomach would devour its own lining if you went to bed hungry, as my mother said.

* * *

The charnel house of the meat market felt cold as we stepped in from the blaze. The butchers sat cross-legged on stone platforms, behind carcasses dangling by their heels from hooks. In bloody drains, I spotted hooves of cows, the hairy ends of their tails, brown glinting eyeballs, and sometimes a bladder, still bouncy and yellow. They rapped prices: "Beef, four rupees," "Pork, eight rupees," "Mutton, ten rupees kilogram." (Chicken, the most expensive meat, was, like crab, bought live.)

Prices reflected demography. Beef was the cheapest meat; not many ate it since cows are revered by Hindus, who make up eighty per cent of India's population. While some Hindus (known as "non-vegetarians") eat meat, fewer eat sacred cows. Fundamentalist Hindus decried cow slaughter as an evil of a rapidly secularising society (which, nevertheless, remained so conservative in my girlhood that one rarely saw a kiss or nudity on the heavily censored screen or, in real life, an adult woman's knees! If adults touched in public, it was girls holding their female friend's hands and men linking arms with their mates.) Pork was *haraam*, prohibited to India's fourteen per cent Muslim minority, otherwise avowed "non-vegetarians," who have contributed Mughlai cuisine–biryanis, kormas, kebabs, and some say Tandoori and Butter Chicken–to India's cuisine. All "non-vegetarians," Hindu, Muslim, Christian, and Parsee, ate chicken and lamb: "mutton," though people suspected that "mutton" of being goat or dog. I remember my Jesuit Uncle, Fr. Theo Mathias, summoning the restaurant's owner to complain, "You call this mutton? It's stringy old goat!" Chicken was the most expensive meat, everyone's favourite, served at every festive occasion in bright pilaus and biriyanis.

Organ meats lay heaped on stone slabs–kidney, liver, heart, tongue, and brains, more expensive because more coveted. My mother filled her plastic shopping bag with slippery pink kidneys, large beef tongues, liver, and white, soft, mushy brains, for we loved home-salted tongue, fried lamb's kidneys devilled with onions and tomatoes on deep-fried toast, and tolerated tender brain "cutlets," croquettes. According to folk wisdom, eating brains made you brainier! (Fish was another universally accepted brain food, as were almonds.)

Nothing was wasted, nose to tail. We returned with inexpensive bags of *rathim*—meaty bones and scraps—for our German shepherd Brutus, which we served boiled with huge-grained brown rice, the cheapest rice, the food of the poorest, just as *atta,* brown flour was. White rice and *maida*, refined white flour, were more expensive. (Our dietary mores ironically favoured the health of the poor, as in *ancien regime* France, where peasants ate crusty brown bread, and the aristocracy bread baked from the lightest, whitest, most devitalised flour).

My family were thoroughly carnivorous; a meal without meat or fish was not a meal. The archetypal dishes of Mangalore, my ancestral hometown, were pork: *vindaloos*, thick gravies dimpled with floating circles of fat, and, most famously, *sarpatel*, pork curry in blood sauce. Jamshedpur's pork came from "*jungli*," free-ranging pigs kept by the enterprising who allowed them to roam backstreets, nosing into drains and rubbish heaps for food. Since people also relieved themselves in those drains, those flavourful *jungli* pigs were notoriously infested by tapeworms, which they transmitted to humans--a nightmarish parasitic infection, tricky to eliminate.

Father Theo Mathias, my father's brother, (whom I called Theo the Great) had become preternaturally health-conscious while he represented India at the General Assembly of the United Nations, which he addressed in 1975 and 1976; he dreaded meningitis and encephalitis, thought to be transmitted by pigs. Theo gazed longingly at the red-ochre *sarpatel* and *vindaloos* and then asked, severely, if the pork was factory-raised or *jungli*. "Factory raised," the hostess rapidly, glibly assured him. (But since we lived in Bihar, among India's least developed states, accepting this claim of a sophisticated food supply required the willing suspension of disbelief). Theo ate the pork, remembering the *sarpatel* of his youth, then told us why the Almighty forbade the ancient Jews pork. "They had such good lives with all those wives and concubines, and all that honey and wine that God said: 'I must withhold one good thing from this people.' And He chose pork."

Poultry were sold live from large round bamboo baskets, the rope netting confining a squirming, ammoniac mass of agitated feathers—iridescent-feathered ducks, brown speckled hens, gay-plumaged cockerels. One could increasingly get factory-raised birds in my childhood, snowy white leghorns, or "broilers," which had snob value because they were expensive, though they were, ironically, fatty, bland, and savourless compared to the lean, flavourful *junglis.* "It's a leghorn," people would say, faux-casually, code for "an expensive, classy meal from the "cold storage" has been provided for your delectation." We gradually realised that the tastiest hens were not factory-farmed leghorns, but the little brown speckled hens left to forage for themselves and grow full-flavoured on worms and chance scraps, and so we reverted to eating those plucky, wandering fowl.

Bending over the wriggling feathery birds, I inhaled the warm, pungent, comforting smell of fowl. "This one:" we pointed out orange-brown chickens with beautifully speckled feathers and sweet dispositions, or sometimes, a snowy-white hen of showy beauty; a duck with a gleaming blue-green chest, or a bright-plumaged cockerel who'd enliven our mornings with triumphant car-olling. My mother poked the chicken's chest--a firm chest being a sign of youth in hens as in women. The chosen chicken was then trussed and handed to our cook to be carried through the market upside down and squawking, struggling to hold its head up. I protested, often tearfully, but the *murgiwallah*, chicken man, my mother, and the cook all assured me, with some magical thinking, that the chickens did not mind, that it did not hurt them, and that, in fact, this was *the* way to carry chickens

Roast chicken with stuffing was the consolation of Sundays, its succu-lence compensating for the boredom of Sunday Mass. When a hen we'd loved appeared on the Sunday table, roasted, I was sad but dispassionately did not see why I should not eat it since it was already dead. When I informed my sister, not without mischief, that this had been *Coco Baccha* or Betsy Hen, she burst into tears and refused to eat. "It's no longer the same creature," I said as I ate her share. We had competing areas of toughness. I was afraid of ghosts; she was not. She ate *capsicums*, red peppers, in sandwiches. Their seeds resembled chillies, so I was afraid to, after my father mischievously told me, with botanical accuracy, that capsicums were giant chillies. I watched my father and little sister eat them in sandwiches with a kind of wonder while remaining too cowardly to try.

* * *

Acrid drains in which bloody innards and iridescent fish scales glinted led to the cacophony of the fish market. The sure knowledge that fish not sold that day would (given the rudimentary refrigeration of blocks of sawdust-coated ice) begin to stink gave the voices of the fisherwomen that edge of desperation that makes "yelling like a fishwife" a multi-lingual simile. "Pomfret, ten *rupya seer*, *bhangra*, mackerel, eight *rupya seer*," women outshouted each other; fish was oddly sold by the *seer*, one and a quarter kilogram. Whole catfish, carp and *mah-seer*, Indian salmon lolled on ice, prawns occupying the pride of place. It was vital to buy fresh fish, as all the fishermen assured you theirs were. Those initiated in the housewifely kabbalah inspected eyes and gills with a frowning show of caution, brushing the flesh to gauge its firmness.

Crabs in wicker baskets, covered with rope netting, crawled over each other, trying to escape. We pointed at the biggest, who were hauled out, had their legs snapped off with pincers, and were poured, still alive, into our plastic shopping bag to be curried. I screamed in empathetic horror as the crabman broke their legs; he laughed, assuring me that the crabs felt nothing. The casual cruelty of the marketplace! Once, just in front of our car, a man relentlessly beat a mule overladen with bags of grain which was too exhausted to take another step, despite the beating. I burst into hysterical tears. My father offered the man a rupee to stop.

My mother, my sister and I sat in a circle on the veranda that evening, shelling peas, painstakingly extracting crabmeat from its shell for crab cutlets, and deveining prawns before they were cooked with potatoes and tomatoes, or pickled—time-consuming tasks that would have derailed the cook's finely-tuned schedule, for he still needed to serve our multicourse dinners on time.

* * *

The heavens operatically burst during the monsoon, roads transformed into muddy rivulets, torrents racing past our ankles in rippling chevrons, bearing mango peels, sugarcane stalks and dung from overflowing gutters. We dashed to the used bookstore for shelter.

Books in the town's only public lending library, my father claimed, had chunks of the most thrilling pages ripped out, and their dirty pages transmitted disease. We never entered them but instead exhausted the children's bookcases at our two private clubs, furtively borrowed from the adult shelves, and used the second-hand bookstore as a *de facto* lending library. The town had no bookstore!

I traded the paperbacks I'd read and didn't want to reread at the used bookstore. The man exchanged two of ours for one of his, almost unquestioningly, judging books by covers and condition rather than by author, title, or content. He'd buy tattered paperbacks with resale potential and rebind them, pasting on the cropped cover, but spurned hardbacks: they took too much space, and people, assuming they were intimidating and boring, never bought them. The dealer seemed just about literate and probably did not read the English language books he traded but, nevertheless, stayed in business by instinct, shrewdness, and a good memory.

Books were treated with respect in India, covered with old calendar pages or brown paper. Some of my classmates kissed any book they inadvertently dropped or touched it to their heads, as if making amends for this trespass against learning. It was a crude habit of *babus*, semi-educated clerks, the nuns at boarding school said, to bend a book in half to keep your place, or to dog-ear its pages as a rough-and-ready bookmark, or, heaven forbid, to moisten your finger with spit to rapidly leaf through it. To throw a book into a dustbin was unthinkable; books accumulated in heaped bookshelves, in cupboards, every-where; were lent or given away but never ever thrown away. So we sometimes acquired antique books that had floated around since the British Raj, which ended fourteen and a half years before I was born. I love old books, the fading cloth binding with gold lettering, the thick yellowing pages with rough-cut crin-kly edges, the conquistador pleasure of slitting uncut pages, the first time human eyes had read *those* words on *that* page. I checked publication dates, both the word "antique" and actually handling one, filling me with sensuous pleasure.

With a mixture of ambition, drivenness, perfectionism, the thirst for knowledge, and the love of reading, I–impractically–wanted to read *every* classic ever written. When I finished a book, I wistfully studied the lists of "Also Pub-lished By" at the back, exultantly ticking off those I had read and fiercely longing to read those I had not: Rabelais, Cervantes, Erasmus... I studied the floor-to-ceiling stacks of books, hunting for high culture, steadily upgrading any fluffy or "low-brow" book in the house. My father marvelled at the speed at which I could find a good book among hundreds in the stacks of the library or second-hand bookstore, which I did almost instinctively, my heart leaping at beloved logos: plump penguins, puffins, and pelicans; the sprinting torchbearer, a frowning sun, the medieval pilgrim, the signet ring, steadfastly choosing the classics I thought I "should" read, independently evolving a code resembling Matthew Arnold's: "Life is too short to read much more than the best that has been thought and said."

I discovered in that little second-hand bookstore *The Cloister and the Hearth* about the parents of Erasmus, for heaven's sake (started many times, never finished); *Kenilworth* by Walter Scott about doomed Amy Robarts, pushed down the stairs by Leicester, who hoped to upgrade her for Queen Elizabeth herself; Stevenson's *The Master of Ballantrae*, *The Admirable Crichton*, a strange sex-ually charged play by J. M. Barrie (and a sort of precursor to *Lady Chatterley's*

Lover!), and Somerset Maugham's spiritual *The Razor's Edge* which I adored—flotsam and jetsam of our colonial heritage! And thus, by stealth, I assembled an aspirational library of classics in my teens and actually read them, in defiance of the snide definition of a classic: "a book which everyone wants to *have* read, but no one wants to actually read."

Not so were most customers. Chauffeured cars stopped outside, and portly matrons, great bunches of keys, betokening household responsibilities, jingling from their waists, dashed in with a large paper bag of Mills and Boons, formulaic romances from the British pulp factory. And dashed out again, having traded them for Denise Robbins, Barbara Cartland, or Harley Street doctor-nurse romances—that tsunami of syrupy, sappy novels that engulfed girls as they reached puberty. Some women lingered at the Mills and Boon stage, still reading those sweet, sentimental romances, identifying, in wish-fulfilment fantasy, with the insipid, conniving heroines who netted Tall, Dark, Handsome (and, of course, rich) men who were besotted with them. (TDH, we schoolgirls mocked the typical Western romance hero with unconscious irony, for we ourselves, in unquestioned prejudice, favoured somewhat lighter-skinned men). Reading: the opiate of the literate.

* * *

My mother sometimes stopped at the jeweller's to browse, for Indian women are obsessed with jewellery. We watched women bring in their heavy gold jewellery to be weighed and refashioned and drunk in the array of necklaces, bracelets, earrings, and toe rings glittering on their bier of azure or scarlet satin, the ancient beauty of sapphires, emeralds, rubies, diamonds, and gold sinking into the blood.

We each had a jewellery box for our costume jewellery, a dazzling panoply of rings, clip-on nose rings and bead necklaces, glass bangles, and stainless-steel bracelets, which my parents played at over-valuing. Once on hearing them fret about my erratic boarding school bills, to which I had charged frivolous things, Shalini sadly and valiantly appeared with her jewellery box: "Don't worry about Anita's bills, Ma and Pa," she said. "You can sell my jewellery."

* * *

To skip the last and sweetest shop, the reward for all our labours, was unthinkable. My heart raced as I entered the sweet shop–dazzling geometry, bright neon rainbowed tiers: diamonds of *kaju burfi,* cashew nut fudge; squares of leaf-green pistachio *burfi,* a rich milky sweet; spheres of golden-brown *besan burfi,* a comforting golden sweet made with chickpea flour; and rectangles of carrot halwa, oozing ghee and studded with slivered almonds and raisins.

I pointed in barely contained excitement, wanting one of *everything* in the store, which I sometimes got when we ordered mixed sweets. "A moment on your lips, a lifetime on your hips," my mother warned, smirking with delight at the witticism. My father scowled at the neon pink, red, yellow, and orange colours: "Most food colouring is toxic!" Ignoring Cassandra words, we chose the brightest sweets. So what if we poisoned ourselves with infinitesimal swirls of colour! Children believe they'll live forever.

My father always scraped the thin leaf of beaten silver off the *badaam burfi,* almond fudge, with his fingernails; the "silver" was toxic aluminium, he feared. "They wouldn't waste money on real silver when people would never know the difference," he snorted. Once we reached home, my father happily headed for the white paper carton of sweets in the refrigerator the moment he woke up in the morning, before going to work, before lunch, after lunch, when he felt like a snack, at tea, before dinner, after dinner, and before going to sleep—a habit I acquired from him, though now, in middle age, I no longer lead myself into temptation by bringing anything sweet home.

Indians have a national sweet tooth, and every celebration, congratulatory occasion, or surge of goodwill is marked by gifts of *dudhpedas,* a milky fudge, or *rasgullas,* light, super-sweet milky balls floating in cardamom-flavoured sugar syrup. Sugar is deemed a necessity, a *de facto* food group, and both sugar and *gur,* jaggery, rich-flavoured, unrefined sugar, appeared, along with rice, wheat, lentils, oil, and harsh soap on the ration card—heavily subsidised essentials available to every Indian, rich and poor alike. It's used daily–to make sweets or siphon into the immensely sweet fragrant tea served in little clay disposable cups in makeshift tea carts and dark, grimy *dhabas* and consumed around the clock as a quick energiser.

My mother sent the cook to the ration shop to claim our family's rations; we then traded with him, exchanging our ration of stuff we did not eat—large-grained brown rice and grains like bulghur or *ragi,* millet--for his share of what he considered pricey, even at ration prices: white rice, and white flour or *maida,* more expensive than the coarse whole-wheat flour*, atta.* (As far as health was concerned, Durga got the better of the bargain!) *Gur,* full-bodied as molasses, which came in golden brown lumps, we did not trade. I loved *gur,* which my mother rationed, and I declared that, when I finally grew up or went to heaven, synonymous states in my mind, I would eat as much *gur,* condensed milk, and chocolate as I wanted. Heaven, not as the land of eternal, ecstatic worship as in the Prophet Isaiah, but as the land of Cockaigne conjured up by the medieval imagination in the hunger years–where roasted piglets pranced, squealing "eat me;" grilled geese flew into your mouth, and the skies rained cheese. I sometimes checked on the commodity prices of cocoa in *The Statesman,* looking forward to the day when chocolate would be cheap and I could eat as much as I wanted. The day eventually came, and I did–but no longer.

* * *

An iridescent halo of flies, occasionally shattered by impatient hands, buzzed around the vendors and their little pushcarts at the entrance to the marketplace. We'd have *nimbu pani,* lime juice squeezed in front of us while we watched, or sugarcane juice. The glasses were retrieved from a tin bucket into which they were dunked to clean them between customers; the ice was chipped off a sawdust-coated block, but if we were thirsty enough, we drank anyway, trusting in immune system miracles. The vendor placed fat stalks of sugarcane between the iron jaws of his juicer and muscles bulging, turned the handle, extracting every drop of juice, then offered it to us, nectar with a twist of lemon.

Men, squatting above little coal stoves, sold skewered *kaleji*, liver kebabs. ("It's probably dog's liver, not lamb's," my father said). There were deep-fried *pakoras*, vegetables in chickpea batter. ("Careful. That oil has probably been re-used so often it's rancid. It can give you hepatitis," my father cautioned.) We sometimes got bright red ice lollies from little pushcarts over my mother's objections; she claimed they were made from filthy water scooped from gutters—since the slum-dwellers who sold them didn't have access to municipal water—and would give us urinary infections (which, to be fair, I did develop.)

On the way home, we filled up at Esso, the local petrol pump owned by Mr Gabba, just a few litres because petrol rapidly evaporated in the heat. His promotion: On filling up, the child of the family drew a bead from a bag; a red bead earned a prize, sometimes no more than a bar of Lux Supreme, a pricier scented soap. I invariably drew the red bead, and the one time I didn't, asked the mechanic to let me try again and remember his cross, darkened face when, sure enough, once again, I drew … a red bead.

And, almost daily, the market came to us. Clank, clank: At the peremptory banging on our green wrought iron gates, children, dogs, and servants rushed onto the veranda. Both etiquette and ubiquitous guard dogs forbade entering a garden without this ceremony. A visitor sometimes, or a vendor. The breadman brought a daily loaf of fresh sliced white bread. The milkman cycled up with large clanging tin cans on either side of his bike, full of rich buffalo milk, still warm from the udder, which we boiled to pasteurise, skimming off the cream to make ice cream or *ghee*, clarified butter; nevertheless, he was suspected of watering down his milk. When the cook boiled down the pot of saved cream, the house filled with a tantalising aroma as it reduced to *ghee,* the ambrosial crème de la crème, butter of butter, which, like a magic spell, made everything–pilau rice or Indian sweets–taste even more delicious. Ghee was considered obscenely decadent and, illogically, more fattening than butter (perhaps because it made food "morish"), and food cooked with it was both loved and dreaded.

The *andawallah,* egg man, brought fresh brown eggs, and an Adivasi tribal man brought hives, gathered from the forest, and smoked out, from which he had to squeeze fresh honey in front of us, or else my mother suspected it of being adulterated with sugar water. Nevertheless, the honey solidified, which it should not have, and the tell-tale film of grainy crystallised sugar revealed that he had, indeed, doused his hives with sugar syrup and let them dry out before his rounds.

The *kachrawallah,* "rubbish man," appeared, offering to buy scrap paper, rags, old tin cans, or empty bottles, which led to crises of conscience, for sometimes pristine perfume or liquor bottles were filled with an adulterated simulacrum and sold as new. Sometimes conscience won; sometimes, we took cash.

The *dhobi,* the washerman, collected heavy clothes and grimy whites, which he flayed on rocks by the river; the lighter ones, the *ayah* hand-washed at home. The *mochi,* cobbler, came around, aesthetically mending ramshackle slippers and sandals and even resoling shoes, using old tires. The magazine man delivered *Femina, India Today* and *The Illustrated Weekly of India.* Afghans, Pathans, "Kabuliwallahs," sold dried fruit and nuts straight from the deserts of Arabia, they said. My father gaily pronounced them to be cheats but bought anyway; he adored dates. And, during the Indo-Pakistan war, refugees from East Pakistan, then morphing to Bangladesh, arrived at our gates, begging, bringing tales of rape and torture perpetrated by the Pakistani army. We listened, wide-eyed and appalled.

Animals visited: Wizen-faced monkeys apparelled in little dresses or trousers and waistcoats pranced and leap-frogged over each other for small change. A Himalayan black bear in female clothes, led by a heavy metal ring through her nostrils, tottered onto our front lawn on her back paws. "See, she's dancing," the trainer said. The hysteria of dogs alerted us to a gaily caparisoned tame elephant ambling down our street. It came up to our veranda, knelt on his front legs, and curled his trunk upwards into a salaam. "He's saying Namaste," the mahout said, offering us a ride, which I was too scared to accept. And once: a cobra in a basket raised his hooded head and swayed at the charmer's flute. I screamed.

Once home, my mother unlocked her cupboard to store her staples in the tidy rows of bottles or tins, which had once housed store-bought jam or Bournvita, the caramelly malted powder without which we refused to drink milk, while we, still unsated, begged handfuls of *kismis*, raisins, nuts or *gur*.

Shalini and I each had "treasure chests," now emptied of the much-loved imported Quality Street chocolates; on them, an elegant, overdressed Georgian couple promenaded beneath a parasol. Into these, with a proud sense of thrift, we poured our "savings:" Phantom cigarettes with false red glowing tips; tiny technicolour candies with a cumin centre; Chiclet chewing gum, Lacto Bon-bons, or waxpaper-wrapped Parlé toffees. We headed for these tins after meals, munificently offering everyone supplementary dessert. Sometimes, we stored a piece of Cadbury's chocolate or moist fudge-like *burfi* there, and everything melted, and the colours ran, and we opened our tins to tearfully survey a shape-less mouldy rainbow. And once again, I renounced thrift and all its works. But initiations are not easy, into shopping or housewifery.

Parks, Restaurants, and Things Bright and Beautiful

"You wake and hear the birds cough," people said of Jamshedpur. But as children: Air pollution? We never considered it. For us, Jamshedpur was the city of parks and gardens: the Locomotive Park in the neighbouring company town, TELCO (an acronym for The Tata Electric Locomotive Company), with the locomotive we'd "drive," saying *Locomotive, locomotive, put on steam;* the airplane in Aeroplane Park we "flew;" the Clock Park, with a clock made of flowers, whose moving, flower-planted hands accurately told time.

And, above all, glorious Jubilee Park, which people pronounced as one word: *JubliPark!*, created to celebrate Tata Iron and Steel's fiftieth anniversary. We wandered through headily scented mazy rose gardens, beds of rainbowed colour, blood-red, violet, improbably blue or near-black roses. Dancing floodlights transformed the fountains into molten jewels: ruby, sapphire, sunflower, then orange, leaping leopards, burning tigers.

Bridges arched over streams; I gazed down and felt dizzy. "Perhaps you suffer from vertigo," my father said. *Vertigo, vertiginous.* I liked the sound of the words.

From little wheeled carts, we bought groundnuts, "monkey nuts," we called them, freshly roasted with salt and chilli powder, still scorching from the coals. A compulsive reader, yearning for mystery and excitement, I read the handmade paper bags, made of old magazines or scrap paper, as I chafed off their wispy red coats. Would I read a neighbour's secret love letters or their version of meticulous household account books my parents kept? And, since we sold our old exercise books to the vendors who came door to door, I secretly hoped that one day I'd be told by a friend or their parents, "I read your school essay on my peanuts bag. It was brilliant." Fame!

* * *

My father and I sometimes walked alone by moonlight around the lake in Jubilee Park, now glazed silver, until I felt a stitch knot my sides and whimpered. "Keep walking," my father said. "The lactic acid will dissipate. Your second wind will come."

"Impossible," I moaned. "Impossible," until the blessed second wind came.

My father imparted basic training, survival skills.

"When *goondas* and bandits waylay you, and say, 'Your money or your life,' *always* say, 'Take my money.'"

"Huh! And what would you say, Pa?"

"Take my wife. Please." He chuckled.

* * *

As we walked past the lake of liquid silver, long after dark, my father said, "This is dangerous, you know. We could get robbed; we could get murdered." People feared terrorist attacks by the Naxalites, far-left radical communists. "Don't worry, Pa. I'll protect us," I said and took the dagger, *kukri*, with an intricately carved sheath, which my parents had bought on their honeymoon in Kashmir.

As dark shadows loomed in the distance, I charged at them, whooping threats, my beautiful *kukri* carving circles in the air.

"*Bacchao, Sahib, Bacchao,*" voices yelled in good-natured faux terror. "Save us, Sir. Save us." The shadows were *rejas*, female manual labourers, walking miles to their villages after a hard day's work at the steel factory.

Everyone laughed.

Except me.

* * *

On an island in the centre of this lake, clever impracticality, was a restaurant, overpriced, and so a treat. Row, row, row your hired boat there.

And there: golden *masala dosas*, South Indian delicacies, restaurant food, eighteen-inch-long crisp paper-thin rice-flour crepes, protruding far beyond the stainless-steel plate, bursting with their stuffing of oniony, turmeric-bright, mustard-seeded potatoes, served with little stainless-steel bowls of coconut chutney, coriander chutney, and *sambhar*, spicy *dhal* with vegetables and large red chillis.

Dosas demand the sensory pleasure of being eaten with one's fingers: a multi-phasic ritual. Crack the crisp crust at the centre; pour *sambhar* over the potatoes; spoon in coconut chutney, then tear off bits from the edges of the *dosa* and use them to scoop up fingerfuls of soft potato with piping hot *sambhar* sauce, and cool leaf-green coconut chutney: a magical mouthful of flavours.

I had a restaurant ritual: I seized the pepper shakers and sniffed and sneezed, sniffed and sneezed, chanting like Lewis Carroll's violent duchess, *"Speak roughly to your little boy/ And beat him when he sneezes/ He only does it to annoy/ Because he knows it teases."* "Stop it!" my mother said sharply. But I only did it to annoy because I knew it teases.

* * *

Sometimes, when my parents longed for the foods of their childhood, we drove miles to the town's only South Indian restaurant in Sakchi, dark, crowded, and scruffy, my father, glancing around, frowning and furtive. He was Controller of Accounts at Tata Iron and Steel, Senior Management, and, since Jamshedpur was intensely class-conscious, did not want to be spotted at so down-market an establishment by the clientele: TISCO's manual labourers, clerks, and secretaries from South India.

However, the crisp comfort of the *dosas*, almost impossible to mimic at home, compensated for his embarrassment at being seen among the throngs of voluble working-class South Indian families out on a Saturday morning treat; bachelor workers who ate all their meals there, or the man of the family, splurging his earnings on himself.

My parents nostalgically ordered the tastes of their South Indian childhood, which now, in memory, have become the tastes of *my* North Indian childhood. South Indian food totally differs from the foods of the North; besides dosas, there's *upma*, semolina fried with split peas, colourful chopped vegetables, and spices, pleasing to the eye and palate; *uttapam*, a spicy rice-flour pancake; *vadas*, spicy lentil cumin-flecked doughnuts; *masala vadas*, spicy patties made from split lentils, and *idlis*, tasteless ovals of ground steamed rice, that compensated for their blandness by their baptism with spicy *sambhar*.

The waiter brought scalding, very sweet coffee to the table, which he cooled before us by pouring the fragrant, steaming coffee river from a stainless steel "tumbler" in one outstretched hand to one three feet below, tumbler to tumbler, until it was drinkable. Not a drop was spilt. He beamed with pleasure at his own dexterity. Coffee by the yard, my father said, *soto voce*. Coffee is *the* drink of the South with its coffee plantations, while North Indians, with their tea plantations, drink tea, *chai*, for breakfast and at teatime, often grabbing little clay cups of tea from *dhabas*, shacks, or roadside carts with their always-bubbling brass cauldrons of sweet milky tea, doctored periodically with more milk, sugar, or tea leaves.

* * *

The restaurant of my heart was Frank's, the oddly named and only Chinese restaurant in town, run, equally oddly, by Chinese Catholics. It was green-walled and green-lit by little dim hurricane lamps on a filigree base, illuminating tables on which cruets of soya sauce and red seed-speckled chilli sauce lay like promises of better things.

We pored over the old greasy menu, whorled with soya-sauce thumb-prints, reading blissfully, like Dennis the Menace and Joey, who, claiming, "We can't read", get the waitress to read each of the ninety-seven flavours of ice cream; listen joyfully, and then, choose, once again--plain vanilla. And the wait-ress sighs: "They always do it."

But I knew what I wanted, and I wanted nothing but it: "Franks' Special Chow Mein" and "Franks' Special Fried Rice." They *were* Chinese food to me, and I had to have both.

"You always order the same thing," my mother said. "You can't just have starch. We need a main dish." She ordered sweet and sour pork and sweetish chicken chop suey, fried crisp, which I refused to touch. Things should be either sweet or savoury, and meat, fish and vegetables should *never* be sweet, I believed. Laodicean in-betweenness was heretical!

Then the restless, intolerable wait. The sound of steel on wok, the scent of soya sauce and aromatic oils sharpened my senses with anticipatory hunger and reduced all thought and conversation to a single, oft-repeated sentence: *"When will it come?"*

And with a flourish, the meal came: to my taste buds, perfection--steam-ing platters of wriggly noodles, glistening with flecks of oil, soya sauce and *ajinomoto*, or MSG, and rainbowed with... our forks explored: slivers of pork, beef, prawn, chicken, onion, red and green bell peppers, delicate Chinese vege-tables, and slithery black mushrooms, slippery unctuous pleasure.

Indian Chinese food, I'm told, is not like everyday Chinese food; it's closer to Chinese banquet food--spicier and far richer. The fried rice was all the colours of a pastel spring: green onions, carrots, pink shrimp, bacon, and slivers of omelette. We flecked the whiteness with soya sauce. I ate rapidly, ecstatically.

Everyone, including my mother, liked prawn best, so she offered hers around, on fork tip, and we accepted, greed conquering guilt.

Finally, I absolutely could eat no more. And always, the same wonder: I entered the car satiated, then realised as it pulled into our driveway that I felt hungry again. How could this be?

* * *

On Sundays, once we had got Mass–our family's non-negotiable habit–out of the way, we picked up four white square fragrant cardboard cake boxes of Chinese takeaway from Franks and drove to a "beauty spot," often by the still waters of Dimna Dam, the boxes sitting warm and comforting as a hen in our laps, leaking soya sauce and oil, the tantalizing aroma of Chinese food filling the car, present torture for future pleasure, making me agonizingly, unbearably impatient.

In Manjooti Square at Dalma Hills, after lunch and after my sister and I raced to collect *manjootis*, pretty, red black-eyed seeds, nature's beads dropped from the coralwood tree, the family sat on the grass or on the concrete seats around spreading banyan trees and played Scrabble, a game I loved. My father and I played impetuously, sacrificing long-term gains for a present buzz, while my mother played circumspectly, competitively, suspending us in a limbo of hope and dread, while she stealthily went for triple word scores, word domination, the kill. Lexicon, like Scrabble but played with a pack of cards instead of tiles, was our other picnic word game.

We once took our neighbour, Anne Cherian, on a picnic to Riversmeet at the supposedly sacred confluence of the Subarnarekha and Kharkai rivers, a beloved picnic spot. After a favourite picnic lunch of chilli chicken, a mixture of soya sauce, ground chillis, ginger and garlic, I slipped away with Annie while my parents rested on *dhurries* in post-prandial sluggishness. We walked across the beach of hot glittering sand, across the sandy spit that had appeared in the centre of the river at low tide, to the other side where the *rejas,* female labourers, were making bricks from sand and red clay, like a Pharaonic punishment; Jamshedpur was rapidly growing. We watched while the tide came in until the slender bar of sand was no more. The setting sun bathed the river a glowing orange. And somewhere, on the other side of the bridgeless river, were my parents.

I was excited. Lost, lost! Marooned. An adventure! The dusk chorus stepped up: chirping crickets, buzzing gnats and mosquitoes, crows cawing as they winged to high trees. With curious glances, the *rejas* left. "Annie, let's run away," I said, heading *away* from where we had left our parents on the opposite bank, and so we did until our legs filled with lactic acid, and the fun went out of it. Annie cried.

And then, hearing footsteps, we turned around to see a dark figure loom in the dusk. But it did not say, "Your money or your life." For, I realised, my heart sinking, it was my father, his face threatening Egyptian plagues. He was in his mid-fifties; his gait betrayed exhaustion. And though he did not want to talk about it, now or ever, I later learned that he had walked for an hour until he found a spot shallow enough to wade across in the rising tide. Annie stopped crying. Had I been prescient, I would have started.

"Come," my father growled. "We were running away, Pa!" I said brightly. I was safe in Annie's presence. Outsiders were sanctuary, no dirty linen, or skeletons on display outside the family, just sweetness and light. We drove home in ominous silence until Annie was dropped off. And then, vengeance, I forget the precise instrument, a belt, perhaps.

"See how upset Pa is. See the veins stand out on his forehead," my mother said. "I hope he doesn't have a heart attack." And I felt terror at the thought of my father's early death, a terror repeated through the dramas of my annual trip to boarding school, "Pa's veins... Heart attack…" and I'd go to school petrified and pray for my father's life at Mass…

But I still tried to run away.

* * *

Wedding invitations arrived through the year, singly or in floods: on whimsical, handmade woven cloth paper, gilt-edged, gold-lettered, gold-tas-selled, addressed extravagantly, Shri N.J. Mathias, Family and Friends.

Weddings: A time for generosity. A time to show off, a time *not* to lose face. (Why wasn't So-and-So invited? *They couldn't afford it.* Nobody wanted that said.) So, hosts invited comprehensively, wildly, full of forgotten-fairy terror: yhe bad luck, the wagging tongues, the instant enmity. Social ambition, pride, fear, and conformity lurked behind the profligacy, hundreds of guests at weddings, many of whom the bride and groom barely knew. And this heedless, magnificent potlatch burned up years of saving commenced at the birth of a daughter or started a new cycle of paying down wedding debts. A disconsolate dog barking near the *shamiana*, the wedding marquee, is meant to bring bad luck; how much more to turn "a guest" away. Two of my teenage cousins, Sunil and Dennis, invested in a suit and tie and showed up repeatedly at Bombay weddings to which they had not been invited, at the Taj and Sheraton and Sun and Sands, for the meals of their lives.

"Let's go, Pa," we'd say as invitations arrived. "I don't know who the hell they are. Never heard of 'em," he muttered. TISCO had thirty thousand employees whom my father, head of the crucial Account Department, knew slightly, if at all. Showing up at the wedding of people he didn't know? To what favours might that obligate him? Sometimes, however, we prevailed.

Hindu weddings were unlike our Catholic weddings, which were borrowed from a Western playbook--"Here comes the bride, all dressed in white," "given away" by her father, "something old, something new, something borrowed, something blue," and then *sarpatel* and waltzes in the church hall. Here: jingle, jingle, comes the bride, all dressed in red, queen for a day, wearing the traditional bridal necklace, the *Navratna*, gold with nine traditional precious stones: ruby, emerald, pearl, coral, garnet, blue sapphire, cat's eye, yellow sapphire, and diamond. With rings on her fingers and bells on her ankles, nose rings, earrings, toe rings, an armful of bangles, a clutter of necklaces, and a *maangtika*, a string of gold and jewels, tumbling down her centre parting marked with red powder (indication that she was now a *sumangali*, a woman of good fortune, that is: married!). Happy hennaed patterns on hands and feet, bright make-up, and the glitter of jewellery made the plainest woman dazzle.

Garlanded with hibiscus and marigolds, almost obscured by their finery, the bride and groom sat on a flower-decked dais, radiating nervous excitement. They had probably exchanged no more than perfunctory courtesies if it was an arranged marriage--as it almost always was. The few love marriages then, which the town regarded frowningly, often involved girls from poorer families, with more beauty than dowry, whose mothers put them up to it, other families bitterly said.

Crowded parking lot, crowded hall. Hundreds of guests sat at tables in long rows, or sometimes on the floor, women on one side of the hall, men on the other. Relatives bustled around, puffed up with importance, cauldrons balanced on their hips. From this apparently bottomless cornucopia, they coax, cajole, almost force people they do not know to eat, eat, eat up, offering seconds, thirds. A runny mass on the banana leaf: Fish out the chicken from the chicken pilau, the mutton from the mutton biriyani. Eagerly await the dessert: *jalebis*, a crisp orange mouthful bursting with flavourful syrup. Gleefully accept seconds.

Then we children, self-importantly and self-consciously, went up to add our present to the pile in front of the couple, a cheque, or one of the multiples of bedspreads, vases, ceramics, and brass knickknacks, more than a lifetime's worth, so that the couple were set for the wedding gifts *they* would give for the first few years of their married life--and it was for life. Divorce, in our small town, was almost unheard of: women made the accommodations, and, anyway, small-town life, lived in the public eye, was not conducive to affairs. Marriage was a financial transaction between families, the bride's family handing over as large a dowry as they could afford on the understanding that the groom would look after their daughter for the rest of her life.

Children raced around. *Hijras* arrived, members of India's storied transgender community—powerful bodies, masculine jaws, bright, slattered make-up, carelessly draped sarees, long hair bleached or hennaed orange, loose or in buns. They danced, swaying, singing, clapping hands while banging their *tablas*, hand-held drums. They were given money and sent on their way. The song and blessing of hijras at a wedding or the birth of a child, poignant events for people called "the third gender," was meant to bring good luck. Children were cautioned not to stare or comment (though they mimicked the *hijras* once they left), for a *hijra's* curse was reputed to be as potent as their blessing.

* * *

My father enlivened my childhood with anecdotes of his eight years in England—the cosmos of the books I read, *Alice in Wonderland, Winnie-the-Pooh, Peter Pan, The Wind in the Willows,* and Enid Blyton. England was the land of my imagination, and if I had a choice, I would have transported myself there--instantly. I wished Jamshedpur libraries were well-stocked with the books I longed to read and the town had the theatre, opera, and ballet my father had seen in England. But I did have riches, not the cultural smorgasbord I then yearned for, but what destiny chose for me—all the riches of a multi-religious society.

We celebrated Holi, India's spring festival, along with Easter, which co-incided with it; it was, essentially, a naughty child's fantasy. People crept up to each other with brilliant powders in their hands, water pistols with coloured water hidden behind their backs, or flung water balloons that spilt bright dampness on unsuspecting friend, foe, or stranger. On this one day, everyone was supposed to be "sporting." Norms and consequences were suspended; it was the controlled explosion of mischief that societies need to persevere in a dreary existence.

My mischief-loving soul delighted in Holi, though, often, mischief melted into malice. Someone flung a bucket of stolen weather-resistant silver paint used for railings onto our cook, Durga, which caused a painful rash, and did not scrub off for days. I was in Calcutta one Holi, catching a train for boarding school, and remember a bucket of water—was it clean? was it even water?—poured on us from an upper floor and the spirit-shrinking shock of the malicious laughter. We had forgotten the cardinal rule of Holi: Wear old clothes.

During the season of *pujas*, worship and celebration of gods from the Hindu pantheon, posses of young Hindu men appeared on our veranda, asking for money to celebrate Durga Puja, the festival of the Mother Goddess; Ganesh Puja, celebrating the Elephant God, remover of obstacles; Saraswati Puja, for the goddess of knowledge. Our contributions were ostensibly to fashion a larger-than-life clay idol, meticulously painted, gaudily dressed, garlanded with marigolds and frangipani, with a scarlet *tikka* on its forehead. The idol on its platform was carried aloft through town in a procession of the poorer townsfolk from the slums, *bustees*, beating drums, chanting, revving themselves up into manic religious excitement, before being ritually drowned at Riversmeet.

The money also went to *prasad*, sweetmeats offered to the idol, and, creditably, given free to anyone who enters a Hindu temple. Annoyed about spending money to celebrate gods whom I did not believe existed, I tugged at my mother's sari, muttering, "They shouldn't be asking us; they know we are Catholics," but my mother gave anyway, intimidated, and averting danger, "the arrow that flies by night". Also, she did not want to appear stingy, for the gangs recorded each family's donation in a lined exercise book, and she could see our neighbours' contributions as they could see ours (though we suspected that much of this extorted money would be spent on *paan,* betel leaves stuffed with psychoactive areca nut, or *bhang,* moonlight alcohol laced with drugs).

Diwali, the autumn festival of light, which, ironically, ushered in colder, darker days, celebrated the universally longed-for triumph of good over evil, light over darkness. Every house and shop was decorated with *diyas,* little earthenware lamps, wicks floating in oil.

Not to celebrate Diwali, the Hindu New Year, would have been too cruel to non-Hindu children. In fact, we celebrated it whole-heartedly—we lit earthenware *diyas,* beautiful in the evening, and created dazzling *rangoli,* literally coloured circles in the patio of our backyard, tracing complex spirals with gold, silver, indigo, scarlet, and sun-bright yellow powders, which we bought in sets in tiny bottles.

Diwali's twin joys: fireworks and sweets. Our Hindu friends and people who owed us favours (or hoped to! —perhaps my father had hired them or promoted them or might do so) came around with little boxes of melt-on-the-tongue Indian sweets, on which we pounced with jubilation: *peta,* a traditional Diwali sweet, crystallized, almost translucent, pumpkin; *sohn papdri,* made of crisp, golden filaments of sugar, cardamom and chickpea flour; and, for children, *mishri*—shiny little rocks of pure sugar.

On Diwali evening, beneath our parents' vigilant eyes, we lit fireworks on the little concrete patio outside our house—holding *fuljadis,* sparklers, literally flower-sticks, at arm's length, proud of our grown-up caution. "Keep them away from your hair. So-and-so's hair caught fire one Diwali," adults said. The *fuljadi* burst into sparkly stars, iridescent flowers, and we joyously swirled those starbursts of crackling light. There were boxes of tiny squibs, *patakas,* red paper concealing a fragment of explosive; squatting on the patio, we hammered them with a flintstone–a pop, a flash of light. Coiled firework serpents spun, hopping around the floor in indignant circles. Catherine Wheels whirled, rings of mystery; a rocket sped starwards, then meteored down in rainbow sparks.

On the day after Diwali, my parents read aloud newspaper accounts of fatalities: fireworks exploding in people's faces or burning spectators caught beneath their descending canopy; fires as stored fireworks ignited; workers, often children, killed in factory explosions as they toiled long hours producing pyrotechnics for a nation's delight.

Dimna Dam

Dalma Wildlife Sanctuary Guest House. Jamshedpur

With our mother and Uncle Ronny at Riversmeet

Brutus, The Honourable Dog, and Other Enchantments

I loved dogs passionately as a child, as today, believing that I instinctively understood all dogs, and they understood me. Most dogs in India, however, are working dogs, guard dogs, not pets, chained by day, and released by night, the terror of burglars. Strictly outdoor dogs, never petted. "Beware of the dog," a placard many houses sport is, alas, an injunction that it's safest to take literally.

However, I discovered that I could tame even the most savage dog—going up to their locked gate, talking to them kindly but at a distance, approaching ever closer over days, putting my hand almost within biting range, and then, when the dog wagged its tail, I tentatively extended my hand to pet it. My sister and I wandered the neighbourhood, learning the name of every watchdog whom we befriended, and charmed, so that they bounded up to us when called.

The bungalows of the three Directors of the company, down the street from us, were doubly protected by a bored guard at the gate, and an Alsatian, the most common watchdog. We fell in love with a magnificent, luxurious-furred Alsatian called Jai (Victory) and visited "Jai's house" every day, where the watchman, recognising us, let him play with us. "Jai, Jai, Jai," we called, and the dog raced up with unprofessional delight. His powerful sinuous body wriggled in excitement and wagged along with his overjoyed tail as he leapt on us, paws on our shoulders, a glorious mass of joy and fur, nearly knocking us over as he licked our faces.

I gradually tamed my first dog, Rover, a stray. I spotted him hovering in the shadows of our long banana-tree-lined backyard walkway and called to him, but he, used to evading sticks and stones, cowered, and slunk away. I set out a bowl of bread and milk stolen from the fridge for him each evening and sat reading on the stairs leading to our back garden, waiting for his visit. During my parents' parties, we stole titbits to lure Rover to the back patio, and, gradually, the aroma and our goodwill tempted him ever closer until, on a magical day, he allowed us to pet him. He visited more often and stayed ever longer, and my mother began buying him *rathim*, cheap scraps of meat, gristle, and bone from the butcher when we shopped, and Rover became definitely, undoubtedly, our dog

Rover was a brown dog with a chest of soft, thick white fur we called his "puff," perhaps because it reminded us of a powder puff, or perhaps we confused it with "ruff." Rover was our only subject of conversation once we finally tamed him; my father's colleague, Mr Pannikal, whom we called Mr Parkles, often recalled how we ran up to him in the United Club library, saying, "We have a brown dog. His name is Rover. He has a white puff." Rover was the sweetest and most gentle of dogs, and I called him my best friend. Though we were not supposed to feed Rover at dinner, I slipped him food under the table, where he positioned himself beneath my feet. Mrs Domingo once visited us with four chocolate Santa Clauses she had handmade. Rover, whose head was on my lap as I sat on the veranda steps, looked up with enquiring, melting brown eyes. I could not bear to eat the Santa while he watched it intently, so I gave it to him, and, loving chocolate, then a rarish treat, was very sad when he sniffed it, licked it, and then rejected it! As, squeamishly, I did too.

Before I left for boarding school, aged nine, I sat on the steps leading from the veranda to the garden, overwhelmed with sadness at leaving Rover, stroking him, talking to him, while as he lay with his head on my lap. While I was away, he was bitten by another dog in a fight and slowly died of his wounds in our garden, a horror I am glad I never witnessed, though the thought of it is searing.

* * *

Desperation, pushiness, dumb luck, dumb love: these helped me acquire the pure-bred Alsatian I called Brutus.

My father's brother, Eric, who lived in Bombay across the country, asked us to pick up a free puppy for him from the litter of the pure-bred Alsatian guard dog of the American Jesuits who ran XLRI. He would arrive the next day on his free ex-Railway employees' pass and retrieve it.

In an astonishing error of judgment, my father took my sister and me along to choose a puppy for Eric.

A whole litter of soft-furred, sharp-eared Alsatian puppies! I cuddled one. The little creature wriggled in my arms. It leaned into my chest, licked me. And activated the ancient, instinctive bond between dog and human.

"Can we take him home, Pa?" I asked.

"No. No. Anita put it down," my father hissed.

"Please, Pa. I want it." Both my sister and I pleaded, "Pleeeease can we have one too?"

"No! Ma can't stand dogs. And I *hate* them. No!" he said.

"Oh, let them have it," said the kindly Irish-American priests. "A family dog. It's part of childhood," they said, recalling a golden time, American suburbia of the fifties…

Public scenes and being the centre of attention were the definition of torture for my shy father.

"Pleeeease, Pa. We love it already," my sister and I repeated. Unable to withstand this enveloping chorus, he assented.

* * *

We returned home, ecstatic. "Two puppies?" said my horrified mother, who had no time for animals, for whom one night with *a dog* was more than enough.

"One is for us!" I said triumphantly.

"What rubbish! Noel? You're joking. *Noel?*" my mother squawked, looking plaintively at my father.

"What to do, Lovie?" my father said helplessly. "Those idiots."

* * *

Would they return it in the depths of the night? I slept that night with the puppy in a cardboard box on the floor next to my pillow, letting him bite my dangling fingers, so I would instantly wake up if they took him away.

They didn't. Brutus became the King of our hearts, never out of sight.

Commercial dog food was then unheard of in India. We fed the just-weaned pup boiled rice and meat, upon which he had violent diarrhoea. My mother, remembering the dysentery that had killed my newborn brother, and almost killed me, looked after the pup. And as Antoine de Saint-Exupery says: You become responsible forever for what you have tamed.

* * *

I called him Brutus, The Honourable Dog. I was enchanted when I was eleven by the magical rolling rhythms of *Julius Caesar*, to which my father had introduced me. *Friends, Romans, Countrymen*, a staple of elocution contests in India, was also the first Shakespeare speech I memorised. *But Brutus is an honourable man,* Mark Anthony persistently maintains as he persistently disproves it. How I loved the irony!

Our games now revolved around Brutus. I cast desperate spells of my own invention on Brutus, so he would always remain a bandicoot-eyed puppy, but he grew, grew, becoming temperamental, snappish, nipping me when, on holiday from boarding school, wanting to pet him, I dragged him out by his paws from under the bed where he had retreated from the heat. A one-man dog, he was devoted, principally and ironically, to my father, who still professed to hate dogs but brushed his luxuriant fur and, early each morning, threw a ball for him across our three front lawns, a good half-acre, so the beautiful Alsatian remained sleek, sinewy, and strong.

We had Brutus for just three years. My father retired at the mandatory age of sixty from Tata's and got a new job at XLRI. A flat came with the job, a three-bedroom flat after our sprawling four-bedroom, fifteen-roomed house and, according to the rules: No animals.

Asking for exceptions or favours was anathema to my proud, reserved father, so we gave Brutus to his colleague, who coveted a watchdog for his bark and bite, not as a pet. The man was vegetarian and flatly refused to buy Brutus the scrap meat, *rathim,* on which we had reared him; he could not stomach the thought of touching body parts of dead animals, he said, but he did promise Brutus plenty of fresh milk from the buffalo in his backyard, a promise I hope he kept.

Inevitably, the scrawny chickens we bought live from the market (and called *cocos* in onomatopoeic imitation of their song) who roamed our garden to fatten themselves up for the day of slaughter became pets. I sat on my red wicker chair in the middle of the front lawn--virtually a secret garden because of the high wall surrounding it--and watched the chickens explore the grass with their beaks, discovering worms and grubs invisible to our eyes. Occasionally, I captured a fluffy white leghorn, or a brown-speckled hen, and placed it on my lap, stroking its fat, soft body while I read; its familiar warm chicken smell was comforting. They offered us the early morning excitement of hunting new-laid eggs and joyously banqueted on our plates' scrapings, musically clucking as they ran up to eat. And whenever I remembered to the delight of feeding chickens, scattering the uncooked rice grains in far-reaching arcs, watching them dart to retrieve them, clucking in excitement.

Our self-possessed, busy ducks had more personality. Donny—named, of course, for the cocky cartoon duck, gleaming in his iridescent peacock blues and greens, strutted pompously around the garden, his plump chest leading the way, totally absorbed in his endless search for worms. He was self-confident and busy, full of gusto and the joy of living. I was fondest of gentle, equable, brown-speckled Daisy, his plainer, sweet-faced, good-natured partner who agreeably sat on my lap while I read, a placid, warm, contented bundle. They were, for a long time, spared the early morning tryst with destiny.

I had a white rabbit when very young. My mother said, "You were so cruel to it. It ran when it saw you coming." And I felt sad though I could not imagine myself being cruel to an animal since I've always loved them passionately. Having since nurtured children, as well as rabbits, dogs, ducks, and chickens, I've realised that all small animals are reflexively wary of small humans, who may not have learned to hold them gently.

There was world enough and time, time unscheduled, eternal, which we squandered in a dream. Badminton on the lawn all morning, counting as we struck the stiff, white-feathered shuttlecock, striving for ever longer rallies, as if keeping the shuttlecock aloft forever was the purpose of badminton. Mutual self-improvement, not conquest! Skipping rope, counting skips before we tripped, trying to have every session up there among our personal bests, a self-competitiveness I've continued, recording the number of books read each year, the number and pace of miles walked, always seeking to best myself (now increasingly difficult).

Play is the work of children—Ludo, Snakes and Ladders, and endless rounds of Beggar-My-Neighbour, simplest of card games, and later Rummy,

Draughts, and Chinese Checkers, which I loved, as I did Whist, played far into the night, with a gambler's fever. Monopoly was our favourite game, played obsessively, all afternoon, all evening, ricocheting between exhilaration and despair as, in plutocratic euphoria, we gained and lost fabulous London real estate, Oxford Street, Bond Street, Park Lane, Mayfair, playing deep into the night until our father, impoverished, exhausted, made reckless trades, declaring utter bankruptcy. And at our backs, we did not hear, time's winged chariot drawing near.

* * *

When I was six, I decided to collect *all* the knowledge in the world. (That this had already been done in books called encyclopaedias, I did not know.) With crushed grains of rice or a homemade glue of flour and water that my mother had thickened over the stove, I pasted into my scrapbook snippets of information from the children's and adult magazines in the house—creating pages on Australian mammals, extinct woolly mammoths, dragons, giraffes, or fossils, besides things I thought I *should* know—I have a pasted entry on engineering!! I requested General Knowledge books as gifts, imprinting odd facts on my mind, reading–memorisingly–*Ripley's Believe it or Not* and *The Guinness Book of World Records,* hungry for *all* the knowledge in the world, and believing that this too was it!

Collecting embodies our longing for completeness and perfection. I had trivial collections–scented erasers imprinted with a calligraphic letter of the alphabet, and a bestiary of animals, beginning with that letter. They cost seventy-five paise each, devouring the pocket money I'd painstakingly earned through small academic, domestic, or gardening tasks. I longed to collect all twenty-six but never earned enough to. I gathered, too, a little menagerie of plastic animals which came with Binaca toothpaste, again never corralling a complete one—a desire manufacturers deliberately thwart by producing a surfeit of some toys and a dearth of others, keeping children purchasing, purchasing. And I had a postcard collection of faraway, glamorous places which family friends and their friends had visited on their holidays, cards I constantly reorganised in my album.

But the passion of my childhood–eclipsed only by reading, was my stamp collection, flowering from a nucleus inherited from my maternal grandfather, a gentle, shy, sensitive man who loved poetry, and was the Assistant Collector of Customs in Bombay. (King George VI collected stamps, making it fashionable throughout the Empire, even among those who lacked his spare change.) I had rare stamps from countries which no longer existed, having changed their names—Tanganyika, Aden, Malaya, Zanzibar, Ceylon, Siam, my little stamp collection tracking the morphing kingdoms of the world. I read the unfamiliar names with a thrill of pleasure–*Helvetica, Sverige, Norsk, Hellas,* or *Bundesrepublik Deutschland.*

I treasured stamps given me by our Parish priest, Spanish Father Jesus Calvo, during the 1968 Olympics, in Mexico City, when I was six and as gripped by philatelic fever as the rest of the world was by the Olympics–line drawings of athletes running, swimming, cycling, skating, *Citius, Altius, Fortius.* We asked the Belgian, Spanish and American Jesuits in town for the stamps from their letters; we bought little packets of stamps at philatelic exhibits at the Clubs. I traded with friends and spent innumerable quiet hours pasting stamps into my album with cellophane hinges, in pages for each country, and then thematic pages–butterflies, birds, flowers, space exploration, Nobel prize winners, Christmas, or shapes: round, oval, diamond, triangular or square, pondering, rearranging–theme or country?-creating bright, beautiful, dreamy pages.

Shalini, three years younger, did not have a stamp collection, but my mother gave her a stamp album the Christmas I turned ten. I burst into tears. Stamps that entered the house, hitherto mine by divine right, would now have to be shared. I would never have the perfect collection; instead, my mother had again interposed herself into and asserted power over my private treasure island and would control the distribution of stamps, playing politics, favourites, divide-and-conquer, and, undoubtedly, the best stamps would go to my sister. What had been a deep source of joy, self-forgetfulness, absorption, privacy, and quietude had been stolen to become a province of scenes, nagging, drama, power-plays, and stress. And my collection would be holey, wholly incomplete.

Impulsively, in a gesture I later regretted, bitterly, I gave my sister my two precious hardbound stamp albums, grey and green, with their plush leather covers; she could have them, I said, since I would now never have the greatest stamp collection in the whole world. My mother, pleased for Shalini, and lacking empathy for me, did not intervene or stop me, and so I lost my beloved collection, and watched her arrange stamps in my albums with a sad little twist of my heart. Once when we fought, I demanded them back, and she returned them, quietly and mournfully. "Give a thing, take a thing, dance around the Devil's ring," my father said. However, seeing the stamps she had pasted in them, I realised that they had become as much hers as mine and returned them, though I still yearned for the albums I had impetuously given away, which had so many hours and days of my childhood pasted into them. The time I spent rearranging my stamp albums I now spent reading, which, of course, is how I now spend my days, green shoots of grace steering me through the bitterness of that loss to my true calling.

Gentle Teacher Ekka, the Hindi teacher, was a thin, bespectacled lady, an Adivasi, who dressed in worn sarees, her salt-and-pepper hair in a messy bun; she was always kindly towards me, amused by my mischievousness. Once, when I was sent to stand outside class by sadistic Miss Subhadra, my nemesis, she stopped to comfort me, "Don't worry. I saw your story in the school magazine. You will be a great writer. You will be famous one day. Perhaps you'll become the Prime Minister of India, like Indira Gandhi." I considered it.

"Teacher Ekka says I will be famous one day," I told my father. He snorted. "Why not?" I said, "I am only six, but the naughtiest girl in the school. Everyone in school knows me." "Are you saying this with pride or shame?" my father asked, his usual response to my chatter. "You will be famous if you want to be. But for what? If you burn down our cinema hall, you will be famous." Oh!

Perhaps I would invent something? Our ballpoint pens continually ran out of ink…why not invent the world's first refillable ballpoint pen? I pried the nib off a ballpoint pen refill and tried to pour my favourite turquoise fountain pen ink into it. However, the glutinous indelible ballpoint ink coated my fingers, my clothes and the desk, and the bright ink I poured spilt everywhere else. My mother was infuriated! The death of an inventor!

I decided to relearn forgotten arts. I read that the ancient Chinese made paper from rotten rags, and so I tried to make parchment, soaking rags in water, which, alas, never rotted sufficiently. Making papier-mâché –soaking newspaper in water and sculpting the wet goo--was more successful. Once when I changed the water for a cut rose in a discarded condensed milk can on my windowsill, I discovered a green slime at the bottom, which I licked off the tip of my finger. It was sickly-sweet. So roses left in water exude a delicious green sludge? I had discovered something new, unknown to science. Could I patent this? But when I could never replicate it, I realised, sheepishly, that I had probably not scraped off all the condensed milk before placing my rose in the tin. No, I would not become a famous scientist.

* * *

Though we did not get official pocket money, we could earn theoretically unlimited sums by undertaking extra academic work, doing domestic tasks, or growing vegetables to sell to our parents, money we used to buy sweets, toffees, or scented erasers. We could sweep and mop the veranda for ten paise a shot, a waste of time, actually, since the ayah swept it every morning and evening anyway. I was bilingually literate by six and could earn ten paise a page by translating fairy tales in English, my beloved language, into Hindi, my dreaded one. For translating a page of Hindi into English, the animal fables of the *Panchatantra*, say, or the stories from *Champak* magazine to which my parents subscribed to improve our Hindi—an easier task—I earned seven paise. I enjoyed translation and loved getting "rich" in the process. My handwriting was wobbly, so I could earn five paise for simply copying out a page of English prose in my very best writing, which (accidentally) improves prose style.

I sometimes put the money I had earned into a cardboard box sent by my mother's Jesuit cousin Father Stany Coelho in Kohima in Nagaland, who was eminent in the Holy Childhood Society, which runs orphanages for abandoned children. In exchange for donations, you could name the next orphan, always female, left on their doorstep. I liked the name Angela (and wished I had been named Angela rather than Anita) and so chose it each time I donated my pocket money, and if there are today middle-aged Angelas in North-East India put it down to my Anglophilic reading!

I could also earn ten paise by describing a painting with detail, precision, and flourish; (my mother considered flowery writing good writing, as I did then). I studied paintings by the Old Masters, Botticelli, Leonardo da Vinci, Raphael, Fra Angelico, and Michelangelo from the calendars of the Salesian fathers that my grandparents sent us with glossy reproductions of famous Christian paintings on every page--the Virgin and Child, the Holy Family, saints, and angels. I instinctively loved these artists, loved the sweet, serene faces and the rich, bright colour long before I realised how fame-freighted those names and images were. And so, accidentally, though it was but a means of keeping me quiet, I learned to look intently, to really see, and to try to capture in words the dreaming hills of Umbria and Tuscany, the elegant, tiered buildings, inviting arches, and brilliant infinity scarves. Learning to sink into the dream of a painting proved as vital a future source of pleasure as learning to express myself precisely and, if possible, lyrically. And seeds of a lifelong love of art and writing were sown into my life, while my mother got some peace—the golden thread of grace runs through life.

A girl and her bunny

Triumph! Brutus and Bonzo

Uncle Eric and my father with us and the puppies, Brutus and Bonzo.

Brutus and Donny, our pet duck

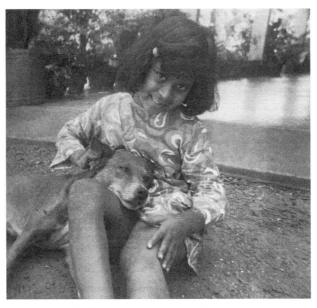

With Rover, the stray dog I adopted off the street

My Secret Garden: When Time Held Us Green

And I grew up fostered alike by beauty and by fear. Wordsworth

When time was green and infinite, my sister and I spent all morning perched on our wrought iron garden gates, studying the faces of all who passed us.

As neighbours, servants, and passers-by approached, walking, cycling, or in rickshaws, I scanned their faces and predicted: "Smiler." Shalini scowled at them. If they smiled back, I got the point; if they glared, she did. Then she predicted "Grumpy Face," and I tried to make them smile, for a point. Most smiled back; some self-consciously jerked their heads upwards and glared at us. A point for a correct guess. We were accidentally training ourselves to gauge character from faces, a skill which has now become second nature.

Twin white star jasmine shrubs bloomed like guarding angels on either side of the green gates, their exhilarating scent welcoming us when we returned snack-satiated and almost asleep from late-night movies at the clubs. Night-blooming Jasmine, *rath-ki-rani*, or Queen of the Night, relying on moths for pollination, released its sweet, heady fragrance in the evenings, when the heat chased us out to sit on the veranda or to sleep on the lawn behind the high, white-washed walls of our garden, which concealed a magic enclosed kingdom, an unsuspected riot of colour.

Our driveway was gravelled with *murram*, tiny misshapen beads of iron ore, refuse from the smelting of iron into steel. I sat on the driveway, sorting this gravel, fascinated by the snail-shaped curls, the fossil wriggles, and globules of iron. "The ayah asks: 'Why are *Budha Baby's* (the Big Baby) clothes so dirty, and *Chotta Baby's* (the Small Baby) so clean?'" my mother said, repeatedly, dishing out shame with relish.

On lazy or busy days, my father left his beloved silver Fiat in the driveway instead of in the garage. Once, on seeing the keys in the ignition, I jiggled them, yanked the handbrake, and the car inexorably rolled backwards towards the gates. I screamed; my father ran, stopped it, and then slapped me. Terror and exhilaration merged. *"I have driven a car!!"*

Though we continually transformed it, the garden was designed and created by the British and American executives who had lived there before and just after India achieved Independence in 1947. It was an earthly paradise to me—an acre with a front garden with three lush emerald lawns edged with borders blazing with flowers, separated by gravelled paths and arches on which roses rambled; an orchard of about thirty fruit trees and bushes; vegetable plots at the sides and back of the house, and some areas left wild and unplanted to dreamily muck about in.

Our driveway was separated from our neighbours, the Cherians, by a long bed, with a curb of large flint and quartz stones cemented together and filled with tropical foliage plants with variegated, speckled, dappled, or dark-spectrumed leaves--coleus, plumbago, corkscrew crotons, philodendrons, and bleeding-heart caladiums. I disliked most of these, feeling conservatively that leaves should be green. It was a bed of tropical clichés, layers of poinsettia, hollyhocks, hibiscus, bougainvillaea, and canna whose extravagant overblown shape I did not like, no more than I did the showy, ubiquitous marigolds, made into garlands offered to the Gods; their musty, pungent smell repelled me. I was already a creature of my reading, visualising the jocund company of a crowd, a host of golden daffodils long before I saw them.

A privacy hedge, thick as a wall, rendered each garden invisible to its neighbours, though, ironically, my mother and our neighbour Elsie Cherian subverted its purpose by shearing an oval archway into the hedge, from which, once or twice a day, Mrs Cherian's stentorian voice echoed "*Cel-line.*"

To me, Mrs Cherian, a six-foot-tall, blue-eyed, Jewish American woman, was as exotic as the specimen fir trees the previous British owners had planted beneath our veranda stairs, at the entrance to the garden, which did not thrive, whose tops we lopped off and requisitioned as Christmas trees. She had five children–Son, Claudia, called Sissy, lovely, gentle Selma, called Penny, Annie, my near-contemporary, and Paul. At her heels were two sausage dachshunds, Chips, brown, short-tempered, and snappish, and Lena, with silky, glossy black fur, placid and sweet-natured, who waddled comfortably–and an irritable black cat who repulsed my overtures with a spit and scratch, and ever since, I see cats and shudder.

My mother went to the hedge when Mrs Cherian hollered for her, and the women talked for half an hour…about everything and nothing, standing the whole time. It was a hedge friendship; they rarely entered each other's houses or shared a meal or a cup of coffee. The hedge chats were a guilty pro-crastinatory break from the crushing mundanities of running their households. Besides, we inhabited different worlds. They socialised with the few Jews and Syrian Christians in town; we, with the Catholics. "Roman Catholics are rat-catchers," Annie, the youngest Cherian, informed me when her brother Paul came over to show us his scrapbook about Israel, into which he'd pasted every clipping he'd found.

"Ma," I'd yell when I wanted her, and Mrs Cherian yelled back, "Anita! Don't scream for your mother; come to her." "Ma," I shouted again. "Don't go. She should come to you," Mrs Cherian said. "*Maaaa*," I hollered, until even-tually, crossly, and perhaps for her own reasons, she came.

My mother's precious rose bushes, on which she had painstakingly grafted clippings from her friends' roses with old strips of cloth, bloomed in the bed bordering the driveway and lawns. We grew tea roses, apricot, orange, red and–oh perversity of experimenting gardeners!–blue, and eventually, after a long period of experimentation with her flower snippers and rags, my mother bred a midnight black rose.

When a kindly African-American, James Greer, who was visiting TISCO on business, came over, my sister and I were enchanted by our visitor, who had gentle, courtly manners and was the first Black person we'd seen. I wrote to him when I was a nine and ten-year-old at boarding school, and he had returned to the States, and he always wrote back. As we showed him the garden, our pride and joy, my parents froze as they heard my little sister point out the pitch and velvety black rose and brightly confide, "My mother calls this a Negrette Rose." But James Greer sensed her love and innocence and just laughed.

* * *

Our two large rectangular front lawns mirrored each other, like butterfly wings, separated by a gravelled walkway, bordered by red, orange, and white bushes of Ixora or Chinese woodflame, each flower a cluster of many tiny flowers. Delicate gerberas, African Daisies–scarlet, burgundy, ruby-red, orange– swayed on their long stems in the bright borders around the lawns; they were interplanted with lupins, zinnias, petunias, snapdragons, gigantic dahlias, cosmos and whimsical corkscrew-petaled chrysanthemums.

I slipped my fingers into the snapdragons or antirrhinums whose name sounded importantly grown-up, wearing the blossoms like fake nails to scare my sister. When the red and white Easter lilies bloomed, my sister and I jousted with the stamens, trying to decapitate the fuzzy brown T-heads. We often went to school hidden behind enormous bouquets for our teachers or visiting dignitaries--roses, gerberas, larkspur, and delphiniums, cradled by maidenhair and lacy ferns.

Our *ayah*, Kamala, cut the grass with a hand-sickle, squatting on her haunches, moving methodically across the lawns, scything. The grass piled up beside her in heaps which we gave my father's colleague for his backyard buffalo, or the gardener burnt with rubbish from the house and garden, sprinkling the fertilising ashes over the flower and vegetable beds.

* * *

In those days before ambition, when time was infinite, I tried to construct a dam beneath the brass tap in the garden, around the little hollow created by the dripping loose hose–inspired by Jamshedpur's Dimna Dam, a favourite picnic spot. I banked mud around the hollow, let the tap drip, drip, drop into my dam, watched the waters rise, frantically strengthened the mud walls, delighted when it held, resigned when the waters dripped over the walls, and the dam burst. Then I'd begin again. Or I would aimlessly dig with a hand spade, a *kurpee*, since my father said that those who dug deep enough might find antique treasures of ancient civilisations–old coins, old jewellery, the myriad odd things lost in gardens, and eventually hit secret life, groundwater, your own private well.

Our third smaller diamond-shaped lawn had triangular rose beds like photo hinges at each corner. A rock garden sprawled between it and the garden wall: a heap of jagged flintstones and rocks, interplanted with cacti--small bristly phallic ones; wide-armed showy ones, pencil tree cactus, cyclamen, begonias, crotons, and *euphorbia milii*, cerise-blossomed crown of thorns, as contorted as bonsai.

A prolific row of tomatoes propped up by mulberry twigs grew virtually untended between the lawn and the hedge separating us from our neighbours, the Vazifdars, whose spinster sisters lived with them; my mother made these into tomato chutney, tomato pickle, tomato jam, "tomalade" -a marmalade made from tomatoes and lemon rind, and even our own tomato ketchup, though we snobbishly preferred the store-bought version.

A massive *Jamun* or rose-apple tree, *Eugenia Jambolaya,* far too tall to climb, towered over all this, and each summer, we waited for it to shake down its bounty across the lawn and over the garden wall, covering the garden, the pavement and road with thousands of little luscious, very sweet *jamuns*—like purple cherries—which we devoured, crimsoning our lips and teeth. Once we grew bored of them, my mother converted the rest into sweet *jamun* wine. In the evenings, when my parents went to parties or adult movies and we were guarded by the ayah, I lay on my bed in our playroom, watching that immense, perhaps virgin, tree roar and toss in the wind. Its crown resembled a man in a top hat, the logo of Dean and Company, which had published my beloved Enid Blyton.

In a burst of horticultural enthusiasm, a previous owner had planted specimen fruit trees along the gravelled path between the house and the three lawns; their erratic yields marked eras. There was the *chickoo* tree, *sapodilla sapota,* which yielded its brown, nectary fruit on Aunt Joyce's only visit; the pomegranate, which exquisitely flowered on Uncle Mervyn's only, equally mythological visit; the fig which fruited when Uncle Ronny stayed in some dark abysm of time; a custard apple tree, and a *pomelo*, like grapefruit. We probably needed two of each for reliable cross-pollination, I now realise.

I loved to climb the gnarled branches of our *champak,* a frangipani tree on the boundaries of our garden and the Vazifdars, threading the petals of its flowers, a creamy white with a daffodil-yellow heart, back into the stem and tucking them in my hair. Hidden among its large glossy dark green leaves, high above the world, re-reading my beloved *The Swiss Family Robinson,* I daydreamed about living in an island treehouse like the Robinsons who, shipwrecked, tamed animals and birds, planted gardens, and achieved self-sufficiency in the middle of the ocean. With my entrepreneurial imagination, I plunged into an involved and detailed dream about being marooned like Robinson Crusoe or his literary descendants, The Swiss Family Robinson, on an undiscovered island I'd name after myself, the exquisite flowers I would discover, the nectary fruit and delicious edible plants I'd grow from harvested seed, the flocks I'd raise from eggs pilfered from birds' nests, the herds of goats I would tame and breed, and the complex, ingenious, self-sufficient economy I'd construct in the wilderness through sweat and brilliance, ingenuity and optimism.

The right side of the house had a concrete patio for the ayah to wash clothes, squatting on her haunches, scrubbing them with bars of harsh yellow washing soap, and soaking the whites in Robin Blue indigo, which counterintuitively turned them whiter. Then, wringing each garment into a tight serpentine coil, she flayed it on concrete, haloed by iridescent soap suds, before rinsing and hanging them up, cascades of colour dancing in the wind.

It was perpetual dusk at that side of the house, beneath the dense shade of the towering mango and jackfruit trees, and the air whined with mosquitoes. We'd swat our arms and slay several. We had a play area here--twin swings in which to hurl ourselves high and higher and a homemade sandpit in which we idly let sand shimmer through our fingers. It was the only shady area of the garden. Elsewhere the sun shone even when it rained, and during these sun showers, we said as our classmates did, "In the forest, foxes are getting married."

Spring winds littered the garden with tiny white mango blossoms, slowly replaced by fallen paisley-shaped midget fruit, while the survivors grew through storms that hailed down scores of green mangoes, which we ate raw with salt and chilli powder or had the cook pickle. And then, the mangoes glowed orange, ushering in a season of plenty—mangoes for breakfast, after lunch, for tea, after dinner, mango ice cream, mango lassi, mango jam. My father, mango-starved after eight years in England, woke at five in the morning and, after his yoga, sat on the veranda, a basket of mangoes on his lap, devouring them, then tossing the seed across the lawn and over the garden wall, revelling in the power and accuracy of his toss, a trick we greatly admired, along with his ability to peel an apple, without breaking the skin, producing a single triumphant spiral. However, as the season wound down, there were fewer and fewer garden mangoes, and we resorted to *buying* the now scarce mangoes, which we divided carefully. My mother gave us children the fat cheeks; my father took the fleshy side clippings, and she had the *bata*, the seed. "It's okay. You have the mango. I'll have the *bata*."

Nestled high among large glossy leaves, oval-shaped jackfruit with their prickly yellow-green exterior grew and grew, to fifteen pounds, twenty—the largest known fruits, their large seeds covered with sweet yellow flesh. They were welcome, at first, when they bountifully ripened overnight, but as the abundance continued, week after week, the soft, slithery, fibrous flesh felt difficult to swallow, the distinctive overripe scent felt oppressive, and we refused them. My parents then sent baskets of mangoes, papayas, bananas, and jackfruit to their friends and to the nuns at school and gave some away to the servants, who pickled the jackfruit seeds, and curried the jackfruit and fallen green mangoes or papayas to eat with rice for lunch and dinner.

The white scaly bark of the three guava trees– "tourist trees"–at the side of the house flaked in stiff slivers to reveal red trunks. I poked the sharp flakes beneath my fingernails with an odd stab of pleasure. We happily ate guavas, yellow fruits with a pink core, when they first ripened until, again, surfeit led to disdain, the almost-delicious became commonplace, and my mother and the cook frantically converted the surplus into guava wine, guava jelly to eat on buttered bread at breakfast and tea, and our favourite: guava cheese or *halwa,* much like the centre of Turkish Delight.

Perennial vegetable-bearing trees and bushes grew in a largely wild patch behind this shady mango, jackfruit, and guava grove—*bimli,* bilimbi, the Cucumber Tree, a tasteless vegetable I hated; a tamarind tree; a spicy mango-like vegetable called *ambade,* or hog plums, eaten in curries or pickled, and drumsticks, *moringa*, whose long pods we curried, squeezing out the marrow between our teeth. Each year I was startled afresh when a wild purple epiphytic orchid bloomed high on the tamarind trees—lavish beauty lurking high up, inconspicuously, solely for the eyes of God and those who look upwards.

The absurdly enormous leaves of banana trees swished bordering the gravelled walkway from the house to the back gate that was used only by the servants and the postman; their pendulums of clustered fruit were always in season, again more than we could eat, so we disdained all but tiny *elaichi* bananas. A little grove of papaya trees grew in a field between the outdoor kitchen and the Cherian's garden—ridiculously easily, even from stray seeds tossed in the rubbish pile waiting to be burnt. Their orange smile and cluster of slippery mucus-coated black seeds were–familiar story–welcome at the outset of the season; then, how sweet its fruit, though, soon enough, we wearied of their plentifulness.

Gooseberry bushes, whose fruit too tart to eat raw, but which we made into jam, hard seeds and all, grew here, and roselle or *Hibiscus sabdariffa* with tart rose-shaped fruits, another brilliant jam plant. There was a productive Malta lemon tree and a cluster of mulberry trees, whose black, sweet fruit we ate raw or made into unbelievably delicious jam and wine. They grew unstoppably; when we cut off mulberry twigs to stake tomatoes, they, astonishingly, rooted— yet more mulberry trees. In summer, during every spare hour, my mother and the cook steadily converted the surplus from the vegetables and the thirty fruit trees into goodies with a longer shelf life—wines, jams, jellies, preserves, squashes, pickles, chutneys, cakes, *halwas*, and *burfis,* fudge-like sweets—time-consuming labour, which explained the many unplanted areas of the garden

A tidy and bountiful vegetable garden had rows of *bhaji* or Indian greens, turnips, ladies' fingers (okra) and pumpkins, which did not interest us since, on principle, we disliked vegetables. Wisps of seeded cotton wafted down from the silk cotton tree; we joined the ayah in gathering it to restuff our old lumpy pillows. We nibbled the almost sweet, deep purple berries of the gay yellow, pink, and orange-flowered lantana bushes that separated our back garden from the Cherians, though warned that they were toxic, but death then seemed implausible. With the infinite patience of childhood, we let the nectar of wild orange honeysuckle drip on our tongues, infinitesimal drop by drop. In fact, much like the earliest humans who discovered the edible by sampling everything, we experimentally tasted most things in the garden, even nibbling tart oxalis, called *kutti-meeti,* or sweet and sour.

Shalini and I each had little beds to cultivate at the sunny left of the house with our names embedded in the earth with large white flintstones. We called this our "Sister-Sister Garden," since we'd illogically go there and play at being sisters. Here we boiled tea for Sister-Sister tea parties in an old tin pan placed on top of two bricks, beneath which we gathered a pile of sticks and leaves, which we lit by striking two flintstones together until the friction created an electric white flash, edged with blue and orange.

In that fertile ash-enriched soil, the radish, lettuce, coriander, or mustard seeds Shalini and I planted germinated in a day; on the next day, green shoots grew; a few days later, we were eating the crisp lettuce or radish in sandwiches--or so memory reports. We pressed the yellow mustard flowers and the tiny white coriander flowers between the pages of our books to dry them and sold the vegetables to our parents like budding entrepreneurs—one *paise* per leaf of lettuce, three *paise* per radish, and ten *paise* per tomato, using our garden earnings to buy sweets: colourful jujubes coated with grains of glistening sugar, or orange slices at a paise a sweet.

When my mother was bored or disgruntled, she reproached my sister, "You're playing with *Anita?* But you become naughty whenever you play with Anita. And when you were born, she held your head underwater in the bath. She put a pillow over your head. She pushed your pram down the stairs."

"I was three then," I should have said. "Go away. You are not my guardian angel," I did say. Whereupon she slapped me.

And my sister looked at me tearfully and went off to join my mother in her domestic duties, later writing them a promissory card, "I prums you I will never be naughty again."

I then scooped up our brown hen, Betsy, and read motionlessly for hours in a chair on the lawn or on an outdoor rug, a *dhurrie,* occasionally looking up to watch shape-shifting dragon, angel, or elephant clouds. When weary of re-reading, for I had read the books we owned multiple times, except for some of the glossiest and best-looking, which my mother locked up to keep them nice, I took the bow I'd made with a bit of elastic on a supple twig, and ineffectively aimed at birds with a homemade stick arrow, having watched *"chokra"* boys as street urchins were called, use catapults to down birds for fun or food. I kept trying to create a boomerang, which should magically return to my hand... but did not.

The well-inhabited garden had concurrent kingdoms—our pets possessed it, as did birds, insects, God, angels, and death. The continuous cawing of crows dominated the soundscape. Their sharp, shiny beaks, cold beady eyes, and glossy black feathers scared me. We heard the high song of *bulbuls,* nightingales; *koel,* Indian cuckoos, and *mynahs,* starlings, within the trees and sometimes found the intricately woven cocoon of weaver bird nests blown down by the wind, their eggs intact after the fall. Occasionally, a baby bird, blind and featherless, which we watched sadly, at a distance--for I once picked one up, and my parents scolded me. Its mother, repelled by the human smell, would reject it; other birds, sniffing the alien odour, would peck it to death. The next day, I saw it shrunken, almost defeathered, red ants devouring its eyes.

In a shoebox with punched air holes, I captured insects: scarlet velvety bugs, ladybirds, and jaunty green caterpillars, their bodies speckled with orange, red, and black eyes. I sometimes picked up *kambli buchi,* blanket insects, caterpillars that were all fur and bristles, and broke into a rash. I longed to see a chrysalis, which I'd read was golden, and watch it morph into a butterfly, spreading resplendent wings. No doubt our garden, full of caterpillars and butterflies, was rich in chrysalides, but not knowing what to look for, I never saw them, and the caterpillars, immured in the shoebox I'd lined with mulberry leaves and grass, lacking moisture and the right host plants... all died.

It was the kind of garden you could enter in the morning and leave in the evening, its enchantments undimmed. We sniffed the intoxicating tuberoses, checked on our vegetables, nibbled mulberries, climbed trees, tracked ants to their hillocks, sand and time sliding through our fingers. A thumb on the nozzle of the hose created a silvery fountain. The dog followed us at heels. Our pet ducks and chickens followed us, clucking. When I was sent to boarding school, I cried myself to sleep when my mother sent me pressed mulberry, coriander, and mustard blossoms, because I consciously missed only two things about home, my dog and my garden, the very word a hieroglyph of happiness.

Shalini and I in our backyard swing

Me comforting a distraught Shalini

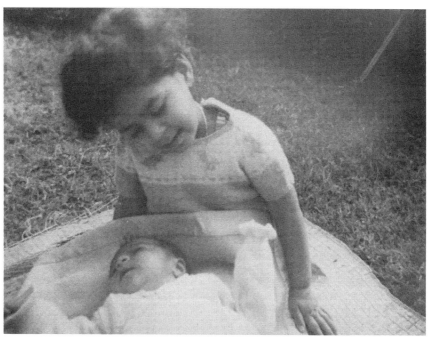

With my father and Uncle Ronny on our favourite gate

The Rooms Have Their Stories:
Wonderland, The House of My Childhood

6 C Road East, Jamshedpur, my first address, was alphanumeric, like all the addresses in that planned city on a grid. Trees joined like praying hands over C Road on which our large white house stood--eucalyptus with its white peeling bark; *neem* or Indian lilac whose twigs our servants used as toothbrushes, and *golmohur*, Royal Poinciana, the flame tree with fierce orange-red flower bursts. Earliest of memories: me, aged three, still an only child, walking down C Road East at night, between my parents, holding their hands, the air golden with stars and streetlights, and my mother saying proudly, "Father McGauley calls us 'The Holy Family'."

Our house, like most houses in that company town, belonged to the Tata Iron and Steel Company. It was among the larger homes, originally built for British executives, and lived in by American executives after Independence: twelve high ceilinged rooms, cool stone floors, quiet, bright and airy, and surrounded by a garden of an acre, with an additional outdoor kitchen and two rooms for servants in the garden, and a detached garage.

We spent most of our day on the long sunny veranda, which spanned almost the entire length of the house. My father sat there in the early morning, eating garden fruit, and reading *The Statesman*, and, in the evening, on returning from work, settled into his comfortable green wicker armchair with his much-loved *Time* magazine (gallantly setting it aside to read to me when I climbed into his lap and presented him with a children's classic). Or I'd sit on his knees and say, "Let's play rodeo, Pa," and he'd vigorously buck, trying to unseat me. Or he'd teach me to box, to execute fancy footwork, with one guarding hand in front of my stomach, while I kept imploring, "Remember to pull your punches, Pa."

We did our homework on the veranda and entertained guests there–using the "drawing room" only for formal visits or guests to impress. The veranda walls had bucolic village scenes and lurid sunset seascapes painted by a family friend, Hector Crasta, in the heart of metropolitan Bombay, and oils of sunsets over Naini lake that we bought from hopeful artists, who arranged their paintings over the pavement in the Himalayan tourist city of Nainital where I went to boarding school, sensing that seeing the glorious hill-surrounded eye of a lake reproduced on canvas would induce a purchase. It did!

On summer nights, we slept out on the lawn behind the garden walls or on the veranda beneath a carved silhouette of a deer; bright wild geese positioned diagonally as though in flight, and a large clay butterfly with iridescent deep blue dust on its wings, things grown dear through familiarity which we once returned from a holiday to find stolen, after which we got our friends, the Athaide's teenage sons to sleep on the veranda when we travelled. Amid the ornaments were fawn-coloured lizards, *chipkalis,* which, with infinite patience, clung motionlessly and unblinking on the wall, virtually part of it, their beady, almost lidless eyes open. Then—a quick flick of a long tongue, and the mosquito or fly which strayed too close was no more. I was afraid of the *chipkalis*: A spider or a lizard's urine dropping into your eyes could blind you, people said.

Twice a day, in our eternal battle against dust, the *ayah* Kamala swept the entire house with a soft broom, a *jhadoo,* of split feathery twigs. And each evening, she poured buckets of water over the veranda and swept it out with a broom of stiff twigs bound together with wire, after which, squatting on her haunches, she moved across the floor, mopping or "swabbing" it with rags cut up from our old clothes, leaving great wet arcs which slowly vanished.

Kamala periodically waxed the stone floors with Johnson's Red Floor Polish. We were forbidden to walk in socks or barefoot on those floors since our socks turned a deep stubborn red, or the soles of our bare feet stained the bedsheets. And that favourite position of children, lying on the floor on your stomach, reading with your legs right-angled in the air, meant red-stained clothes and being scolded by my mother (though I absent-mindedly did all those banned things!)

And sometimes–horror!–I forgetfully walked with red-polished feet on the treasured living room carpet–a mazy flower garden, all twirls and tendrils, bought by my parents on their honeymoon in Kashmir, staining it: a minor domestic tragedy in those days before carpet shampoo or vacuum cleaners. "The ayah's son, Viju, carefully walks around the carpet when he's sent to the big house to bring us our letters. What good manners that little servant boy has! Why can't you do that?" my mother nagged.

Red floor polish was a baleful idea!

My mother, the green-thumbed, lined the veranda with a row of potted plants--caladium, coleus, maiden-hair ferns, and cacti which unpredictably bloomed crimson, orange and purple. Clustered at their base, warming the soil, were white flintstones, which I struck to produce a flash of blue-edged light, which burned the edges of paper. The thrill of conjuring fire from stone never faded.

I lay dreamily on my stomach, watching the busy chain of ants scurry to their mountain castles on the edges of the veranda, a crumb of bread or pink coconut fudge in their mouths, provender for their ant citadels. I placed a Brobdingnagian finger in their paths and watched them pause, regroup, and find an alternative route. Even my shadow heightened their agitation. Time felt eternal.

My father said I used to race after them on all fours, swipe one, and devour it, whooping "Atta," my baby name for myself—and, apparently, ants. My mother and grandmother let me; according to folk wisdom, eating ants, full of formic acid, improved eyesight!

* * *

The veranda led to the drawing room, tacitly reserved for visitors and, therefore, unlit and unappealing during the day. Hours spent on the red furniture around the floating flowers of the Kashmiri carpet, listening, in semi-boredom, to adult conversations–for visits were family affairs! –have imprinted it on my mind. A formal room, a room for show; crystal and silver given as wedding gifts to my parents or grandparents; souvenirs from my parents' foreign travel; our school trophies; highbrow or handsome books; like all drawing rooms, it was a pastiche of who we were, or, mainly, whom we wanted to seem to be.

There was a dusty, distinguished and never-wound cuckoo clock, a souvenir from my father's work trip to Switzerland, on which my mother had accompanied him. We loved, in those dreamy days, the Swiss clock with little ballerinas trapped beneath glass, exquisite in white lace tutus, white satin toes extended, who twirled and pirouetted upon the hour while music tinkled. "I want to be a ballerina," I told my father, another unachievable ambition, like my other declared ambitions: the first woman on the moon, or the first woman to climb Everest.

On a display rack lay a little wooden shoe from my parents' trip to Holland that doubled as a pin cushion; nearby, a still joined clam shell from Hong Kong, contained within its jaws, oh wonder, a miniature countryside with an intricately carved watermill. We shook a glass paperweight, and dervish snowflakes submerged a dreaming London. In the display cabinet smiled a bride doll in her exquisite white lace wedding gown and veil, which my father had bought me from a work trip to Japan when I was four. My mother refused to let me play with her, probably fearing I'd soil the white lace, and she remained, sleeping beautifully under glass throughout my childhood, forever forbidden to me, though I often gazed at her wistfully. *Noli me tangere, do not touch,* a theme of our house.

A framed parchment from Rome, with an exquisite illuminated floral border, granting Noel and Celine Mathias and their home a Papal Apostolic Blessing from Pope Pius XII, ornamented the centre of the living room. Above it, the Sacred Heart of Jesus smiled, pointing at his bleeding heart, paintings inspired by Sister Margaret Mary's vision of Jesus, "revealing His Heart, with all its treasures of love, of mercy, of grace." Jesus' eyes followed me. His kindly, slightly poignant gaze—was it sad, reproachful, or perhaps commiserating? — was always on me, which seemed to me astonishing. Christ magically looked at me, no matter where I hid in the room: Could this be proof of the existence of God? I childishly wondered, ignorant of artistic technique.

My father once flew to Mangalore from Jamshedpur's aerodrome with my little sister when I was six, leaving me at home, which was patently unfair since I was older. "No. You will misbehave, and tell everyone family secrets, and people will gossip," my mother said. Shalini, however, would behave impeccably and conventionally, and garner the praise she coveted.

I was really sad as I wanted to fly, which I never had; to go to Mangalore, where I had never been; and to meet my grandmother and my father's three sisters whom I'd never seen; and, especially, to meet that almost mythical character, whom I had never met, Julianna Lobo, my father's beloved grandmother, my great-grandmother, who was partly Portuguese and then nearly 102-which I never did, for she died soon afterwards. And then, when left alone with her, my mother pinched my face in a rage with her sharp nails, tearing the skin; I piteously showed the Sacred Heart the wound and told him my sorrows and scratched the torn sliver of skin every day to keep it raw to show my favourite nuns at school, and my father when he returned. A faint scar remains!

Ferocious water dragons writhed across the rosewood alcohol cabinet bought on my parents' honeymoon trip to Kashmir, carved in the ancient tradition of the grotesque protecting the precious—like cathedral gargoyles or the gnome which scowled on the handle of the bottle-opener that came with the chest. The intricately carved cabinet, made by Muslim craftsman-to whom, ironically, alcohol was banned-looked like a decorative chest. However–slip your fingers beneath almost invisible handles mid-chest and pull, and out popped bottles of alcohol ensconced in red velvet circular holders. This cabinet proved useful when Bihar instituted Prohibition, which meant that people bought alcohol on the black market at extortionary rates (though our friends in the army, fortunately, provided us with good, cheap, and newly illegal alcohol). People hid alcohol beneath piles of clothes in their cupboards or *almirahs* since, acting on a tip or angling for a bribe, the police were rumoured to raid houses and parties looking for contraband alcohol. We, however, continued to store our alcohol in our drawing room, guarded by carved rosewood dragons.

Being a child meant alcohol was doubly prohibited—and so, a double draw. While my parents politely walked the guests to their cars, my sister and I dashed back to savour the last sips left in glasses or to pour ourselves a forbidden inch, deciding that beer and whiskey were unpalatably bitter, even the coveted, smuggled Scotch; brandy was nice in little sips, while rum and coke, which my father said was *not* a drink for ladies, was rather lovely. Our favourites were wine, always homemade, usually *jamun* or mulberry, and liqueurs, precious bottles of Drambuie, Cointreau, Chartreuse, and Tia Maria, bought on the black market, *ssssh,* in Bombay, or gifts from friends' foreign trips, while my enterprising mother experimented at home, and made Amaretto and guava and papaya liqueurs.

My mother still owns the red sofa and matching red armchairs of my childhood. My parents were married in Bombay, an "arranged marriage," before my mother visited Jamshedpur or her new home. She looked around her large new house in delight—a new silver Fiat; new matching furniture, a massive new radio!! "What a beautiful red sofa set!" she gushed, to which my father, unskilled at lies, secrets or silence, said: "Fifteen rupees a month!" My father had returned from Britain with an English professional degree, rare in India at that time: Fellow of the Institute of Chartered Accountants, England and Wales, but, being generous and free-spending, with little in the way of savings. However, wanting his new wife to have the best of everything, he had, with a mixture of male vanity, love, and goodwill, bought everything new, on instalment plans. My mother now viewed her new habitat with new eyes--the car, a hundred rupees a month...

My father's imported radio, a large EKCO, a serendipitous acronym for E. K. Cole, an English firm (five rupees a month!), dominated the largest rectangle on the display cabinet. Beneath it lay the record player on which he played the precious records he'd brought back from England–Schubert's *Trout Quintet,* Mozart's *Jupiter Symphony*, or Beethoven's *Moonlight Sonata.* After dinner, my father retreated to his newspaper or sat quietly, listening to his classical music. I picked up my book; my sister did her homework, and my mother produced her perennial basket of mending and sewing. "Why don't you read books?" I'd say, for she rarely read books, though she had studied English Literature at Sophia College in Bombay, but she said she *could* not. Once she started reading, she could *not* put the book down until she had finished it, no matter its length. Mrs Cherian once lent my mother *The Valley of the Dolls* by Jacqueline Susan, a tale of drug addiction and sex in Broadway and Hollywood, which she read right through, neglecting the ticktock of domesticity, her sewing, and giving the cook ingredients for our snacks, proving her self-assessment correct. I no longer urged her to read.

Sometimes, my mother insisted we say the Rosary together, twenty minutes of sheer torture by noise. She led the recitation of fifty-three Hail Marys, her long-lashed eyes closed, and face scrunched with intensity, and then she looked imploringly at the picture of Jesus, adding overwrought prayers, imploring "Our Lady of Perpetual Succour" to protect us "from schisms and heresies and the malice of enemies," adding too "Hail Holy Queen, to thee do we send up our sighs, mourning and weeping in this valley of tears." Gabbling those prayers by rote had no spiritual value to me; it was intense, almost-screaming boredom, and I felt sheer relief when it ended. But my mother relished having the audience for her dramatic performative prayer, though she knew the other three would rather have been reading or studying

And then she said, "Let's have a family hug," and we were all to hug the person closest to us. She once observed, "Being hugged by you is like being hugged by a bear; being hugged by Shalini is like being hugged by a doll." "Well then, I will never hug you again," I said. And did not.

We had just a few children's LPs, *My Fair Lady, Mary Poppins* and my favourite, *The Sound of Music,* of which, through long repetition, I had every song by heart…*Edelweiss, edelweiss…Auf Wiedersehen, Goodnight.* Another record I knew "by heart" was my father's Malcolm Sargent's *Messiah* performed in the Royal Albert Hall, to which I listened until I could sing the whole thing–as I still can! I was not allowed to play the imported records myself but had to wait for my parents to put them on, for they feared I might scratch them, an infantilising prohibition that lasted as long as I lived at home. *Noli me tangere.* As our friends emigrated and gave us their records, we slowly acquired a collection of American contemporary music--Joan Baez, Paul Anka, and Connie Francis… *"Lipstick on your collar, told a tale on you."*

The display cabinet housed the P and T (Post and Telegraph) phone—black and boring with a rotary dial, a colonial survival, and a white TISCO phone provided free to the company's employees, each with different ringtones. "TISCO" we'd call out perkily as the phone rang, or "P and T" --with less enthusiasm. When I was shy on the phone, my father said, "Just say what has to be said, and then stop," a tip I passed on to my daughters (and, incidentally, an excellent writing tip!)

Not everyone had a telephone; people still walked, drove, or cycled to your house with questions, requests, or invitations. When, in 1976, we moved to the campus of XLRI, the Jesuit Business School where my father taught post-retirement, my parents decided to forego a private phone, relying on receiving messages through the telephone operator at the university. A home phone on campus was still such a rarity that it became a nuisance rather than a convenience, they were warned--a *de facto* public telephone. People knocked at your door at all hours asking to use your phone; neighbours gave your number as *their* contact number; their problems and emergencies became yours.

On the display cabinet, too, were the oversized hardbacks my father had brought back from England: a *Complete Home Encyclopaedia* with puzzlingly foreign and irrelevant household hints, and what was a greater draw to me--*The History of Art* and *The History of Literature* by John Drinkwater, into which I repeatedly dipped, fascinated by the progression from Lascaux to Monet, from hieroglyphs to Virginia Woolf. I'd surface with quotations I memorised like Pascal's, "Had the nose of Cleopatra been shorter, the face of the entire world would have been different," or "The heart has its reasons of which reason knows nothing."

Which books should live on the drawing room shelves? According to my father: the books he brought back from England, *The Complete Works of William Shakespeare*, and the old orange Penguins--Valery, Huxley, Gide, Camus,

Galsworthy; we had an eclectic collection of what was avant-garde when he studied and worked in England in the forties and early fifties.

My mother wanted to display the series of handsome hardback series, given us by our neighbour Elsie Cherian, whose parents sent them to her from California--Earle Stanley Gardener's Perry Mason courtroom dramas, most of which I read, and glossy gold-lettered leather-bound sets of Reader's Digest Condensed Classics, embossed gold lettering on the spine: a history of Nicholas and Alexandra and the brutal slaughter of the Grand Duchesses and Tsarevitch; *The Three Faces of Eve*, about split personalities, and a biography of Wallis Simpson, whose only remembered utterance is her quip: "One cannot be too rich or too thin."

My father sighed to find his old Dickens and Dostoevsky superseded by handsome kitsch. "People judge you by your books, Lovie," he said plaintively. "They can, at a cursory glance, tell the kind of person you are." His eyes travelled to people's bookcases, appraisingly, as mine do. So Andre Gide's *The Pastoral Symphony* and *Strait is the Gate,* which I read, finding them beautiful and troubling, were reinstated, less conspicuously, in the barrister bookcase along with my father's old copies of Lytton Strachey's *The Eminent Victorians* and Woolf's *Jacob's Room.* Here too, eccentrically, was a beautiful hardbound *Aesop's Fables* I was not allowed to touch for fear I'd soil it, and a new puzzle book from her childhood she capriciously would not let me solve, though I then loved puzzles–"Once you write in it, no one else can use it," and so I didn't and probably no one else did. *Noli me tangere.*

The drawing room led to our parents' bedroom, one of those rooms with too much furniture, leaving only a walkway between the two large single beds joined together, their bedside tables, the three grey steel Godrej cupboards, and the wall-mounted bookcase.

The two large steel cupboards, his and hers, were always locked; to leave valuables unlocked was to tempt servants to steal, my parents believed –thefts which would, morally, be our responsibility. I discovered *Cheiro's Book of Palmistry* there, identifying the major lines in my palm—life, head, heart, fate, determining fame, luck, wealth, or scandal, which my father snatched when he caught me studying my life line to see if I would die young. I later set up a booth as a palmist at the Fun Fair at boarding school: "Anita Mathias will read your palm. Two Coupons"–sheer fakery; as a manic reader of fiction, I constructed destinies based on faces and demeanours.

I skim-read my father's contraband books whenever he, the absent-minded, left his cupboard unlocked: Harold Robbin's *Stiletto*, John O'Hara's *BUtterfield 8*, James Hadley Chase, and an Alfred Hitchcock anthology of short stories I read wide-eyed aged ten—"*Paaaa*, he strangled a naked girl with her own stockings," which, looking red-faced and frightening, he snatched from me, growling, "Your books will take you to hell,"—rather unfair since they were *his* books. He proudly told me that he owned books on the Vatican's Index of Banned Books like Marie Corelli and Marie Stopes, allowing me to peek at but never handle them, greatly overrating my speed-reading abilities.

Random books were jammed on the wall-mounted shelf in my parents' room—Christian meditations such as *Just a Minute, Please,* and *The Imitation of Christ;* a book on The Dead Sea Scrolls; *The Enemy Within*, Robert Kennedy's account of busting organised crime by going after Jimmy Hoffa, leader of the Teamsters, who on encountering Kennedy would transfix him "with a stare of absolute evilness," and then *wink*. At my father's suggestion, I read a biography of mischievous Field-Marshall Montgomery, whom he admired; to his amusement, Monty's emotionally distant mother would tell the servants, "Find out what Bernard is doing. *And stop him.*" And here lay classics whose fading blue or ochre cloth binding and indistinct gold lettering disqualified them for inclusion with the pristine books of the drawing room, such as *The Pickwick Papers,* which I unsuccessfully started several times, whose humour I found tedious, and which, surely unfairly, put me off Dickens.

The magazine compartments of my parent's bedside tables were filled with old letters and Christmas cards, which I read in idle hours, discovering my name on cards from people I had never heard of, guessing from people's responses the bright contents of the public relations letter they must have received. My mother said, "My cousins in Australia, in Kuwait, they love me; they are begging me to come visit them," so I read saved letters seeking verification.

Magazines built up, the next issue always arriving before we'd read the previous one, which we unrealistically still intended to–*The Illustrated Weekly of India*, like *Life* magazine; *India Today* from Calcutta, then a start-up, much like *Time* magazine; *The Catholic Herald,* and *Mangalore* magazine, my parents being inordinately interested in the doings of our small ancestral community of a hundred thousand people. There were issues of both *Eve's Weekly* and *Femina,* women's magazines, with fiction, recipes, household hints, articles on frippery like ikebana, and flower arranging, as well as on specifically Indian topics like arranged marriages, dowry, "bride burning," mother-in-law problems, "servant problems," and amniocentesis, then beginning to be widely used—the abortion of a female foetus being the frequent corollary.

My mother subscribed to *Femina,* and my aunt Joyce in Bombay to *Eve's Weekly;* each swapped their copies when they visited or sent them in "a parcel" with a friend. When an acquaintance visited a distant city or country in which you had family, they volunteered or were recruited to deliver "parcels" (and, consequentially, bring one back in return!), people thinking nothing, in those more leisurely days, of visiting the house of a stranger, who, with customary hospitality, entertained you with tea and snacks. We, with our full-time cook, sent homemade prawn and pork pickles and assorted sweets to my mother's family; they, in Bombay, with labour hard to come by, rushed out and bought expensive "Bombay halwas" for us.

My mother sat on a low stool before her dressing table, with its full-length mirror with folding wings, powdering, and rouging her face. She never left the house without makeup: "I'd feel naked without lipstick!" Across this mirror spread a crack—scotch-taped.

Dreading the humiliation of complaints against me, my mother refused to let me participate in the extra-curricular activities that my sister did--Girl Guides, oil painting, mirror-work classes, band, guitar lessons, *Bharat Natyam* dance lessons; art classes, French lessons from a German lady in town, swimming lessons, cycling lessons and driving lessons—activities I would have loved to, eager then, as now, for broader horizons…. "You'll misbehave. There'll be more complaints," my mother said, with the little delighted, almost triumphant smirk she had when she thought her statements were wise or witty, and she was getting her own way, asserting her will over mine, and knew I could do nothing about it.

However, they did send the five rupees to let me join the Benji League, a club run by *The Statesman,* our newspaper from Calcutta; children sent in answers to puzzles for points and rewards. Overjoyed at getting to join *something,* even if just a club for child readers of *The Statesman,* I danced in front of the mirror, chanting, "I. Am. A. Member. Of. The. Benji. League," and then tried to leap onto it, scale it, dive into and through the looking glass into wonderland. I slipped and fell, upon which a large crack spread diagonally across the mirror, and, worse, I fell onto and broke my mother's Bohemian rose crystal bowl from Czechoslovakia, a treasured wedding gift, at which she wept heartbrokenly. The crack in the mirror remained for the rest of my life at home, a silent reproach. *Seven years of bad luck,* she said grimly.

The first nine years of my life were a maelstrom of minor illnesses–chickenpox, measles, mumps, fevers, crippling abdominal pains, which required hospitalisation, urinary tract infections and skin infections, my rashes and sores bathed with cool purple potassium permanganate solution, or painted with iridescent red mercurochrome. So I spent many sick days in Jamshedpur, resting on my father's bed which had a lumpy coir-stuffed mattress, though he suffered from backaches and lumbago until he took up yoga. On going to boarding school, however, where the healthy Himalayan air was free of pollution, and escaping the emotional stress of the daily blaming, shaming, nagging, scolding, mocking and disfavour of my relationship with my mother and the angry fights, I enjoyed eight years of almost perfect health. My mother kept me quiet on sick days by propping me on my father's bed with a clipboard and polysyllabic words beloved by children, "Elephant," "Hippopotamus", or "Rhinoceros," challenging me to find a hundred little words within it. And so, I ferociously wrote, Pet, hat, ant, pant, peal, eel, the happiness of words vanquishing viruses.

My mother's bed, adjoining my father's, had unlike his, a comfortable Dunlopillo mattress made of latex from the sap of rubber trees and a Dunlopillo bought for her when she fell pregnant with me, her first living child after seven years of marriage and the death of my brother Gerard. Though she was always on her feet, active and energetic, both she and my father insisted on her frailty. She was hospitalised once when I was six, about which she was utterly secretive. When I told a mean nun at Sacred Heart School that she was in hospital, she replied, "Your mother is in the hospital because you were so naughty and gave her so much trouble," which my mother repeated often, with delighted enjoyment, though it was said to make me feel guilty, sad, and scared. I coveted a Dunlopillo too, and she promised me one if I achieved some impossibly stellar rank in class... which I never did!

It was hot. "It's forty degrees." "It's forty-five," my father read out each morning from *The Statesman.* Though the window air-conditioner cooled my parents' bedroom and ceiling fans whirred, our German Shepherd Brutus still crawled beneath my parents' bed for refuge (in general, if you wish to know the coolest spot in a hot house, watch the dogs).

The heat made you torpid. On sweltering summer days, my sister and I filled a bathtub with cold water and all our plastic toys and spent the afternoon in "a soak," leaving the bathroom door which led to the garden open to keep the room cooler. In winter, however, you had to switch on the hot water geyser with its red Cyclops eye twenty minutes before you planned to bathe and then be there punctually to siphon off steaming water. Once the geyser ran out of hot water, that was that!

* * *

"The Black Room," a small, dark, high-ceilinged storage room, lay off my parents' bedroom. Here, in the large grey steel Godrej cupboard, my mother stored our lacy party dresses and our Easter bonnets and parasols, all of which came from America, and—along with wrapping paper and ribbons, sometimes saved and reused—"white elephants:" brass elephants and peacocks, vases, wall plaques and ashtrays given to us, which she'd regift, as probably the recipient would too, gifts *someone* had *bought* once, but which were now decorative encumbrances, Trojan horses, clutter.

And here, on a clothes horse, lay the sarees my mother was currently using, while the rest lay locked in the cupboard. She summoned my father and me to help her fold her sarees in the evenings, and when I told people she needed both me and my father to help her fold her clothes, she snorted indignantly, claiming she only did it to make me (us?) feel important.

During the Indo-Pakistan War of 1965, sudden air-raid sirens signalled a blackout. We stood in a circle in the Black Room, holding hands, every light in the house compliantly off, loudly singing hymns to keep at bay our fear of darkness and bombs. Did my parents really believe a bomber would be more likely to miss us if we hid in the darkest room, singing–or was my father trying to add excitement to my childhood? He had been an air raid warden in London during the Second World War and proudly showed us his badge, telling us stories of air raid drills and dispiriting blackouts.

When she got angry with me, my mother locked me, without my books, in this dark storage room which had just a single high skylight and one shadeless bulb, triggering a lifelong discomfort and anxiety in dark rooms. "I hope you have a child just like you; then you'll know what it's like," she'd say. Alone in the gloom, I read magazines the American Jesuits had brought back from their furloughs and given us, *Family Circle, Better House and Garden, Chatelaine*, and outdated Catholic journals, *America, Commonweal* and the *Catholic Digest*, and then, taking a break from dark and too-adult articles about LSD trips, drug addiction, mental illness and police brutality, I retaliated, in impotent rage, by "paving" the floor with those old magazines, arranging them like crazy paving stones, the stack growing ever higher until I was released. My puny revenge was to refuse to pick them up. I knew my mother would do so herself, for she would be mortified if the ayah saw the mess–and so I had a mini-victory of sorts.

Sadly, if I had been allowed to read my favourite books on my own rather than have to wait for my father to read them to me, books locked up because "You'll dirty them," my Aesop, my Grimm and Andersen, my beloved *Alice in Wonderland*, I would have been quite angelic, flying on a magic carpet, to a private treasure island of my own, and perhaps, that was the unconscious point of locking up those books, my doll, the children's records; perhaps my mother felt I did not deserve that free and expansive joy, that escape to a Neverland of books and music when she was constantly so infuriated by me.

The emotions I remember as I paved the floor with books were rage and desire for revenge. Out of pride, out of spiritedness, and defiance–anger was the main emotion I expressed, and allowed myself to feel towards my mother, though in boarding school, I felt intense love, and affection too for nuns, teachers, other girls, and Mickey, the school sheepdog. But locked alone in the darkness, which always made me stressed and nervous, powerless, without books to read, or my diary to write in, locked in for an indeterminate time, without water, toys, or anything to do, there were surely other emotions which I did not permit myself to feel, but instantly transformed into rage–fear, abandonment, loneliness, sadness, boredom, hatred, helplessness, the sense of rejection, the sense of being all alone in the world with no one to really rely on except myself, which, in many ways, was true. Would my father have taken my side if I complained to him? He was too wary to do so in her presence or absence, for his own reasons ("You should have seen Ma's nightie on our honeymoon," he said to me once. "It was *see-through*") though once, unable to sleep, I heard voices and crept to their room and heard him say, sadly, "Why can't you be a mother to her?"

But eating rage at capricious injustice exacts a price; the anger is greater for its long suppression. They once took me to a psychiatrist in Bombay who gave me such a strong dose of sedatives that I was utterly pliant; however, to their credit, they soon took me off them. Feeling my feelings…I did not know how to then, and still am learning now.

* * *

Our parents' bedroom opened onto the bedroom my mother always made me always share with my sister–quite unnecessarily, for we had a four-bedroom house with a large unused guest room, as well as a "Toys Room." Our beds were covered with crazy quilts, sewn by our mother and grandmother from our outgrown dresses, giving them a new sentimental incarnation. There was a rocking chair, a rocking horse, and an old Singer sewing machine on which my mother made our dresses, and nightdresses and almost all our clothes.

I loved the floor-to-ceiling bookshelves my father had constructed in an alcove here where I stacked my books--birthday presents from family friends, books our American neighbour Elsie Cherian passed on, such as *Freckles*, *Charlotte's Web*, and the Bobbsey Twins, and books which my mother asked childless relatives to pass on to us--Scott, Stevenson, George Eliot's *Silas Marner*, Hardy's *Two on a Tower* and *Under the Greenwood Tree*. For in India, books are rarely discarded; they yellow in dusty heaps, part of the décor, like wallpaper.

Though generally fearless, I was terrified of ghosts and darkness, thanks to too much reading and the ghost stories I'd been told by my father. For a while, I was afraid of entering my room at night and noticing my fear, my mother sung gleefully, her humour laced with sadism: "Midnight is coming, the ghosts are getting fat. Please put a ghost in the old ghost hat," riffing on "Christmas is coming, the geese are getting fat; please put a penny in the old man's hat," sung by street urchins on Bombay street corners in December. My terror increased. Just the word "midnight," the ghosting hour, unnerved me then, though, for much of my adult life, I've been midnight's child, reading far beyond it.

* * *

The large ensuite guest room, on the other side of the drawing room, was called "The Boy's Room" because my mother's youngest brother, Ronny, and my cousin Paul had stayed there in prehistoric times–before I was born. (My father remembered, with amusement, how Ronny, a little ten-year-old in shorts, ran after the train, crying, as it pulled out of Bombay's station, the Victoria Terminus, bearing away his newly-wed eldest sister, my mother.) We didn't, however, have many house guests in out-of-the-way Jamshedpur--my father's brothers, Eric and Theo, and Uncle Ronny, who brought expensive *sohn halwa* from Rajasthan, an exceedingly rich sweet, like hard toffee, milk-chocolate-brown with little flecks of gleaming ghee gleaming, made from the milk of camels, commonly used for transportation there, even by postmen.

Watching Ronny on the lawn, I whispered urgently, "Pa, I've decided to marry Ronny. Should I tell him now?" "Girls can't ask men to marry them," my father said magisterially. "Then what can we *do*?" I asked. "Girls *hint*," he said. "But I don't *know* how to hint," I wailed (still don't!) upon which, to my mortification, Ronny, who, sitting motionlessly on the lawn, had overheard the whole veranda conversation, laughed out loud.

Me and Uncle Ronny

The unused "Boy's Room" was inviting, a hideaway, a refuge, a place of privacy, freedom, and solitude. This multi-purpose, no-purpose room provided the undesignated space which gives homes a sense of spaciousness, an invitation to dream. I went there to read, losing myself in other worlds, occasionally, through slightly parted curtains, hearing the conversations in the living room. My father's subordinate came to complain about something I had said or done to his daughter at school. He was shy, hesitant, his speech soft and halting, his head bowed, evidently sent by his wife. When he left, my father, drained, evicted me from the guest room and lay down in the darkness, an eye mask over his face.

We had a piano in our guest room, stored for an elderly Catholic gentleman whose post-retirement house was tiny, but who impractically dreamed of someday, somehow, retrieving it. He occasionally visited to nostalgically tune the piano and fill our house with music. My sister and I taught ourselves to play simple tunes like "Three Blind Mice" and "Happy Birthday" through trial and error, pencilling in numbers on the piano keys, experimenting until we produced a simulacrum of the tune, upon which we memorised the numbers. *("Do-re-mi,"* was 1-2-3; 1-3, 1-3)! We composed songs and produced "concerts" for our parents, singing and accompanying ourselves on the piano, making "concert programmes," books with facile rhyming poems accompanied by drawings or stickers.

I had my Hindi tuition here—torture, and here too, my father tried to teach me Math, flying into inchoate rages if I could not understand (or he could not explain clearly). "You idiot, you moron, you twerp," he'd sputter in helpless exasperation. "You have the brains of a sheep." Once, in an altercation, he got so angry that he hurled his beloved Olivetti typewriter at me. Astonishingly, I caught it and threw it right back at him, and, in the save, he sprained his little finger, which he clutched sorrowfully, then went to lie down. When asked if my parents spanked me, I'd say, "Wellll, I have been typewritered and picture-framed and slippered and belted" (depending on what lay closest to hand).

My father kept locked an album with black and white photographs of himself and his thirteen brothers and sisters in the guest room. As the longed-for first-born son, born after five girls and then, equally improbably, the eldest of eight male Mathiases, my father was coddled by his mother, who refused to cut his long ringlets until he was six. We saw younger incarnations of his sisters and brothers during the colonial period when they looked decidedly less pre-possessing (the sari lends a dignity to all but the sloppiest)–plump ladies with short, bobbed, and curled hair and knee-length dresses, men in tennis whites. (With the changing social mores in the first decade after Independence when to ape the British became déclassé, Mangaloreans took Indian names, grew their hair, wore sarees, and did not bare their legs, for, in the sixties and seventies, adult women who wore dresses and exposed their legs ("bacon and eggs," the cognoscenti said in Cockney rhyming slang) were suspected of being Anglo-Indian, Indians who had English blood, or claimed to, and who immediately lost status in independent India. (Some Anglo-Indians in Jamshedpur were ru-moured, by our visitors, of being the product of the Saturday night escapades of drunken British Tommies.)

And we saw pictures of my father's father, particularly dark-skinned, se-vere, and balding (who died in 1932 when my father was sixteen, two days after the birth of his fourteenth child, my Uncle Joe). One day, my father opened his filing cabinet to find that silverfish had devoured much of this irreplaceable album of memories. He cried.

I occasionally searched for chocolate beneath a large brown wood cup-board here, above which unfading bouquets of crepe paper red roses with green paper leaves and paper-wrapped wire stems were stored, along with a mandolin in a black case lined with red velvet, which my mother claimed she could play. We had invited my teacher, Berna D'Cruz, a spinster who lived in the school's hostel for out-of-town teachers, to spend the day with us when I was eight, and since I was reputed to be a girl genius, she gave me a terrifying book, *The Com-plete Stories of Edgar Allen Poe*. ("The Fall of the House of Usher," and the claustrophobic "The Tell-tale Heart" and "The Cask of Amontillado" became the stuff of nightmare, Fortunato bricked-up alive, his jester bells still ringing.) Berna organised a treasure hunt for me, hiding chocolate around the house, Gems, the Indian version of Smarties; Five Star, like Milky Way; Krisp like Kitkat, and as she left, said airily, "There's one more. You haven't found the Cadbury's Fruit and Nut bar. Keep looking." And I never did find it, though I sporadically hunted under beds, and beneath piano pedals, for months, years. It remained a minor mystery. Had she invented that bar of chocolate? Or did a servant or my father eat it?

* * *

In the small playroom, the Toy's Room, off the veranda, we stored our playthings, which weren't abundant, in a green wooden chest—an inflatable penguin, a stuffed rabbit, dolls, a Meccano set which had once belonged to my maternal uncles; a Doctor-Doctor set with a stethoscope, bandages, and injection syringes to inspire ambition; paper for Connect the Dots, and naughts and crosses which we played endlessly. There we decked, in a variety of paper costumes, paper dolls that Aunty Olga had given us on her emigration to Australia (called Aunt in the smarmy Indo-Anglian habit of calling everyone in one's social class and of an older generation, Uncle or Aunty). "A sad tale's best," we felt as we marshalled them through never-ending sadness, Little Princess scenarios: destitution, deaths, serial divorces, yours-mine-and-ours families, and unbelievably cruel step-mothers, though we knew no step-mothers (only mothers-in-law; in India almost the same thing!) and few divorced people. Divorce was a dark scandal among Catholics, no less than Hindus—a mortal sin leading to excommunication, the nuns said, and only whispered of, in the presence of children.

The laundry, hand-washed and dried out of doors by the ayah, was starched and dumped on the ironing table here, waiting to be ironed. I once lovingly decided to iron my Uncle Ronny's shirt from Bombay Dying, made of Terrycot, a new, expensive, and then-coveted fabric, but got distracted and wandered off, leaving the iron on top of the shirt. I remember Uncle Ronny's shocked, darkened face when we saw the burnt hole in the shirt, and though he said nothing, my mother never let me forget the incident. And see...I haven't!

* * *

The house was like a three-layer cake--the veranda and toys room facing the front garden; the living room, two bedrooms and two bathrooms in the middle layer, with our bedroom, the dining room, indoor kitchenette, and pantry in the third layer, facing the back garden. The main kitchen, eccentrically, was outside, in the garden, to keep the house free from the smell of cooking.

The long dining room off the drawing room had prints of classic art brought back by my father from his eight years in England--Leonardo's *Last Supper* and Jean Francois Millet's light-filled paintings of French peasants pausing to pray the Angelus at noon. In a china cabinet, its glass embossed with carved wooden swirls, our collection of English china grew as my mother bought pieces from the Catholics of Jamshedpur who emigrated to Canada, England, Australia, or America. As they added to it, my parents recalled staying with relatives of a local Jesuit missionary, Fr. Durt, in Belgium, whose blonde children did the washing up, saying wistfully, "We wish *we* were *Indians* and could eat with our *fingers* on *plantain leaves,* and then *just throw them away."* My father kindly confirmed that he never washed up, not adding that we ate with the correct knives and forks on imported china, and the cook and ayah washed up.)

A curtain at the far end of the kitchen screened off a work area where a clay water jug, a *surai,* with a perpetual wet leaky circle around it, kept water refreshingly cool and thirst-quenching. No one drank water straight from the fridge; that was considered undrinkably cold. Round wooden bowls on the shelves held onions, garlic, and potatoes to be doled out to the cook as the recipe demanded. And here, in an always locked built-in wall cupboard, my mother stored dried fruits, nuts, spices, and rows of little bottles of essences, vanilla, almond or orange, which gave her cookie and cakes their intensity, and food colourings such as cochineal, made from the cochineal beetle, which turned sweets blazing red. Whenever my mother unlocked this, my sister and I appeared, asking for cashew nuts, pistachios and *kismis*, raisins to be poured into our cupped hands. And there were rows of coloured medicine bottles, green glass bottles of Phosfomin, a "nerve tonic" for my mother "because you give me so much trouble," and blue bottles of my father's Pepto-Bismol for indigestion, Optrex eye drops, and much-detested slithery castor oil, cure for constipation. There were also little bottles of sugary homoeopathic remedies which my parents, who oddly believed in homoeopathy, ordered from Father Muller's Homeopathic Pharmacy in Kankanady, Mangalore; I loved the taste.

While the cook prepared our daily meals in the outdoor kitchen, in a coal-fired built-in stove, my mother used the little kitchenette off the dining room with a small electric stove, brought from England on their ship voyage, to make fancier things--trifles with layers of sherry-soaked cake, jelly, custard and jam over which she and my sister laboured for hours; and a rotation of treats like *nankatis*: butter cookies, cashew nut macaroons, carrot halwa, and beetroot or pistachio burfi, soft milky fudge-like sweets.

The wall shelves of the indoor kitchen had neat rows of homemade pickles--mango, tomato, bamboo, lime, brinjal, prawn and pork. Oversized jars held my father's favourite: homemade ginger preserve--pricked ginger, simmered in sugary syrup, sucking which soothed, and perhaps cured, coughs and sore throats. My father sliced the ginger preserve onto toast for breakfast, slathering it with thick gingery syrup, or sucked pieces as a treat.

And here were rows of homemade jams—roselle, mulberry, gooseberry, tomato, marmalade, tomato marmalade, and guava jelly. The heady comforting smell of simmering fruit and sugar pervaded the house on jam-making day.

When we volunteered to help, we importantly stood on a chair, constantly stirring the thickening jam in a stainless-steel pot on the small boxy electric stove—placed on a chair to bring it to an adult's height—to ensure it did not stick to the bottom and burn, while skimming off the variegated and oddly beautiful circles of pink and white scum, impurities that rose to the surface. Bread and jam, eaten at breakfast and afternoon tea almost daily, was a staple.

This rarely used kitchen was an eccentric repository—steamer trunks from my parents' trip to Europe; golf clubs from my father's gay bachelor days; and, on the walls, stray prints and postcards he brought back from Europe: armless Venus de Milo; Michelangelo's horned *Moses*, and *David*, capturing the moment the youth became a man; on gay blitheness descends the weight of thought.

* * *

Beyond the kitchen was a dark, windowless pantry always locked—against us children, the cook, the ayah, and the depredations of my irredeemably sweet-toothed father who, like me, could not easily stop eating sweets or salty snacks once he started. Here, in rows of neatly stacked round stainless-steel containers, or in tins which had once held Ovaltine or Cadbury's caramels, my mother stored the sweets she made, bringing out pieces of fruit halwa and burfi fudges that everyone had long forgotten. After the free-for-all day of their creation, my mother rationed sweets— two at tea-time, one after main meals. However, my father sometimes colluded with us in stealing my mother's pantry keys and rootling there for treats. We opened tins to find forgotten pink coconut *burfi* covered with specks of green mould, and fudge with suggestions of white fungus, sweets we'd have relished when freshly made. And I, once again, renounced thrift and all its works.

A dirt path connected the main house to the servants' quarters in the garden, located behind a concealing white-washed wall, a relic from the colonial era when the English occupant did not want his view of the lush garden obstructed by the natives who served him. Beneficently, the wall also offered the servants privacy.

Our outdoor kitchen, built at the end of the garden to keep coal smoke and spicy aromas out of the house, lay here, sandwiched between the rooms of the cook and the ayah. We occasionally rambled into this dark room where our meals simmered on the large clay coal oven, which protruded from the wall and watched pink spaghetti strands of minced meat emerge from the cast iron meat grinder mounted on the table. The kitchen was in continual use, the cook walking back and forth, bringing in, steaming beneath steel lids, a cooked breakfast, lunch, dinner, and cooked snacks for tea or elevenses.

A narrow open-air corridor between the shielding white wall and the servants' rooms functioned as their outdoor living room where they relaxed, bathed, cooked their meals on *chulas,* small clay stoves, and scoured our dishes with coal ash. As was common in the municipal design of the period, the company did not provide a bathroom in the servants' quarters; the servants, like all those who worked in company houses, relieved themselves in the open air, in the drains of the back lane behind the big houses.

The facades of each company house in Jamshedpur faced each other, with an asphalt tree-lined street between them, immaculately maintained by the Tata Iron and Steel Company. The servants' quarters at the back of each house also faced each other, with a dirt lane between them, faeces in the drains, and chickens pecking through the trash. The rubbish from each home was dumped here in open concrete receptacles, an overflowing heap smelling of banana skins and rotting fruit, surrounded by a haze of flies, occasionally rooted through by roving cows, goats, or rag-pickers who salvaged paper, cloth, bottles, tins, anything recyclable. When the rubbish piles grew too high, they were burnt.

I had never ventured to the lane at the back of my house until, as a volunteer with Mother Teresa's sisters in my late teens, I drove there in the mobile dispensary and was appalled by the faeces, the flies, the foetid drains, the rubbish (our rubbish!) heaped in square concrete dumps waiting to be burnt. This shadow lane had always been there, behind my house, but I had never peeked there. The poor, the hungry, the sick and tired servants came with complex health complaints that needed more than the iron, B complex, Vitamin C and aspirins we handed out gratis. They sometimes just needed the medicine of more and better food.

* * *

Our lives were undergirded by the labour of three live-in servants, who lived in the servants' quarters in the garden, and who created order, beauty, and leisure—a full-time cook, a full-time *ayah*, and a part-time but resident gardener.

For most of my childhood, our cook was a short, stocky Hindu man with just one name, Durga, whom we had hired from a Mangalorean lady, Mrs Britto, who, like everyone, had left Jamshedpur on retirement. She had trained him to cook Mangalorean favourites with ease—*sarpatel,* vindaloo, *sannas,* toddy-fermented mildly sweet, steamed soft rice dumplings or sweet vermicelli with fried raisins and almonds-and my mother treasured his services.

The *ayah* of my early childhood, Kumari, an Adivasi, had a daughter my age, her skin bumpy with prickly heat and covered with sores which dripped pus. Fascinated, I reached out my finger to touch them, and my mother and visiting grandmother ran out to stop me, refusing to allow me to play with the girl lest I got infected too, for I once had "prickly heat" and itched until my skin tore and festered, whereupon my grandmother bound my hands in little scratch-proof mittens.

So we were kept apart. I lived in the big white house. She lived with her parents in a room in the servants' quarters. When my parents went to movies or parties in the evenings, Kumari slept on a sheet on the floor of my room, guarding me, an only child then. She once brought her feverish child, who was usually left to play alone while her mother cleaned our house, washed our clothes, and bathed me. When she thought I was asleep, she tried to put her child on my bed. I woke up. "No, it's my bed; take her off." The red polished stone floor beneath the sheet was cold. So Kumari kept placing her daughter on the bed each time she judged me asleep, and I, just three, kept waking up and insisting that the other child be removed. Though she was gentle and calm, as all our Adivasi servants were, she resigned the next day, which my mother forever held against me (though I was just three at the time!), for Kumari was her favourite servant. She reproached me for years: "And it was all because of you…"

Kumari was succeeded by Kamala, mild, soft-spoken with a homely, pockmarked face, who serenely went about her work. Twice a day, she swept the whole large house, mopped the floor with our cut-up old clothes ("swabbed," we called it), dusted, washed clothes, and hung them out to dry. She and her husband, a rickshaw driver, lived at the back of the garden in one room of our servants' quarters, while the cook got the other—a perk which came with the job, costing the employer nothing while being invaluable to the servants.

One morning, during my boarding school vacation, my mother announced that Kamala had had a baby boy during the night. I was astonished. She'd worked as usual throughout her pregnancy, and I had not realised that, beneath the folds of her sari, she had been pregnant. "Haw," I said, our boarding school exclamation of surprise at the shocking. "Haw, haw!" I had just learned the facts of life at my girls' boarding school and felt squeamish at this evidence of *that* activity in our servant's quarters, just across the garden path. "You mean she was *pregnant* all this time? Haw. You mean she had *a baby* in our servants' quarters. Haw!" For us girls, insulated at boarding school, sex, honeymoons, pregnancy, all seemed comical, slightly obscene. It became a family joke, my childish shock at reproduction in our garden.

Kamala's husband, the rickshaw puller, had fierce parental ambition. He would have been a rags-to-riches hero in a land of opportunity but, in India, was limited by caste, class, and illiteracy. The family's ambition, all their hopes and dreams, were invested in their only son, Raju, whom the rickshaw-wallah dreamed of sending to Loyola, the best boys' school in town, run by American Jesuits.

The fees at Catholic schools, deliberately kept affordable for professionals, were prohibitive for manual workers. So, the rickshaw-wallah, as everyone addressed him, as if it were his name, worked from early morning till late evening, hauling six children in his rickshaw's little two-seated carriage to school, then parked himself in the marketplace, ferrying women and their shopping home, and then back to the schools, transporting the children to tutorial institutions, and then to their homes.

His exhaustion, fear and worry expressed themselves in violence. We heard him yell, and Kamala scream. "He's beating her again," my father muttered.

"He'll never get his son into Loyola," my father said, this boy without access to preschool, with illiterate parents who knew no English, who lived in a one-roomed servants' quarter. How would he meld with children of professionals? Eventually, though, my father did put in a word with the American Jesuits; Raju did get into Lower Kindergarten, and few guessed that the dhoti-clad man who cycled his neat son to school in a rickshaw was, in fact, the child's father, a scenario repeated across India, as some children educated in Catholic English-medium schools grew ashamed of their less-educated non-English-speaking parents. I remember Madhu in boarding school, whose diminutive, sweet smiling mother came to Sports Day. "She's my ayah," Madhu said, which didn't deceive anyone, though it shocked us.

* * *

My mother's friend, Mrs Domingo, who, on retiring, left Jamshedpur for Bangalore, as my parents were later to do, asked us to replicate her arrangement with a short, sturdy tribal man called Shambu-an epileptic, gentle, trusting, vulnerable, and probably developmentally disabled. We let him sleep safely on the concrete corridor of our servants' quarters, and he did some digging and heavy work around the garden. Shambu was a willing worker and a sweet-spirited, smiley, though disconcerting presence. Raw pink skin blotched his face and arms–burns from the fires he had fallen into during epileptic fits, fires lit by the homeless to keep warm during cold Jamshedpur nights. Though he worked as a labourer at construction sites, being illiterate and good-natured, he was routinely cheated of his wages by building contractors who denied he worked the days he did

When we moved to faculty housing at XLRI, with just one room for servants, which we gave the cook, Durga, we had to let the ayah go and regretfully told Shambu that he now needed to fend for himself.

As we were shopping a year later, a disfigured beggar, his face and arms a patchwork of half-healed pink and white skin, repeatedly raised his burnt hand to his head. "Salaam Sahib, Salaam Memsahib. Salaam Baby," he cried, grinning broadly. It was Shambu, now homeless but delighted to see us. He would gladly have traded his strength for work as a labourer, but being continually cheated by bullying contractors, robbed during epileptic fits, and never being able to earn enough to rent a room to sleep and bathe had sapped his spirit. His burns made him look repulsive to prospective employers, though he was still the same cheerful, willing, hard worker. He was left with few options but to beg. We sadly gave him money each time we saw him.

The municipal sweeper, the *jamardhani*, who swept out the drains in the lane behind our house (work traditionally given to women from the lowest castes, the *Harijans*), periodically came to the back door to ask after my mother's health—upon which she received *baksheesh*, a tip. She was old, very thin, in a torn, checked saree, a Dalit from India's hereditary caste of *sudras*, unconsidered untouchable by traditional Hindus, who believed their touch defiled food and communal wells from which they were forbidden to draw. Even their shadow was considered polluting, beliefs which sadly persist in parts of India today.

My grandfather had recently died, and I was particularly sad because my mother chose to visit him on a family holiday to Bombay, where I loved going, while I was at boarding school rather than during my three-month school holiday. When I heard they had been without me, I thought, "I will never see my grandfather again," the first of several prescient intuitions. On his death, my mother plunged into Catholic grief—mortuary cards, rosaries for his soul, giving money to priests to say Month's Mind and other masses to rescue his soul from purgatory.

"*Kaisa hai,* Ma?" the sweeper enquired after my mother's well-being. "My father just died," my mother said. The *jamardhani* collapsed onto her haunches. "*Aaiii,*" she cried. "*Apka baap mur geya.* Oh, Ma, Ma, Ma, your father died," she wept, heartbrokenly and long, in loud, high-pitched wails, her face flooded with tears. "*Hai,* Ma, Ma, Ma."

My mother gave her extra baksheesh.

I was astounded. "How can the jamardhani *cry* for your father whom she has never seen?" I asked.

"She has a warm heart, not like *you!*" my mother said.

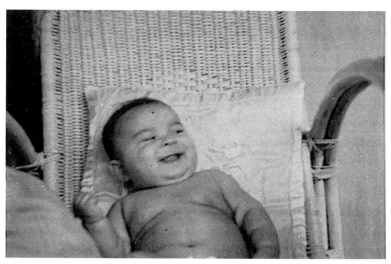

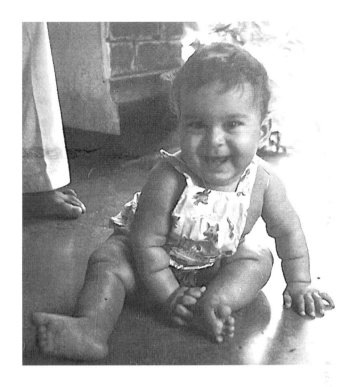

Polyphemus, the Cyclops!
My Father, Noel Joseph Mathias

I used to believe everything my father told me. I lived in a magical world. His cook before I was born was a Cyclops, he said. He had a single eye in the middle of his forehead. And his name was Polyphemus.

Wow! My father had patiently read me the Greek myths. And now I learned that, in our servants' quarters, in our own backyard, at 6 C Road East, Jamshedpur, Bihar, India, we once had living: a Cyclops!

* * *

I took this news to school. I could not "be good" at school, and the nuns could not make me. Every day, after school, while the ayah sent to walk me home waited outside, I was required to record all my transgressions in the Principal's office.

When the list of misdemeanours, which I recorded with legalistic honesty, was particularly lengthy, my parents were called in for a conference. My father, a shy man, who was on the School Board and the school's honorary treasurer, hated them.

Sister Veronique, the Principal, said, "Well, Anita's very imaginative. She's obviously bright, but a little, a little… You know what she told Sister Desiree. That you had a huge one-eyed monster called a Cyclops, living in your backyard, and his name was Poly… Poly…"

"Polyphemus. We did; we really did. Pa told me."

"What nonsense!" he flushed, putting his tongue on his upper lip, as he did when both amused and embarrassed. Sister Veronique, observing him, dropped the subject.

"Anita, what do you mean calling poor Hanif a Cyclops?" my mother said in the car. "The poor man was half-blinded in an accident; that was all."

"But Pa told me. Pa, don't deny it!"

He laughed helplessly, his eyes on the road.

"Family jokes!" my mother muttered, defeated but not about to switch scapegoats. "Anita, why must you always tell family jokes?"

His mythological allusions continued unabated. When invited to dinner with Lancelot and Iris Rebello, he said, "Lancie has a brother called Arthur. They've inherited *the* round table," and I innocently asked to see it. When a new Brother joined the community at the local Jesuit management school, XLRI, he said, "Now they have gone and hired a wizard called Merlin," and so I stared at Brother Merlin with big, awed eyes, awaiting magic.

* * *

My father was born in 1916, the longed-for first-born son, after five daughters to Dr Piedade Felician Mathias, a surgeon, and Josephine. His older sisters, Ethel, Winnie, Jessie, Dora, and Prissie, remembered, resentfully, how they were exhorted, "Pray, pray for a boy," each time Josephine's belly swelled, and how, as girl after girl appeared, their father scolded them, "It's *your* fault. You didn't pray hard enough."

My father, due on Christmas day, arrived on the second of January but was, nevertheless, named Noel (Christmas in French, we'd explain his unusual name to people) and universally doted on. The sisters recited their mother's perpetual litany with an undercurrent of bitterness beneath the mirth, "Ethel, Winnie, put on Noel's shoes; Ethel, Winnie, comb Noel's hair;" his mother, for years, refused to shear his baby curls. He was the favourite of his forbidding bad-tempered father, who "made a fuss" of him and bought him a pony called Paddy and a donkey called Ned to ride with the servant's help, to accompany their two dogs, Togo and Toby. They had six cows, pets, who also provided milk, cream, and home-churned butter for the eventual family of sixteen.

* * *

Since India was then part of the British Empire, the affluent (particularly Catholics and Parsees) rapidly became anglicised. My father and his brothers went to a small elite boarding school–just a hundred boys—Montfort School, in Yercaud, Tamil Nadu, run by a Belgian order, the Brothers of St. Gabriel, and staffed by French, French-Canadian and Belgian brothers. (The girls evidently had learnt to pray, for, miraculously, seven boys were born after the miracle baby boy, my father: Patrick, Theophane, Eric, Morris, Michael, Charles, and Joe.)

Fourteen children meant hand-me-downs. My father and Pat first went to boarding school wearing the too-large overcoats of their older sisters, Ethel and Winnie. As frightened new boarders, they huddled together as a horde of boys surrounded them, tugging at the oversized, baggy coats, first from one direction, then from the other. He told us the story as if it were a joke, making comedy out of shame, humiliation, and sadness, as I, in childhood, learned so well to do. (He was delighted to pass the coat on. People in Mangalore would say, "I saw Theo; he was wearing *that* coat. I saw Eric; he was wearing *that* coat." And so on, with Michael, Morris, and Joe!).

My father's memories of school lingered as one-liners that passed into family oral history. The waiter who caught a boy stealing an extra banana and said, with the common substitution of f for p, "Cunning fella, flicketh the flan-tain, fut in the focket." Two Anglo-Indian boys, tormented by the rest, cling together for comfort; the elder advises the younger, "Burr it up till Tata comes" (Bear it up till Daddy comes). My father's mischievous little brother, Theo

Mathias, later an eminent Jesuit, introduced a goat into the dormitory, to be caught by a sadistic Belgian brother, who twisted his ear, saying–and here we have an imitated accent–"You may larrf, you may gr-ii-n, you sm-ii-le, but we see aff-ter."

* * *

My father loved literature, recounting the plots of his favourite short stories and novellas like Maugham's "The Verger," Maupassant's "The Necklace," or Melville's *Billy Budd*, and declaiming bits of Shakespeare, Milton, Wordsworth, or Kipling from his schooldays, with a trained and retentive memory, which I've inherited. However, as the eldest son in a family of eight clever, ambitious boys, it was unthinkable for him to study something as ethereal as English Literature in college, as my maternal grandfather and uncles had done. He had, unfortunately, the example of his distinguished father, Dr P. F. Mathias, who died when my father was sixteen–an eminent surgeon who was decorated with the OBE in 1929 and was the first Indian Superintendent of the Stanley Medical College and Hospital in Madras.

So, though naturally responsive to words, rhythms, and story, to myths, poetry and literature, my father's education was a conventional one for upper-middle-class Indian men, who in that generation were steered towards lucrative professions–medicine, management, law. My father applied to Medical School and sat on the front porch day after day, waiting for the postman and his admission letter to Stanley Medical College (where a ward was named after his father!). His mother, observing his agony of suspense, had but a single unpitying comment: "Had you studied, you'd be a happier boy today." He laughed, making light of trauma, but often said similar things to me–and I have uttered variants of it–words: an inheritance invisible and real as genes. Sometimes, however, he gleefully detailed his abysmal grades at university (fact? fiction?), and we'd squeal, horrified, for we were ambitious, driven children.

My father never did hear from Medical College; he later suspected an uncle from a rival branch of his father's family, who worked in the admissions office, had purloined his application. At any rate, it had vanished. When the College, pressured by his father's former colleagues, offered him a place mid-term for his dead father's sake, daunted at having to catch up and guilty about subjecting his mother to the cost of the wasted term at St. Joseph's, Bangalore (or he had eight younger siblings) my father declined it, realising, half-relieved, that he didn't really want to be a doctor, for he hated the sight of blood or any bodily emanation. However, still under the thrall of his father's influence, he studied physics and chemistry–in neither of which he had *any* interest.

After he graduated from St. Joseph's College, Bangalore, my father applied to the British Indian Army. The English doctor conducting the army physicals left the love letter he was laboriously composing to the French girl he was courting lying around. My father, who had learnt excellent French from the Belgian brothers at his boarding school, Montford, corrected it in red ink. And was discovered.

And so, he failed his physical, aged twenty-one. A bad heart, the report said. This worried him for years, and rightly so, for he did indeed die of a heart attack, sixty-eight years later, aged eighty-nine.

Meanwhile, India, too, was in the throes of the Great Depression, and jobs were scarce. Friends of his father recommended him to the British Minister, the head of the British Legation in Afghanistan; he worked in Kabul from 1940 to 1943 as a decoder for the encrypted messages that arrived from Delhi and London, highly confidential work for the Empire was teetering. As a Catholic and the son of an OBE winner, he was considered more reliable than a Hindu or a Muslim, for, of course, India was wriggling towards Independence with the Quit India movement. Accommodation was provided for all Legation workers, dormitory style, where he was roused, very early, by a British fellow worker, who woke the grumpy dorm with his bouncy morning chant, *Wakie,* *wakie, rise and shiney.* Or on other mornings, *I have a bordig gold,* a morning cold. Later, a family friend, F. L. Silva, suggested an ideal profession–a Chartered Accountant-and so, using his share of his father's estate, he went to England to acquire a coveted British degree, eventually becoming Noel Mathias, FCA, Fellow of the Institute of Chartered Accountants, England and Wales.

* * *

"This other Eden, demi-paradise, this precious stone set in the silver sea." My father's stories about his eight years in England were as familiar, as repeated, as the stories of my own childhood. He spectacularly wasted time in a way I can't imagine myself doing (for regretting the time he had squandered in his youth, he grew upset at the sight of me "lolling and wasting time," which I cannot do without guilt). A Tube ticket in his pocket, he spent the day, book in hand, circumnavigating the bowels of the ancient city in the thrill of being there among those old famous names: Angel, Baker Street, Barbican, Chancery Lane, St. Paul's, South Kensington. He listened in awful fascination to murder trials at the Old Bailey and, with the sense of opening worlds, to orators in Hyde Park.

My father bought a single cinema ticket and stayed put all day, watching film after film. He saw fabled Shakespearean actors in "the gods" in the Old Vic: Laurence Oliver, Gielgud, Peggy Ashcroft, Michael Redgrave... Listened to Malcolm Sargent conduct Handel. Read the avant-garde writers of the time as their books rolled off the presses. I read, much too young, the orange and white Penguin paperbacks–Virginia Woolf, Andre Gide, George Orwell, Aldous Huxley, D.H. Lawrence, and E. M. Foster– he brought back to India with him, along with his joy and delight: the classical music LPs, Beethoven's *Pathetique,* Mozart's *Jupiter Symphony,* Schubert's *The Trout Quintet,* or Handel's *Messiah* to which he'd listen quietly, dreamily, in the evenings.

When money ran low, my father worked at India House, the High Commission of India in London, repeatedly quitting when he felt flush and financially invulnerable, then returning shame-faced when he had run through and out of money. He was rehired, because of his eminent OBE-winning surgeon father, though Krishna Menon, the acerbic Indian High Commissioner, would ask, "What, Mathias? Is India House a railway station waiting room?"

* * *

Through serendipity and grace (which are, perhaps, the same thing), my father lodged with a colourful evangelical family, the Ponsfords, of whom he always spoke nostalgically! Mrs Ponsford, a rare, colour-blind woman (by choice? by temperament?) in the blithely un-politically correct world of the Forties and early Fifties, opened her heart and home to the waifs and strays who washed up in London, then the heart of the heart of the world. My father told us of Arab housemates who'd arrive at breakfast declaring, "We'll lick them; we'll obliterate them, just you wait and see," even as Jews were being smuggled past the British blockade into Palestine of the British Mandate, and the nation of Israel was inexorably born.

Mrs Ponsford once rented the bedroom of her son Ian, a fighter pilot in the RAF, to a Nigerian lodger who had contracted tuberculosis. Mrs Ponsford's Christian race unconsciousness was far in advance of her family's. Ian, back home on leave, burst into the drawing room, announcing furiously, "Mum has given my room to a tubercular n***er." Each morning, the said Nigerian, yearning for his warm, green continent, rushed down to check the mail cascading through the golden front door slit. "Oh, stop that," Ian snarled. "Who do you know who can write? And, anyway, you can't read." My father described casual racism: walking away rapidly, mortified, when he visited Oxford on Saturday evenings with Hamish, Ian, and Keith, Ponsford sons and their friends; the drunken English boys swaggered beneath the windows of Balliol College (which admitted more foreign students than other colleges) and yelled, "Come on, Balliol; send down your n****rs." In contrast were his Sunday afternoon idylls, when he drove to Cambridge on Sunday afternoons with Mr Ponsford, a Cambridge man, to stroll on the tranquil Backs amid ancient, unchanged beauty.

The Ponsfords took in a Kindertransport German Jewish girl, Anita, of mute, black rages, who often flung her morning bowl of porridge, sweetened with precious rationed sugar, at Ruth, the Ponsford's warm-hearted daughter. "Ignore her, Ruth, ignore her," Mrs Ponsford said, citing a cruel, contemporary cure for tantrums, and so Ruth continued stolidly eating her own porridge, Anita's porridge coursing down her cheeks. (My father gave my sister similar advice when we scrapped).

* * *

To me, who had never left India, his adventures, his vignettes, were magical! West Indians rushing onto the field after cricket matches, flinging jubilant bats into the air, singing, "Crick-et lubb-er-ly crick-et"—or so he said. The English fair-weather greeting, "Nice day, inn't," and the folk wisdom, "Cast not a clout till May is out." Drinking in pubs with his friends, singing, "We will hang out our washing on the Siegfried Line; Have you any washing, Mother dear," or *Alouette, gentille Alouette, Alouette, je te plumerai,* which he translated to our horror.

Air raid sirens wailed as he banged on doors, badge and papers in hand, during his evening job as an air raid warden (part of his mandatory national service), getting the recalcitrant to put off their lights and adjust their blackout curtains to foil the Luftwaffe. Unfortunately for my father, wartime and austerity rationing persisted throughout his eight years in England. While he had to turn over his coupons for butter, cheese, bacon, meat, eggs, milk, tea, sugar, and jam to Mrs Ponsford, who cooked meals for the lodgers, he kept his own confectionary coupons, twelve ounces every four weeks. He consumed all this chocolate in one fell swoop, in a glorious theobromine high, the *only* way to eat chocolate he always maintained, in mood-altering overdoses. (When I went to England, thirty-two years after he left, he said, "I have one piece of advice to give you." I raised an eyebrow, awaiting a talk on sex. But what he said was: "Everywhere you go in England, you will see sweet shops. *Look the other way*." (But alas, I only took his advice in a Damascene moment, four years ago!)

My father picked fruit in Europe with Hamish, Ian and Keith Ponsford for cash and adventure after the War and went as a lark to an International Festival organised by the Communist Party of East Germany in East Berlin in the early Fifties for the experience and cheap holiday. He danced Eastern European folk dances; listened to concerts of classical music; and saluted, proclaiming, ironically, *Freiheit*, Freedom.

From 1946 to 1952, my father volunteered every autumn and winter in the Common Cold Unit near Salisbury for a holiday of sorts. It offered warm, furnished accommodation in a hut, three cooked meals and pocket money in return for submitting to research on what triggered, abbreviated, or cured the common cold. He was injected with coronaviruses and rhinoviruses and walked from a hot bath to a cold room. The food was good, his hut quiet and comfortable; there were plenty of books; he enjoyed his long walks in the Salisbury countryside, and so he submitted to something he would never have dreamed of in his health-conscious middle age.

* * *

The Ponsfords were evangelical Christians, but despite responding intellectually and aesthetically to their faith–he quoted from the King James Bible with pleasure and relish–my father never succumbed to religious fervour, was perhaps too conventional and conservative to do so.

I went to Reformed churches in my twenties and thirties, not *really* believing their narrow interpretation of who enters the strait gate, but, like Pascal's gambler, I explained the theology to my father, 'just in case..." When I tried to explain *Sola Gratia, Sola Fides, Sola Scriptura, Solus Christus* to him, he would have none of it. "Yes, yes," he said, divining my intent. "I am going to hell. And listening to this is a foretaste of it!"

My father began to lose his hair in his thirties; he went weekly to the barber; tried the recommended lotions, potions, tonics, and salves. Finally, the barber said bluntly, "*Now*, there's only shoe polish." He recalled arguing with Mrs Ponsford about inerrancy: "And you *truly* believe Absalom was suspended by his hair in a forest?" Mrs Ponsford snapped, "Leave these matters to scholars, Noel. *Why* do you think it could never happen? Of course, it could never happen to *you*."

Whatever his private thoughts, my father remained outwardly conventional, hating, above all things, to attract attention, be observed, commented on, or judged. For many years, he dated but did not marry an Englishwoman, who took him to the opera, taught him to appreciate Beethoven, Bach, and Handel, and introduced him to contemporary literature. He talked about her with the utmost fondness.

"Why didn't you marry her, Pa?" I asked.

"Oh, it would have been too embarrassing!" he said. "How would I have introduced her to my family?"

Anyway, dating English girls was fraught. On a clifftop weekend walk, his Parsee friend argued loudly with his English girlfriend. On hearing them, sailors from the Royal Navy eagerly ran to her rescue. "Can we help you, Miss?" they asked, to his friend's mortification.

* * *

I once had an extraordinary conversation with my father when he fondly spoke about his English woman friend.

"So, Pa, were you a virgin when you got married?" "I'm not going to tell you." "But now I've got curious. *Tell me*!" "What kind of question is this?" "That's not fair. You kept asking me if I was still a virgin." "Fathers can ask daughters such questions. Daughters can't ask their fathers." "Why not?" He just smiled.

"Okay, at least tell me if you fathered any other children." "No," he said, definitely. "I did not father any children." "How do you know?" "I know." "Did you visit prostitutes?" "No. I was a graduate student when I was in England. Students don't visit prostitutes. They have friends."

"So, you slept with a friend? With whom?" He smiled. "I won't tell you." "Why? If you tell me, I promise I won't put it in my book." *"In your book? My God!"* He flushed, then laughed in horror. "Are you *mad?* Please forget this conversation."

But how could I?

* * *

In his early thirties, he sneezed, he coughed, he blew his nose; he wanted to tear out his eyes. He was convinced he had developed tuberculosis. TB before his coveted Chartered Accountant qualification? The horror! So, every evening, every weekend, he sat in Kensington Gardens or took a bus to Whipsnade Zoo, breathing cool fresh air, so good for tubercular lungs. And sneezed and coughed the more.

In despair, he finally consulted a doctor. It was not tuberculosis; it was hay fever. And his self-prescribed regimen of the pollen-filled air of Kensington Gardens was the very worst thing he could have done

His random gleanings from England: "Learn to see through jealous people. My fellow Indians said, 'Mathias, you'll never become a Chartered Accountant,' as they watched me have so much fun. But though I was slowed down by having to work while I studied, I did not get discouraged. I did it. In the end.

"I spent hours reading in the British Library. Whenever I saw a plain woman with thick glasses and lank oily hair," he said (culturally and mildly

misogynistic, as all his family were), "and peeked over her shoulder at the encyclopaedia article she was reading, it was always about sex." An apocryphal tale,
I suspect, as was

another of his stories from London: A little old lady calls the police: "A man in
the flat opposite is exposing himself. He is stark naked!" The Bobbies appear.
"But Ma'am, we don't see anyone." "Ah, but for that, you need to stand on a
table."

* * *

My father worked part-time in the Accounts Department of India
House, India's Embassy in London, until 1951, when he qualified as a Chartered Accountant, after which he worked for Tubbs, Clarke and Co., Chartered
Accountants. While he liked his boss, who was fair-minded (and had hired him
after all!), he realised that he would always be held back by the petty racism of
the period. When an audit was requested, he heard his boss pre-emptively explain, "One of our accountants is an Indian. Do you mind?" Some did. "It's
always best to ask," his boss said apologetically.

My father's epiphany: "Why be a second-class citizen in someone else's
country when you can be a first-class citizen in your own?"

He returned to India in 1952, eventually becoming the Controller of Accounts and Manager of Data Processing at one of India's largest companies, the
Tata Iron and Steel Company, in Jamshedpur, North India, where he worked
until his first retirement at sixty (following which he was the Financial Controller of the American Jesuit Business School, XLRI until he finally retired at the
age of sixty-eight in 1984).

At his retirement party from TISCO, a subordinate, giving a classically
Indian flowery speech, said, "Sir, you were like Jesus Christ to us." The Managing Director of the Tata Iron and Steel Company, Russi Modi, called out from

the dais where they both sat, "Ah, if you had known him in his bachelor days, you would not have said that." Whatever had he done?

My father, in his youth, was as absent-minded as I was in mine. He told us how, while travelling with his sister Ethel and his distinguished Jesuit uncle, Father Charles Lobo, he stopped off at the station's Wheeler's bookstore, browsing absorbed, while the train left without him (a fate I've often escaped by the skin of my teeth). He asked the stationmaster to radio a message to the driver, who told the conductor, who came huffing and puffing into the first-class compartment to say breathlessly, "Father, Father, your nephew, your nephew," and then ran out of breath. And Father Charles said, "What's my damn-fool nephew done now?" ("This was during the Raj," my father added. "In independent India, no one would have bothered.") His mother promised him his dead father's watch when she felt he was able to look after it—a stage she decided he had reached when he got married, aged thirty-eight.

* * *

Two years after returning to India, in 1954, he married my mother, Celine, fourteen years younger—an arranged marriage. To her annoyance, how-ever, whenever he filled up bureaucratic forms to buy a train ticket, for instance, he recorded that *she* was fourteen years *older* than he was. And then, following seven years of infertility and the death of a son, I was born. He had children while his siblings and friends were acquiring grandchildren, he lamented, being forty-six when I was born, and forty-nine at the birth of my sister; he was some-times taken for our grandfather.

As Manager of Data Processing, he introduced computers to TISCO af-ter study visits to Pittsburgh; the first computer he imported, which he showed me on a Saturday visit to his office, stretched across an entire wall. TISCO periodically sent him to England, Europe, Japan, and America to study the ac-counting and computer systems of major companies, and he returned with gifts and stories. A massive man in Manhattan, leaning against a wall, asked my father to tie his shoelace for him. Unnerved, wondering if the man were crazy or a racist, he complied. The man then gave him a dollar–he was too fat to bend. Everything in New York delighted my father… streets with signs saying, "Don't even *think* of parking here."

* * *

"You take your daughter; I'll stay here peacefully with my daughter," my mother sometimes said on weekends, bifurcating the family. And so, when Shahanshah Mohammed Reza Shah Pahlavi of Iran visited Jamshedpur, my father took me to see him and his Shahbanu Farah drive in their motorcade beneath gaudy bannered and festooned arches, the Shahbanu dazzling in a glittering tiara of diamonds, an enormous, tiered diamond necklace, and long, dangling diamond earrings.

Magic: Escaping out of the house, alone with my father! He took me to the Soda Fountain in Bistapur and bought me a Knickerbocker Glory. "Don't tell Shalini," he'd say, and so I returned, *bursting* with the secret, not realising that he probably told her the same thing on *her* secret trips with him, and *she'd* kept the secret effortlessly.

On Saturdays, my father took me to watch cricket matches at Keenan Stadium, to which I gamely accompanied him, though I barely knew (or know!) the rules of any game. Sometimes, we found a travelling circus—glitz and stardust: sparkly girls flying through air on their trapezes, amazingly tame lions, tigers, bears and elephants who jumped on boxes or through hoops, or we drove aimlessly into the countryside that grew more lushly green as we drove away from Jamshedpur, towards Chaibasa or Ranchi, looking for a *mela*, a fair. My father described the endless adventures, terrestrial, lunar and Fmarine, of Ferdinand the Bull, who, I discovered, in my daughter Zoe's childhood, was a real character from a real book, not a figment of my inventive father's imagination, as I had believed.

On the way, we once joined a crowd of squatting turbaned villagers, betting on a cock fight. The magnificent, brilliantly plumaged birds pecked each other as they fought to the death, maddened by slashes from the knives tied to their antagonist's thighs. The villagers cheered, wildly betting. Feathers flew, and blood gushed from the ferocious, wounded, dying birds. I sobbed hysterically, and we fled to the car.

And finally–the Saturnalia of the *Mela*. Everyone in their best and brightest clothes, a riot of shocking pink, purple, orange... I wandered, bouncing my water balloon by its long rubber string; blowing bubbles through a wire wand; hands full of my loot: kaleidoscopes, whistles, pinwheel games. My arms were now decked with brilliant glass bangles–indigo, magenta, vermilion, and tangerine, flecked with gold, and my palate cloyed and surfeited by *sohn papdri* or *buddi-ke-baal*, old woman's hair: crisp, pale yellow sugary filaments that melted on the tongue like candy floss.

I rode the carousel and tumbling boxes and, once, the Ferris Wheel and screamed and screamed in terror as it vertiginously rose. My father paid the operator to pause it until I calmed down, though the horror of being frozen in mid-air, terrified, screaming, looking down, down, was perhaps worse than the inexorable ascent.

* * *

Getting lost, as Enid Blyton's children did, then seemed the most exciting thing in the world.

"Let's get lost, Pa," I suggested as we returned from the mela. "Okay," he said indulgently.

"Turn right, Pa. Now turn left, go down that road," I directed in the Sixties of cheap petrol.

Our little silver Fiat drove down dirt country roads beneath brilliant orange *golmohur* trees and wide-spreading banyans. Dirt roads beneath green canopies that seemed to lead on forever, nowhere.

"Now, are we lost, Pa?"

"Yes! I have no idea where we are,"

"Really? Are you worried, Pa?"

"I am terribly worried."

"What will we do tonight?"

"I have *simply no idea*," he said.

I sighed at the bliss of being lost with my father. I gave him the ring I bought at the fair, its red eye glinting. "Will you marry me when *she* dies?" I asked. "All right," he said absently, letting me wriggle it on his little finger. "Promise?" "Promise." "We are now engaged?" "Yes." I later gleefully informed my mother and little sister, "Pa and I are en-gaaged. Pa and I are en-gaaged."

And so we meandered down the country roads, and I, too dreamy for a sense of direction, was thrilled–lost, utterly lost!–until I noticed, with horror, the Cherians' house, the Mangrulkars', the Bhargavas', and there we were, I realised, crackling down the gravelled driveway of 6 C Road East. Found. Betrayed.

* * *

I thought midnight a most grown-up moment–the "witching hour" of ghosts, goblins, ghouls, and storybook children, and begged my father to have midnight feasts with me as the children in Enid Blyton's Malory Towers and St. Clare's did.

He sighed. He was in his fifties; sleep was sweet, for, like all TISCO employees, he worked five and a half days a week, including a half-day on Saturday.

"All right, but you have to wake me up." "All right, but you have to get the keys to her pantry."

I lay awake in excitement until–was it really midnight, that sophisticated hour? It felt like it!– I roused the weary man who, with some effort, got up and followed me to the guest room, where we devoured rock *chicki*, caramelly, homemade peanut brittle, and Mysore Pak, a decadent sweet made from crisp yellow filaments of chickpea flour, sugar and ghee, and sipped homemade mulberry wine, only a little happy-making.

As we lay in the guest room bed, my father terrified me with ghost stories, tales of the night during his management training course in Hyderabad when he heard a wraith Ferdoon, who had returned from the grave pining for his lover, Shereen. *Shereen, Shereen,* my father heard a sibilance undulate through the room, he said, and then the answering banshee wail, *Ferdoon! Ferdoon*! He thus gave a local habitation and a name to a story which probably owed its genesis to the one he told after it, *Wuthering Heights,* tortured Heathcliff, and the longed-for ghost of Catherine Earnshaw at the window.

* * *

As a child, I believed everything my father said was gospel truth. He claimed he responded to an advertisement in *The Illustrated Weekly of India:* "All mosquitoes eliminated from your house and garden in a day. Guaranteed to work, or your money back." He sent in his ten rupees and waited. He received two small rocks. *Take the mosquito,* read the instructions. *Place it on the lower stone. Cover with the other stone. Crush mosquito.*

A man finally leaves his wife, who wails as he crosses the threshold, "You promised not to leave, and you've left." He: "I promised to cleave, and I've cleft."

He supposedly saw a country bumpkin in Bombay, craning his neck at skyscrapers. A city slicker marches up, "That's *my* building, didn't you know? You have to pay me a rupee for every storey you looked at.' The bumpkin pays up, then conspiratorially whispers to bystanders, 'I gave him fifteen rupees, but *actually*–I looked at *the whole building*.'"

* * *

"Was that really Professor Mathias?" one of his students asked, observing us banter at the train station. "I have never seen him smile." "You can only talk to him soberly on sober subjects," my cousin Dorothy lamented. However, within the sanctuary of fatherhood, my father was silly. He was my younger sister's passion. Shalini sat on his bed while he was at work, and my mother did her mending and told tales of my father, each one ending on a crescendo of delight. Shalini might say, "Pa proudly stroked his pronounced nose and boasted, "I have a Roman nose. An aquiline nose," followed by "*Deeear* Pa, silly Pa." Or "Do you remember when Pa heard me sound out G-nome," and claimed, '*I'm* actually a gin-nome.' I challenged him and said, 'Okay, if you are a gin-nome, what's your name?" and he said, 'Pixie Silver Cloud,' so happily." And then her voice rose in her exultant, ecstatic litany, "Sil-ly Pa. *Swee-eet* Pa!"

We both adored my father, whom we called Padle, a combination of Pa Dear, Pa Darling, and Pa Doll, and ferociously competed for him. When my father walked with both of us, we fought over which hand we got to hold. "I got the watch hand," I'd say. "I got the right hand," she'd reply. And then I wanted it. (Once we were teenagers, however, my father refused to allow us to hold his hand or link arms with him in public. "People might think you are my child wives," he'd say, surely flattering himself.)

* * *

My father repeated old jingles with such gusto we assumed he'd invented them. When we struggled with a bottleneck of ketchup, he'd say, *Shake and shake the ketchup bottle. None will come, and then a lot'll.* I later discovered that jingle that I was sure my father invented–attributed to Richard Armour, not Noel Mathias.

I tawt I thaw a putty tat cweeping up on me," "You tawt you thaw a putty cat. The putty tat was me," our father would say with gusto, in high-pitched baby tones, inspiring my sister to call him "Tweety Pie". An example of his dearness and foolishness we thought, as we teased him, mocking the jingle we believed he had made up, ignorant of its provenance, until, one day in America, I saw that tag of doomed innocence on a child's sweatshirt, and realised, astonished, that my father hadn't invented Tweety Bird after all.

He interpolated himself into the old chestnuts he told us. So, it was his cousin, Paddy, who rode his bike recklessly, saying, "Look, Ma, no hands. Look Ma, no feet," and then, deflated and bloodied, "Look Ma. No teeth." Once, when required as a forfeit in a game of Pass-The-Parcel to tell a joke, Vatsala told the assembled school, "Once Anita Mathias's father saw a boy ride a bike, who said…" "Nice old joke, Vatsala Khanna," Sister Josephine said later, "But why bring Anita Mathias's father into it?" Both Vatsala and I looked equally stunned.

* * *

During my first year at boarding school, when I was nine, my class was enthralled by the occult. Kunjan and Gunjan, twins and "new girls," claiming to be able to summon spirits from the vasty deep, introduced us to Ouija boards and séances. We placed our paintbrushes in a pile, asked the spirits simple binary questions, and watched the brushes move. We placed our fingers on the cap of a coke bottle, on a simple handmade board, with encircled letters of the alphabet, and commanded the spirits to propel our fingers across the board to the right answers. The little bit of steel moved as if by its own volition. It was uncanny, mysterious, magic.

"Pa, let's call up ghosts," I said on returning home from my first year at boarding school, aged nine. "Okay, let's," he said indulgently. He had been to séances in London, where brokenhearted war mothers groped for the spirits of their sons, and unearthly wails and gusts of cold air coursed through the medium's home.

My sister Shalini, just hearing of our planned necromancy, wanted to join. But whom should we call up? We settled on an aunt who had recently died, and, in the darkness, summoned up her spirit even before we had formulated consequential questions.

And Shalini and I waiting, hearts in our mouths, were astounded when a white-shrouded figure ran into the room, said something that sounded like cheep, cheep, and then vanished.

We were deeply impressed, but when we tried it on our own, without my father, no ghost appeared.

Perhaps my sister was too young to disappoint, and perhaps I, too, co-adventurer with my father, intrepid explorer of misty, mystic realms.

"I wonder if it was Ma," I told my sister later. "And a bedsheet."

"Never," she said. *"Never.* It was a real ghost. I heard it cheep. Ma would *never* do such a thing. If it wasn't a ghost, it was Ayah Kamala."

My father's hysterical, delighted laughter told its own tale, though, always and forever, my mother denied that she had *ever* been a ghost.

* * *

Each of his thirty-two teeth, natural or denture, was sweet, my father said ruefully.

At buffets, he went first to the dessert table, even at the posh Taj Intercontinental or Oberoi Sheraton in Bombay, Delhi, or Madras, which then mainly catered to foreigners and the super-rich, where–along with his Jesuit brother, Father Theo, the Director of XLRI, and his brother Eric–he interviewed short-listed applicants to Jamshedpur's Jesuit business school. Both Eric and my father, still boarding-school boys at heart, gleefully started with Black Forest Gateaux, Banana Splits, and chocolate eclairs before they ate a little roast beef to refresh their palates. And after this token attention to convention, my father returned to the only food he really cared about eating—dessert, devouring mille-feuille and sachertorte until, sweetly tranquilised, he could absolutely eat no more.

Our friend, Father Durt, from Belgium, visited him at his office with a box of Belgian chocolates he had bought on furlough.

Each week, as we met the kindly Jesuit at church, his smile grew more strained. He finally asked, "Did you enjoy the chocolates?" "Chocolates?" my mother, Shalini, and I chirped in unison.

"I…I…I," my father said, flushing, "I… have them in my office." He had eaten a scallop just to sample it, he later confessed, and then decided to nibble at a triton, *just* a nibble, and then, slipping, tasted a limpet, a volute, and the moon-shell until, well, the box of chocolates was…just a box.

* * *

As he approached sixty, the mandatory retirement age from The Tata Iron and Steel Company, my father suffered from lumbago and hay fever, and being financially and emotionally responsible for two young girls, he began to worry about health and death. His eminent father, a surgeon, hospital superintendent and prescient investor, had died suddenly, aged fifty-eight, of an aortic aneurysm. And so, he took up TISCO's offer to senior management of yoga classes at work taught by, ironically, a visiting Australian yogi. My father, aged fifty-six, developed the habit of a daily hour of meditative Hatha Yoga, which he persisted in until he died, robust, competent, and nearly ninety. Yoga changed my father's health, temperament, and the course of his life, bringing him muscular strength and inner calm, swiftly becoming as much of a necessity for emotional and mental health as for physical health, helping him deal with demands, change, stress, and hassles.

Our mornings became dramatic, punctuated by the unnerving roar of the lion pose, *simhasana*, or we would come upon him, legs in the air in a shoulder stand, or apparently dead in *savasana*, the corpse position of deep relaxation.

He gleefully described the position in *Surya Namaskar* in which the guru had Tata executives lie on their bellies, thrust their bottoms in the air, and release any lingering gas in their systems, and the sulphurous stench as the officers of The Tata Iron and Steel Company farted in unison.

My father detoxified during this Yoga course, consuming just vegetables and vegetable juices for a few days, after which he swallowed yards of gauze with water to scour his oesophagus and stomach, which, like a magician, he eventually drew out of his mouth, a procedure, *vastra dhauti*, that, fortunately, he did not permit us to watch. He became a vegetarian, unaccompanied in this heroism by his family, for whom, hitherto and still, a meal was not a meal unless it contained meat or fish. My father refused to allow the full-time cook to make his salads, fearing that Durga might not wash his hands with soap before touching the raw vegetables. My housewife mother had no interest in making salads, and so every afternoon, when he returned home for lunch and his midday siesta, my father made himself a large crisp garden-fresh cucumber and lettuce salad with freshly squeezed lemon juice while Durga recited the scores of the morning's Cricket Test match, India against the Marylebone Cricket Club, which he had listened to on his radio as he cooked our chicken, pork or lamb curries, at which my father now wrinkled his nose: *So fatty.* Similarly, he quietly ate his own totally healthy, totally savourless *ragi*, millet porridge each morning, while we often had bacon, sausages, and fried eggs at which he glared disdainfully: *Fatty.*

* * *

Despite my mother's cautions and precautions, my father was often pick-pocketed when we travelled. Before he and I set off to Mangalore to visit his mother, or to Calcutta, Delhi, or Lucknow, where I joined other "parties" of schoolchildren travelling to Nainital, my mother pinned a confining safety pin over the wallet in his pocket.

We succumbed to the seductions of the journey: *jelebis, samosas,* crisp deep-fried pastry enveloping spicy oniony and mustardy potatoes, and for me, comic books.

And then, in this middle of our giddy mouse-playing spending, my father smote his forehead as he reached for his wallet on spotting another banyan-leaf, twig-threaded container of *gol guppas*: crisp, paper-thin, deep-fried wheaten spheres, punctured, and filled with potent pepper and tamarind water. Once again—he was walletless!!

As we arrived in Calcutta or Bombay, we'd ask someone on the platform for twenty-five paise to phone my mother's sister in Bombay or my aunt in Calcutta, whom my father had decided to avoid because of her reputation for serving rich, fatty food. But there we were, shame-faced, pickpocketed, needing to borrow money, and, of course, with Indian hospitality, she invited us to lunch!

"We look so scruffy," he once said when we were in Calcutta and not pickpocketed, "but there are seventeen million people in Calcutta. We'll never bump into your aunt." I was disappointed since, like all children, I was curious about my relatives and wanted to visit them. And then we meandered into a bookshop on College Street, where, to my triumphant amusement, we noticed my unbookish aunt browsing, and soon we were eating delicious mayonnaise-drenched batter-fried chicken at her house, to my delight and the silent annoy-ance of my newly fat-phobic father.

* * *

Though a rationalist in many ways, my father was not immune to super-stition. My parents would not buy those deep sapphire peacock feather fans, shimmering with iridescent moons, which were meant to be unlucky (providen-tially for India's peacocks). He smiled uneasily when I used the white lie of his illness to escape from a social commitment. "He's sad. Now he fears he *will* get sick," my mother said. He similarly shuddered when he overheard the boasts of his younger brother, Theo, an energetic, brilliant Jesuit (whose assignments ranged from Chaplain to the Allied soldiers in Germany after the Second World War, soon after he earned a PhD at the Catholic University of Leuven, and was ordained at Enghien, Belgium, which my father attended, representing the family; advising on restructuring the educational system of Papua New Guinea after its Independence, and being India's representative in the General Assembly of the United Nations in the seventies). Indira Gandhi, who appointed him, specifically asked him to wear a soutane so that he would cut a striking figure in the General Assembly and give the impression that India was a tolerant, multi-religious society. Theo was later the President of The Xavier Board of Higher Education, and The All India Council of Christian Higher Education (associations of Catholic Colleges in India) and the Director of XLRI.

"Retire?" Theo exclaimed when asked about his plans as he turned sixty. "Retire? I am good for another twenty-five years," he declared (as he indeed was!) "Theo shouldn't show off," my father mourned, for they loved each other. "It's tempting fate." And, sure enough, Theo suffered a retina detachment and was required to lie motionless at the famous eye hospital in Aligarh, across North India, where my father took a train to read to him and spoon-feed him. "I don't know why Theo said that," he said, "I *shuddered* when he said that."

A common dread in India: that if you boast of a ship not even God can sink, it *will* sink; India, where people touch wood when they mention good luck to placate listening deities who may be offended by their hubris, and are sometimes offended if you praise their child, fearing you are enviously giving it the *nazar*, evil eye, provoking malevolent spirits to harm it. The parents quickly touch wood, or in its absence, in self-mockery, their own heads.

* * *

I thought of my father while reading of the French-Canadian described by Thoreau, "so quiet and so happy withal; a well of good humour and contentment which overflowed at his eye. He never tried to write thoughts—no, he could not, he could not tell what to put first, it would kill him."

"I sweat blood when I have to write a letter," my father claimed. Every letter he wrote was drafted in long hand and pondered over and perfected before he copied out the final version. Though my father took upon himself the Gethsemanean duty of writing to his mother once a month when he sent her a support check, he often talked me into drafting it for him so that he had but to mechanically copy it out. "Write me a draft, Anita. I'll tell you all my news. Just write it in my style." And so I did, unconsciously developing the dark arts of writing.

My parents, Noel and Celine Mathias

My father Noel Mathias

My uncle, Fr. Tony Coelho, S.J., a Jesuit mystic, and my father

A girl and her Dad

At the Taj Mahal

Oomphatic:
My Mother, Celine Mathias

My mother loved entering national competitions to invent slogans for products. She poured intensity, effort, thought and longing into her entries and often won a prize--once, most memorably, a Favre-Leuba Swiss watch in a competition to describe Marilyn Monroe in one word. Hers was a neologism, *Oomphatic*, empathic oomph. "What is oomph?" I asked. "Oomph," she said, with a little snide smile, "Oomph is oomph." "Sex appeal," my father whispered.

At home, she spoke an expressive, emphatic English, a mixture of Bombay English and an idiolect peculiar to her and her family. "I do so much for you, and all I get is a bun." I used to wonder what that phrase meant, finally realising it meant a circle, zero, nothing. "Your hair is like the Wild Woman of Borneo's; your thighs are like the rock of Gibraltar," she lamented (though, in fact, I then weighed a mere 113 pounds!). "The costume jewellery you wear is like a gypsy's." A reply to a modest, hopeful request she scorned was, "Your head, I'll do it" (though she occasionally relented). Other responses were Indian clichés. I'd puzzle over her reply to my "Why?": "Because the sky is so high," which then seemed senseless to me; (it meant "Just Because.") Her neologisms entered our family's language—the airline eye masks given by her brother Eustace who worked for Air India, were *blinkies*; aeroplane slippers, ditto, were *shoesies*.

Bihari Buddhu--Bihari fool, was another of her expressions, a term she reserved for me since, unlike my parents who were born in the more sophisticated Bombay and Madras, I was born in Bihar, one of India's least developed states. Or, alternatively, "You goonk," which I think meant idiot or "Donk!" Me: "I'm *not* a donkey." At which she sang out, gaily: "If the cap fits, wear it," or "Tell the truth and shame the devil." In a better mood, she'd sing out gleefully, "How do you solve a problem like Anita?"

My mother was intelligent, educated at Sophia College, Bombay, graduating with a Bachelor's in English Literature, with the highest marks in Bombay University, she often told us. After her arranged marriage, she moved from Bombay, India's gayest metropolis (where she had lived in Bandra, a westernised suburb with a high concentration of Catholics: Goans, Mangaloreans and "East Indians," as Catholics from Bombay and Calcutta were called) to Jamshedpur, which was predominantly Hindu and Parsee, with just a small Catholic community, and where she knew no one, except my father.

Small town Jamshedpur offered few opportunities or challenges for an intelligent, energetic woman except to run her household as diligently, creatively and cost-effectively as possible, and that she did, bustling about in her "housecoat," a colourful, floral duster coat which women then wore at home instead of sarees. She supervised the ayah who washed clothes, hung them out to dry, cut the grass on the three lawns with a hand scythe and twice a day, swept, mopped, and dusted the house. She supervised the cook as he conjured up elaborate meals and, with his help, made homemade wines, pickles, ketchup, squashes, hams, jams, cakes, biscuits, and constellations and galaxies of sweets. She made our clothes on her Singer Sewing Machine, on which she rustled up dresses, nightgowns, boxer shorts for my father and knickers for us children, and created quilts out of our cut-up outgrown clothes. An organised, ingenious housewife could ensure a higher standard of living for her family, releasing

money for better educational opportunities for the children and a more comfortable retirement, and diligent she was, always busy.

Praise, admiration, compliments, and recognition were oxygen for my
mother, indispensable; she loved to be universally acknowledged as the best at
everything she did, and, in that small town with limited avenues for female activity and achievement, she could do many things well, and was proud of her
many excellencies. "Did you hear Father Keogh call me the most elegant and
beautiful woman in Jamshedpur?" Yes, I heard. For her brilliancies were family
dogma.

My mother frequently and joyfully repeated these compliments on her
beauty of which she was inordinately proud, her figure which she boasted was
more youthful than her daughters', her money, her generosity with it, her extended family which was "good," numerous, well-married, and, in Catholic
ecclesiastical circles, powerful; her connections, her intelligence, her literary
style, the excellence of her letters and published columns of "household hints;"
her home, her interior decoration, her cooking and her cook, her garden which
was large and beautiful and won prizes for the most exquisite flowers, the largest vegetables; her ikebana arrangements, her bright charm (gushingly turned
on, usually excessive), her popularity, all the people who loved her, her extravagant hospitality, the food and alcohol bills for her parties exorbitant; her gifts
as an amateur actress, scrabble player, photographer, crossword solver; her
singing voice, her tiny feet, how well she read the epistles in church. The best
singer, the best waltzer at church dances, the best actress, best photographer, a
whizz at quizzes, "Mastermind"--flattery flowed her receptive way. She loved
to charm and dominate a room, control every conversation, answer every question, be the cynosure of every eye, the admired, witty, fizzy one. She was,
indeed, a gifted, creative, and energetic woman frustrated at the limited outlets
for her talents. As I told her often, she should have got a job.

Loving the buzz of entertaining and the accolades it brought her, my mother threw expensive parties at which alcohol flowed, and she served quintessential Mangalorean food, *sannas* and fatty pork sarpatel; *kori kachpu*, chicken with grated coconut, *puran poli*, flatbread stuffed with crushed chickpeas, jaggery and coconut; exquisite crab or shrimp dishes, and, for an *hors d'oeuvre*, her speciality, kidney toast, lamb's kidneys on deep-fried bread.

She believed in lavish hospitality, the table laden with food, three main dishes of meat, fish, shrimp or crab, besides rice and sides. Though she was known as a brilliant cook in Jamshedpur and through the Mangalorean diaspora, and it was an essential part of her identity, she, ironically, rarely cooked herself but had trained our cook, Durga, to brilliance. After taking classes in Chinese cooking, she had him make delicious chow mein and sweet and sour, and through persistent trial and error, they could reproduce anything delicious she had eaten, even the *kulchas* and *chola bhatura*, football-sized puffed deep-fried Indian bread we'd eaten in Nainital, restaurant food really. In a town without a supermarket, competitive housewives sourced interesting foodstuffs from enterprising individuals, and so we bought hand-made macaroni from a lady for pasta mince pies; and noodles, soya sauce and ajinomoto, MSG, from a local Chinese lady; ham and salami from the Beldih Club; barley sugar and Easter eggs from Calcutta, and high-quality chocolate from friends and family visiting from the West.

My mother delighted in creating bouquets of roses, larkspur, gerberas, delphiniums and ferns from our wonderland of a dreamy garden for us to take to school for our teachers. She bought ikebana books and took classes in it, submitting her whimsical arrangements to the United Club's annual flower arranging competition. Whatever avenues a small town offered for creativity or accomplishment, she seized–classes in Batik and Tie and Dye and embroidered mirror work, techniques she used to make our dresses and nightgowns and my school pinafores, as well as mirrored peacocks framed on our walls. She loved to act, both in The United Club's One-Act Play competitions and in St. Mary's Church's annual Passion Play, in which she was Mary, her hair unbound, wailing, "My son! My son!" while the audience, observing her, thought, pityingly, as she knew they would, "Poor thing! She lost her son." She adored singing Carols with the Apostolic Carmel nuns at my primary school, and doing the readings at church, expressively. (My father: "How well Ma reads, how well Ma sings. And "see this newspaper clipping in which Ma is called a well-known socialite.")

Monopolising the family's Concise Oxford Dictionary brought back from England, my mother daily tackled the crossword puzzles in *The Statesman*; she played Scrabble and Lexicon intently, to win, being fiercely competitive over everything, games, feet, or bottoms. When a cousin commented on my small feet, my mother instantly displayed her even smaller feet. She recounted, with an ever-fresh relish, how her friend Hermie Rebello, contemplating both my bottom and my mother's as we processed up to Holy Communion, observed, "The mother's bottom looks like the daughter's, and the daughter's like the mother's!" "And that's because I am such a skinnymalink!" she said, smirking.

My mother spoke wistfully of the seven and a half childless years before I was born when she and my father had lived with great intensity, recording every detail of their lives, listing every book they had read, as I still do; every film they had seen; every lavish dinner party they had thrown with the menu and guest list, so that no guest to our house would ever be served the same food twice. And in account books, they recorded every expenditure of their financially controlled lives.

At the birth of my sister, when my father was forty-nine and my mother thirty-five, all our capacity for love was withdrawn from me and lavished on the baby. In photographs, I turn from a smiling, confident ,lively only child, to a sad, scowling, bewildered, left-out, ignored child, my uncombed hair a messy mop. The bear, she called me, while my sister was the doll. When my mother was bored or disgruntled, she nagged me. "Don't stand bow-legged. Don't stand pigeon-toed. It is better to have a millstone tied around your neck and be cast into the depths of the sea than you corrupt Shalini. Sit like a lady. Durga can see your knickers." "Then I'll close the door," I said. "I won't have closed doors in this house," she said; her control had to be absolute. I sang a rowdy chant in my own annoyance. "Old Mr Mathias had a farm, E-I-E-I-O. And on that farm, he had a MA. E-I-E-I-O. With a nag, nag, here, and a nag, nag, there; here a nag, there a nag, everywhere a nag, nag."

My mother's sense of humour had a bite to it. What she found funny, I didn't. One of her favourite exemplars of wit and wisdom repeated dozens of times with great enjoyment, was when my little sister, Shalini, told my grandparents, "God created the world in six days. On the seventh day, he said, 'Let's create *buddhus*, fools,' and made Anita." And my mother laughed as heartily as if this brilliant observation had just been uttered, with no thought of whether it would hurt my feelings or even that I *had* feelings.

Though she and my father usually presented a united front, on occasion, she abandoned him. After they argued in the car on the way home from a party, she said, "Baby, baby, look in Pa's pockets. He has cake for you." And I hurled myself on him in high excitement and put my hands into the pockets of his Madam-Knows-Best suit (named after the Jamshedpur tailor's stern pronouncement when my father disliked the suit my mother wanted, "Sir, Madam knows best"). And found a fistful of *petit four* wrappers. "Papa, why you ate the cake and brought the *papers* for Atta," I wailed piteously, as she often mimicked, finding the distress and disappointment she had caused hilarious.

My mother's grandfather, Crispin Rebello, was a vet who was sent to Persia with the British army to look after their horses, where he bought ruby and diamond jewellery for his wife, Alice, my great-grandmother, some of which I've inherited. "Horse-doctor's granddaughter!" I'd mock my mother as a child. My father, amused, said, "That's not logical. What she is, you are." "*Koli* fisherwoman!!" I said when her nagging, vocabulary, or tone were too offensive (after the raucous tribe of indigenous fisher-people who fished near her house in Bombay). "Do you hear what she is saying?" she asked my father, affronted. "Big-Fat-Mean-Horrible-Thing; I hate you. I hope you die," I shouted repeatedly as a child, rage flattening my vocabulary. "I am *not* fat," she retorted empathically. And she wasn't, but spindly as a Picasso portrait, all edges and angles, her figure her pride and delight. My sentiments were probably reciprocated, but being the mother, she did not say so. Not all parents adore their children. Not all children adore their parents. Truths universally unacknowledged but ancient as Genesis.

Rearing children was less rewarding for my mother than garnering accolades. It brought no fame, recognition or public reward unless you had a model child who "stood first in class" and made a clean sweep of the prizes, which I did not, and since my mother's greatest terror was any criticism, her buzzword, like her family's, being "What will people say?" she cut off from me all extracurricular activities, every avenue of activity, achievement, flourishing, or life outside the home...everything but reading. She took classes herself, fabric, oil, and glass painting; ikebana, and batik, and let my sister take them, but not me. My sister had a regular upper-middle class Indian childhood–Girl Guides, *Bharat Natyam* dance lessons, guitar and drum lessons, art classes, French lessons from a German lady in town, swimming lessons, cycling lessons and driving lessons, none of which I had. "There'll be more complaints from new people; you won't behave," my mother said, with a little pleased smirk when I wistfully asked to do *Bharat Natyam* or Girl Guides too. And when I desperately promised, "I'll be good," she merely snorted.

My life at home was shaped by my mother's fears of what people would say about *her* parenting. She rarely invited friends over to play with me; she rarely let me play at other children's houses. I had no outlet for my vast energy, my vivid imagination, my intellectual curiosity, my hunger for life and experience. When my troubles at the local school, Sacred Heart Convent, escalated–for, of course, I was an angry child, bored, restless, always in trouble at home and school, defying teachers, in physical fights even–my parents, fortunately, put me in boarding school, aged nine, and chose one of the best boarding schools in the country. The first nine years of my life were marked by constant illness–chickenpox, measles, mumps, crippling abdominal pains so severe I could only crawl, urinary tract infections, skin infections... At my Himalayan boarding school, where the air was crisp and unpolluted and far from the emotional stress of my mother's mockery and criticism, I enjoyed eight years of almost perfect health. I was sick only once, with flu! Going to boarding school, aged nine, was my salvation, the bigger world I've always craved, my opportunity for growth and flourishing. (And, in retrospect, I realise that I would not have been good at the activities on offer in Jamshedpur, and instead, I did just one thing: I read, a pleasure which became a passion, a world, a life—and I sight again the golden thread of grace).

As a teenager, I decided her continual unhappy nagging and criticism was because she had nothing interesting to do; I repeatedly told my father that both she and we would be happier if she had a job. I'd say, "Pa, make her work. Let her start a business. She could sell homemade fudge and milk toffee," always thinking entrepreneurially. "The cheek of her," her sister Joyce would say, "just so she can squander the money." But my father said, flatly, "Our wives don't work," being born in 1916, a generation in which a working wife betokened a husband's failure. In fact, the few things my mother still did–running a Sodality for Catholic girls at my school, helping out with the Legion of Mary and Girl

Guides, or writing a column of household hints for the Catholic Herald in Calcutta, he made her stop after I was born in his late forties. "You wanted children, now be a mother," he said, though this bored her; one night, I heard him ask her sadly, "Why can't you be a mother to her?"

A root memory, I don't remember what I had done, and if she demanded this punishment or my father imposed it; she sat in a dining room chair, and I had to kneel down and kiss her feet. I refused and refused, and my father held a shoe, threatening to hit me with it if I did not do it. The terror of physical pain overwhelmed my pride, and I submitted to the humiliating subjection. She accepted this obeisance extracted from me because of my fear of physical pain without a murmur of protest or empathy. Our relationship never ever recovered.

All our interactions ended in a fight, her attempts at teaching me to cook, or write neatly, or knit; everything had to be done *exactly* as she said, but like her, I liked to do things my own way. I sometimes offered help in the whirling dervish activity before a dinner party while she and my sister made tomato and radish roses; red food-coloured mashed potato roses, or flaked fish in mayonnaise reshaped into a fish with carrot fins with an imported olive for an eye, and a ruff of tiny tomato semi-circles as gills. However, she'd smirk and say definitely, "The Best Help YOU can give me is NO Help at All," and then laugh delightedly at her own wit, continually reminiscing about this putdown she considered a *bon mot*. And so, I went off to read.

"You go out with your daughter," she'd say to my father, meaning me; "I'll stay with my daughter." Which meant I left home without knowing how to make a cup of tea, boil an egg, change a lightbulb, cycle, swim, drive, cook or clean, and lacking all practical skills. And the time in childhood or adolescence which I could have spent on all these things (and also in the decades since then for, dreamy and impractical, I rarely ever shop, cook, clean, or drive), I spent reading, and in retrospect, of course, I wouldn't have traded. God once again wrote straight in crooked lines, which we understand better by and by.

Writing things down is cathartic, as is letting them go. And now, I have done both!

* * *

The postman walked down the garden path every day with a sheaf of yellow stamped envelopes, the cheaper blue aerogrammes of India Post or, more excitingly, foreign blue aerogrammes or exotically stamped envelopes. Like many women of her generation, my mother maintained a vast correspondence, writing several letters at a sitting, keeping up with her own large extended family; with my father's sisters and sisters-in-law; with the Ponsfords, with whom my father had lodged in London; with American, Spanish, and Belgian priests who had once served in Jamshedpur; friends who had emigrated from Jamshedpur, and even with penfriends.

Letter writing was the social media of the day: you didn't necessarily even like those you corresponded with. Instead, you wrote to present a glittering image—writing about your wonderful, fascinating self and family at their shiniest; broadcasting your children's accomplishments and your own, and your wealth, health, popularity, success, good taste, good fortune, whatever envy-inducing status markers you prided yourself on. It was a paper grapevine, much conveyed by implication and innuendo. Letter writing was the province of women. Only the occasional man handled the family's correspondence, for to enjoy writing, especially writing letters, was considered effeminate.

My mother loved writing letters and received many every day. She prided herself on her literary style, her flair and flourish with language, and even corresponded with my friends whom she met on her trips to Nainital. I was ambivalent about this, as were their mothers. When they said, "Mrs Mathias writes such beautiful English," Mrs Oberoi replied, "Well, she might, but *I* am your mother." When, at boarding school, I wrote the compulsory weekly letter home in rhyme, hoping I could get away with a shorter letter that way, an inno-vation which so amused my class teacher, Sister Stanislaus, that unbeknownst to me, she got it published in the school magazine, my mother replied with a six-page letter in facile rhyme, for which I had neither news nor energy, and so I stopped writing rhyming letters.

My mother and her sister Joyce, who, like her, had studied English Lit-erature at Sophia College, Bombay University, had had a claustrophobic intimacy before her marriage, all their hobbies in common—maintaining scrap-books in which they pasted every magazine and newspaper article about Shirley Temple, for instance, or the Royal Wedding of Princess Elizabeth and Prince Philip in 1947. They were each other's best friends and cheerleaders, and con-tinued a girlish correspondence for fifty years, full of detailed, tart, acerbic, gossipy Jane-Austen-like commentary on the goings-on of people either or both knew; menus and guest lists of dinner parties they were invited to or hosted; clothes they made or bought; the prices of purchases, absolute steals or outra-geous rip-offs.

Fat letters from Canada arrived from my mother's penfriend, Barbara Redlich, with whom she corresponded for decades but never met. Barbara, born in Austria, wrote of growing up after the devastation of the Second World War. Everything was scarce; everything was rationed, food, clothing, even, oddly–exercise books. So schoolgirls wrote on the line in blue ink in tiny hand-writing, then at the end of the page, turned the exercise book upside down and wrote in black ink. Having immigrated to Canada, Barbara lived to travel, work-ing a clockwatching job to earn money to travel the world with her female housemate. Lesbians, I now wonder, which neither my mother nor I would have dreamed of then, though my urbane, well-travelled father might have won-dered. I looked at her photographs of South Africa and the Victoria Falls, astonished; I had no idea Africa was so beautiful.

Other penfriends were the German relatives of Father Durt, who once sent us a photograph of their daughter Lorraine, a smiling German girl about my age, standing in a field of sunflowers, as tall as she was, beautiful in her rosy blondness. I carried that photograph everywhere and called her my best friend!

At Dimna Dam

The Winters of the Matriarchs

Bombay: city of danger, city of delight, city of Nana and Grandpa. We visited after a packing of best clothes, letting out of seams of what we had out-grown, my mother and the cook in the kitchen all day, for every relative we were to visit on our odyssey across India from small-town Jamshedpur in the north to Bombay and Mangalore down south was given a box of homemade sweets, *kushwar,* which had to be our very best--milk toffee, almond burfi, fudge, and marzipan. All week we sneaked tastes while my mother concentrated on the fiddly sweets she made "with her own hands," and fiery prawn and pork pickle for her brother Eustace, our bachelor uncle of lavish generosity, who, though indifferent to food, did enjoy maximally pungent pickles. One looked around our house, crystal, cut glass and statues–presents from Uncle Eustace.

To Bombay then we went, a forty-eight-hour train journey, nourished by my mother's chilli chicken, our traditional travel food, and by the fattest book I could find, *Vanity Fair,* which I read by the yellow, wire-caged light, while my young sister snored, then woke, saying dramatically, "I didn't sleep *a wink.*"

And oh, Bombay was a cautionary city.

"In Bombay, goondas speed up on motorcycles alongside auto-rick-shaws, then lean over to yank dangling earrings. If the passenger's ear rips, it rips. *Never* wear jewellery in Bombay: This Sindhi, I read in the latest *Blitz,* laid her arm, *glittering* with gold bangles, on the open window of her car. Men with machetes drove beside her on a dark road, then sped away holding her arm on which those bangles still glittered." Chain-snatchers ripped necklaces off necks;

purse-snatchers grabbed handbags in metropolitan Bombay—as my grandparents, who lived in the safe suburb of Bandra, warned us.

The circus children who soar through the air, spangly and sequined, were, of course, kidnapped. A chloroform-soaked handkerchief slides across the faces of children who stray, you know, just down the road from their parents. Sometimes, their legs are sliced mid-thigh, so they look piteous as they beg, crouched on their little skateboards, their owners watching in the shadows, eyes narrowed on the take. This beggar, in *The Bombay Herald*, died with a *lakh* of rupees sewn into his mattress, "some in rags, and some in bags, and some in velvet gowns."

If you take a taxi late at night, the cabbie aimlessly zigzags through the city, or if he sees you are a clueless *buddhu*, drives around in circles, shamelessly grinning at the meter. Sometimes passengers vanish. And wash up out of the Arabian Sea, sans watch, sans wallet, throat slit. Unaccompanied female women are abducted to brothels at Falkland Road—"Did you see those *Illustrated Weekly* pictures?"—to join the sad prostitutes in their cages.

My grandmother said so. My mother said so.

"What are brothels?" I asked.

"Never you mind."

The air was polluted; crooks and thieves, malice and wickedness, abounded in Bombay, Nana cautioned us. No wonder she never went there. In fact, she rarely left her own home into the terrifying world outside--of drunken bus drivers, bogeymen, beggarmen, thieves. Her fears paralyzed her, like the oppression of an incubus. "But Nana, *everyone* who goes to Bombay doesn't get murdered, robbed or kidnapped," I reasoned, reasonably. "Why should we?"

"Why *shouldn't* you?" they asked, their bleak law of probability.

And the fact that my father was indeed pickpocketed–three times–when we went to Bombay, and we invariably got ourselves lost, and that once, in our haste to catch the subway, my father and I inadvertently boarded a first-class compartment with a second-class ticket and were fined-unreceipted-did not increase her confidence in us, or in the monster city.

* * *

We called my grandmother, Molly Coelho, Small Nana, not just because she was as diminutive and cute as a doll, which--timid and diffident, four feet eleven in the shrinking of old age, always dressed in her mid-calf batik dresses--she was, nor because, as a child might, she ate almost everything: sliced beetroot, tomato, pineapple, pomelo, pancakes, or buttered toast sprinkled with the sugar that was strictly forbidden her, a diabetic. No, we called her Small Nana because she was the daughter of Big Nana, Alice Rebello, my great-grandmother, frail, mild, with a constant gentle smile.

Miraculously on every visit, Alice slipped my mother an exquisite piece of jewellery for us "when we grew up," delicate confections of diamonds, pearls, and Burma rubies with deep depths set in rings and earrings bought for her in Persia by my doting great-grandfather, Crispin Rebello, a veterinary surgeon, attending the British army—or, more precisely, its horses.

These Big Nana slipped to us when unobserved by her son Kenneth and daughter-in-law, Gemma, who had moved in with her, an ex-nun of whom my father said, "She's a virago." ("What is a virago?" "Never mind." Another mysterious word for my childhood Kabbalah.) Jewellery: beautiful and atavistically desired in a culture in which, traditionally, jewellery was a woman's only inalienable possession, yet with the power to rend relationships—for one might have children in multiples, but not jewellery, so every piece given to Petra might make Paulina jealous, for, in the implicit algebra of Indian culture, jewellery—like food—represents love.

* * *

Some time in my early childhood, Nana decided to stop leaving her beloved house. "The traffic, haven't you read of the accidents? The drivers these days, maniacs! Bought their driver's licence with a bribe; couldn't be bothered about pedestrians; expect you to run out of their way; how can *I* run? It's no longer safe to cross a street in Bombay," Nana said with finality.

Within her home, Nana had all she wanted: husband, children, relatives, and family friends who'd drop in, the mountain to Mohammed, with gifts of the sweets, delectable hemlock, which she craved and consumed, ignoring her diabetes. And so she lived contentedly, in ever-narrowing circles, a voluntary house arrest, gradually renouncing parties, visiting, shopping, cooking, her world shrinking to a few rooms.

And in this small world of family, in a strange transmutation, *she* became the child to be petted, protected, and indulged. Three of her five children never married. They lived at home all their lives, gradually losing interest in social life and even their appearances. My sister tricked Nana so often that, surely, Nana was tricking her in turn. Eating a delicacy specially prepared for her, "Bombay Duck" (lizardfish), or Nana's signature split pea and tender mutton dish, she'd say, "Nana, this food is Not Nice." "And Nana's face fell," Shalini crowed. "And then I said 'It. Is. Delicious.'" (Shalini would also wave her hand in front of her mouth in agony, saying, "It's *hot*." "Fire-hot or chilli-hot?" the Coelhos would ask, leaning forward solicitously). And so, protected, Nana floated, so passive she could never remember to cut her toenails; they grew, long, yellow, ridged, gnarled keratin, until the doctor paid a home visit to cut them for her.

But faith can move mountains, and love can move recluses. Nana's two exceptions: Family and God. She left the house on rare and select missions: to visit her mother, Alice, or her grandmother, Flora Coelho, who, in a dizzying swirl of modifiers, was my great-great-grandmother, still alive in my early childhood, daughter of "Dewan Bahadur" Pinto, who received a British Empire title. Flora was famous in the Mangalorean community for her fourteen children, the so-called "The Holy Family," of whom nine became Carmelites or outstanding

Jesuits, known as "the ginger beards," a stray Portuguese gene tinting their beards auburn. Flora's married children, meanwhile, produced a slew of eminent churchmen and churchwomen: Sister Jesuine Marie, Principal of Mount Carmel College in Bangalore; John Prabhu, the Jamshedpur Jesuit Provincial; and Father Tony Coelho, a beloved Jesuit mystic.

Another exception: when Nana's youngest son Ronny (whom my sister called Cubby since she thought he resembled a fox cub) treated us to chop suey, sweet 'n sour, and vast cloying pastries at Bandra's sophisticated, upper-crusty MacRonnels whose green-lit and aromatic ambience made you hungry the instant you entered. Ronny, a Chartered Accountant, sweet-natured, gentle, smiley, was everyone's favourite, the frequent prerogative of the youngest. My mother's only sibling who did marry, late, Ronny still, straight after work, visited his old home, where he was loved-up, lapped up, listened to—and tales of the never-seen characters of his office, like his lame polio-stricken boss, Patrick Saldanha who never missed a day's work, transport strike, monsoon floods, or riots and their fires, provided experience-expanding, soap-operatic gratifications to his mother, his spinster sister Joyce and his bachelor brother Mervyn who traded stocks from home. Late in the evening, tired and talked-out, Ronny finally dragged himself to his own home on the rapidly-decreasing days that he had the energy or desire to, until he basically lived with his mother and three siblings rather than his wife and sons.

Nana's final exception: the perilous Sunday morning crossing of Chimbai Road, all ten steps across it, to massive St. Andrew's Church, opposite her house, its floor, gravestones of glorious mismatched marble—deep peacock purple; pale green onion slices; dark red tree-rings, or sheerest white, a paving of crazy geometry, grieving love and petrified family pride. The gravestoned floor sang belated praises to generations of Coelhos, Rebellos, Lobos, Saldanhas, and Lasradoes, all of whom, apparently, were dearly beloved paragons, exemplary husbands, fathers, wives, and mothers, and if those engraved lauds and laurels were even a little true, the final musing would be all too true, "The earth shall not see their like again."

And in its graveyard, amid amiable flowing-winged marble angels and antique urns, was the oceanside family grave of my elder brother, Gerard, who died in 1960 as an infant, three days old—a spot of fascination, yet dread of the inevitable, dramatic, adult emotion. I was given a photograph of him, a ten-pound baby, looking plump, flawless, and perfect in his long white christening robe. No one would have thought he was dead.

* * *

The sea, the sea! It shimmered, rippling corrugated silver, a two-minute walk across the road from my grandparents' house. Sudden breezes brought the acrid, exhilarating, hors d'oeuvry tang of the "Bombay Ducks," long, silvery fish, and *bhangra*, mackerel, that the Koli fisherwomen sun-dried on the beach—making us feel hungry.

"Yes, sea air makes you peckish," said Aunty Joyce, delighted by slang, as pleased as the German nuns at my hill-station boarding school in Nainital were with *their* elemental dictum: "Mountain air makes you hungry, " hungry even after the table at tea, brilliant with cloying sohn halwa from camel's milk, and orange, red, yellow and green "Bombay halwas" freckled with flecks of ghee, clarified butter, the creme de la crème, which visibly oozed from their pores. Such, such were the joys of our holidays in Bombay.

* * *

Across the road, the ocean, washed gold-silver by the setting sun, battered the seawall. Seagulls screeched on the wings of the wind; breakers and waves crashed as in a dream. But we rarely walked down to the beach. Couldn't go without the adults. *Verboten*, anathema: kidnappers, speeders, and the ever-present, never-voiced danger of rape. And couldn't go with them: for inside, somnolence reigned.

So silver bells and cockle shells, we played in the long, barren front yard, its soil shells from ages past when it had been ocean-floor, or the Arabian Sea flooded it in a forgotten tidal wave. And after years of careful beachcombing, still, the yard was scattered with magic, wentletrap, periwinkle, whelk, shells that sang of ancient seas, aliens and strangers on the earth.

"Look, Shalini, look; I found a joined shell." "But I found a green shell." "Huh! 'She sells sea shells on the sea shore. The sea shells that she sells are sea shore shells.' Now you say it." She couldn't, though her teacher made her daily recite a poem to cure her lisp: "The Ambitious Brussels Sprout," until *ambississ bussles* become a family expression of half-forgotten provenance.

Shells of mystery, shells of beauty, sirens from forbidden seas. We carted them into the house, returned, and still, there were more, numberless as the descendants promised to Abraham—"as the stars in the sky and the sand in the seashore"—the latter, the most staggering metaphor for infinity, for in the sweltering summer nights when we slept on the veranda, I, every night, attempted to count stars to seduce sleep, and it seemed a doable enterprise if one had patience and a system.

Time moved slowly, the timeless time of childhood. Eventually, feeling dazed and dreamy in the sun, we drifted indoors to gaze absently at the pretty-pretty ceramic tiles on the windowsills: an English cottage near a watermill; a plump-cheeked white girl, her face framed by hair spilling from her Alice headband, her cheek against a puppy. Or we sat cross-legged in the dark, lace-curtained living room examining the treasures in my grandfather's display cabinet, an ostrich egg, a delicate English blue and gold doll's china tea set; bowls of rose Bohemian crystal or monogrammed, filigreed silver—while hours passed in the delusive eternity of childhood.

My mother's family exuded languidness. No mornings were marred by the haste and hustle of leaving for work, for only Uncle Eustace visibly worked.

The house: lace curtains always drawn, dusky, drowsy with lotus-eating languor, which hung heavy in the air —"a land in which it seemed always afternoon." Trying to get something done was like swimming through treacle. So, naturally, no one summoned up the energy and resolve to clear that house, full of mystery and surprises, of the detritus of years, to rid the corners of rooms of dust-striped paper piles of delusive good intentions: half-read *Eve's Weeklys* and pious Catholic *Examiners*, and old letters and memorabilia; clippings clipped who knows why, when, and for whom; letters to be re-read and destroyed, whose illicit siren enchantment I rarely resisted, and, besides, the layered midden of generations, old silver, old china, old cut glass, fragile old jewellery, too treasured, too precious to use, all fearsomely tagged—"of sentimental value."

The integrity of my grandfather, Stanislaus Coelho, Collector of Customs in Bombay, was commented on in the Catholic and secular press after his death, so there was not the blind eye, the murmured word, the friend-of-my-friendship which lubricates Indian life, just honest advice on legal circumnavigation of labyrinthine Customs rules offered to friends, and the friends of friends—who remembered him at Diwali with gift boxes of dried fruit and chocolates, ties and tie-pins, crystal vases and clocks, and also at Christmas when my grandfather's house was the place to be. These gifts, in their original boxes, piled up in the corners of rooms, in and above cupboards, under beds or lacy-covered tables--ashtrays and towels, glitzy handbags, imported electronic appliances, full measure, pressed down, flowing over from heaps and stacks, until my grandparents were increasingly hemmed in by their own abundance

Like hobbits, however, my grandparents, uncles and aunt still indefatigably exchanged never-used gifts (*mathoms* in Hobbitish); bronze wall plaques and silk scarves, ashtrays and teatrays, vanity cases and briefcases, perfume, wineglasses, and cuff links passed round and round the inner circle or mouldered in large steel almirahs along with their carefully folded wrapping paper, bows and ribbons, awaiting resurrection at a wedding, christening, or birthday. When he

wished to destroy, we were told, the King of Siam sent a glorious white elephant—too sacred to work, an insult to give away–whose upkeep devoured
one's life. White elephants, white elephants everywhere.

My tall, lanky, straight-backed grandfather, Stanny, wore the small black-
rimmed glasses and baggy tweed trousers and jacket which were the hallmark
of old gentlemen of his school. He had the long, sunken, suffering face of T. S.
Eliot, to whom he bore an uncanny resemblance. Stanny, like my father, could
recite poetry by the yard, Wordsworth, Coleridge, Keats, or Tennyson right into
his seventies when he died. *The world is too much with us; late and soon, getting and
spending, we lay waste our powers…*

Inheriting their ability to memorize easily, almost unconsciously, I
learned entire poems "by heart," reciting to myself, "If I were Lord of Tartary,
myself and me alone/ My bed would be of ivory, of beaten gold my throne,"

"Do you want to hear me recite *Tartary?*" I asked. "I won a prize for
reciting it in school." "Oh, a many-splendoured thing," Uncle Mervyn drawled
in his rich-Burgundy voice. Invitation enough. *And in my court, should peacocks
flaunt. And in my forests, tigers haunt…*

Among the antiques in my grandparents' living room, a book of Master
Plots, soon given to me, and others I desultorily picked up: G.K. Chesterton's
The Everlasting Man, a wedding present to my grandparents, and Victorians, eminent and otherwise: a biography of Lord Macaulay, of Alfred, Lord Tennyson,
by his son, Hallam, and of William Cobbett (who was he?)--undergraduate best
student prizes in English literature that my grandfather, Stanislaus, had won at
the Jesuit Saint Aloysius' College in Mangalore in 1912, 1913, and 1914.

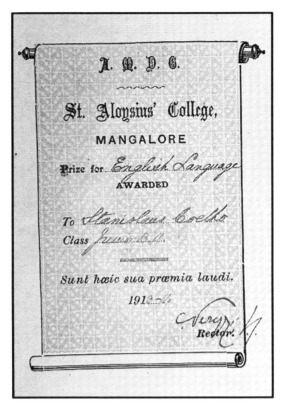

The traditional Biblical trio of tempters–the flesh, the devil, and the world that is too much with us, choking with noise, busyness, and distraction the life of the mind, no less than of the spirit. In another world, another time, my grandfather, gentle, unworldly, nervous, would have been a scholar, but he had twelve siblings, and his father, a landowner, had lost his land after rashly standing surety for a friend.

A man in such a position was expected to earn his living after a first degree (like my father who, aged sixteen, lost his eminent OBE-winning-surgeon father and, having eight younger siblings, served time clerking, and de-coding classified telegrams in Afghanistan before England and his professional degree.) So Stanny Bartlebyied his way to the Customs House, eventually be-coming Collector of Customs and a much-sought expert in the arcana of the Customs Law of British India, and then of independent India.

And so—overwhelmed by the crushing necessity, before women worked, for even the most impractical man to provide for his wife and children—my grandfather, who could sweetly and wistfully recite *In Xanadu did Kubla Khan a stately pleasure dome decree* eventually gave up reading, abandoning the struggle to find a quiet spot, a quiet hour, in a house with a wife and five children and Porlockian friends seeking help and companionship and to beguile an empty hour, his creativity confined to long letters in his spidery handwriting with quirky pen and ink drawings, and infallible recipes like chocolate snowball surprise: mould melted chocolate, condensed milk, and desiccated coconut into balls. Though seeing me leaf through his books, he'd say happily, "I'll teach you to love poetry." Oh, and I do!

I returned home to Jamshedpur with an old suitcase, given by Uncle Eustace, who had given up travelling, full of old books given to me by those who had given up reading. I sobbed over these books with fading cloth bindings and inviting gilt titles, *Silas Marner* or heartbreaking Hardy like *The Mayor of Casterbridge* or *Tess of the d'Urbervilles*, prize books, textbooks, the books of their youth, given to me by my Aunt Joyce's friends, Laura and Chrissie (along with guilty advice: always look up an unfamiliar word, and soon, you'll never meet a word you don't know). Since a college degree in English literature was a tradition in my mother's family, I returned too with school and college literature textbooks *ex libris* of my mother's brothers and sisters, her cousins, her father, Stanislaus, and my grandmother, Molly, who, surprisingly for one so timid, was among the first Indian women to study at a co-educational college, the Jesuit St. Xavier's College in Bombay. Once my mother's first cousin, a sweet maiden aunt, Marjorie, gave me all the Victorian novels in her house, for which her brother, disturbed and mildly drug-addicted Willie, beat her, and I heard this and felt sad and horrified.

In Bandra, I was known as "the girl who's always reading," "who writes so beautifully," and much faded hope and jettisoned longing was displaced onto me by family and their friends who, out of their Saharas of shrivelled ambition, the sky now out of limits, cheered me on as they pointed to bright and morning stars they no longer pursued. So many relatives we visited, daunted by the megalopolis, had made peace with small lives, and with an apparent surrender of aspiration and purpose, just lived to live, each tomorrow the same as yesterday, creeping on at a petty pace.

Is ambition indeed "the last infirmity of noble minds?" Or is it the force that through the green fuse drives the flower, both path and north star through desert days? The boat that swirls you from bogs and swamps into the great river?

One still had ambition. My grandfather's nephew, Alfred Coelho.

Every family had a backstory in gossip, their lives and characters summed up in vignettes and one-liners, a Rosetta clue to everything. People recounted the time Alfred's irate mother marched into the office to berate his father in front of his colleagues. And he, my grandfather's brother, highly-strung, too shamed to return to work, wandered daily by the river, by the weeping willows. A slip of the foot or of the will? He drowned. *Those are pearls that were his eyes. Of his bones are coral made.*

W. H. Auden, in a complicated genetic diagram, shows how a nephew can be the true descendant of an uncle in temperament, physique, gifts, all that matters. That was certainly true of my grandfather and Alfred, who, brilliant and spiritual as none of his own sons were, was sent by his diocese to study at the Pontifical Seminary at Rome.

He returned to pay his beloved uncle a surprise visit. Surprises can be a self-indulgence, cheating the beneficiary of the joy of anticipation. Sometimes dangerously.

My grandfather shuffled to the doorbell. Alfred! His hand to his heart. A mild stroke, a heart attack? The doctor, summoned, said, "You'll have to have an ECG, Mr Coelho." "An ECG?" he protested. "I had one in 1959." It was now 1972.

"The doctor looked at him quizzically," my grandmother said. "He had a very good sense of humour. You could never tell if he was joking."

"Mr Coelho, that was twenty years ago," the doctor said firmly. "The heart changes from minute to minute."

Which became another much-quoted family "famous last word." My father and I went into Bombay after breakfast with an itinerary: purchases enjoined upon us by my mother; Juhu Beach; a visit to my father's cousins, Joy and Gladys. We often walked through the Gateway of India, him courteously offering me his arm, pretending that we were the King-Emperor George V and Queen-Empress Mary, for whose 1911 visit to India the great arch was built. Our travellers' tales, on our return, bore little resemblance to our plans: hunted for the perfect *chola bhatura* and for a hot dog and hamburger (which, in the sixties, seemed to me foreign, glamourous and storybookish*)*, saw *Anne of a Thousand Days*... For even pleasurable adventures, once planned, become a have-to, making me yearn to do something different, spontaneous, surprising even myself. "But, but, but..." my grandmother and Aunt Joyce spluttered. My father grinned, putting his tongue on his upper lip, a tic when extremely pleased with himself. "What to do?" he said. "A woman's mind changes from minute to minute."

Anyway, soon after Alfred's visit and the ECG, my grandfather died. Alfred returned to Rome. And was never again heard of or from. His sister, Diana, in Kuwait, offered rewards; there were sightings. Interpol helped.

Fruitlessly. He had vanished–perhaps murdered, or amnesic following a head injury, or, possibly, in an unimaginable declaration of independence, he had slashed the fraying Gordian cords which bound him to family and reinvented himself.

"And here comes The Ma-ha-ra-ja," my mother's middle brother, Mervyn, drawled as he caught sight of his older brother, Eustace, rolling the syllables in gleeful mockery, his voice suave, melodious, resonant, rich-timbered as port or Christmas cake, a priestly hieratic voice.

His oldest brother, Eustace, appeared, grinning (perpetually cheerful, an anomaly in that family of worriers and fretters) raffish as Rhett Butler in *Gone with the Wind,* whom he resembled down to the ironic glint in his languid, heavy-lidded, deceptively sleepy eyes and his debonair moustache. He was, in the frequent way of siblings, everything Mervyn was not--as lithe as the other was lumbersome, as energetic as the other was torpid, and visibly successful, whereas the other wore the sad odour of failure. With the truth embodied in nicknames, Mervyn called him The Maharaja–after the Air India logo, a red-turbaned endomorphic Maharaja in an outmoded sherwani and red-striped, plumed turban, deeply bowing, on his mystic flying carpet, his courtly right angle bow to any pleb with a ticket. Eustace, a senior executive at Air India, often flew around the world on plush assignments--and was indeed princely in his free-spending carefreeness and careless largesse, his indulgence of his family, his friends, and himself.

Uncle Eustace strode into the house after work, asking me, "What *musti* have you been up to? Have you created a *shindy?'* (Only my father, grandfather, and Uncle Eustace were amused by my outspokenness and mischievousness). 'Want to see the new Boeing 757? The Hanging Gardens? Elephanta Island?" He spirited us away to Juhu beach, where he let us race fully clothed into the salt of the waves, scorning the fuss of swimsuits. Once he was stung by a jellyfish and went limp in paralysis, and we laughed, believing him to be faking and did not even try to drag him in.

When he took us to Bombay's Zoo in the Victoria Gardens on a sweltering day, I burst into tears to see the hippopotamus lying limp and gasping in a thin, filthy film of water and cigarette butts. The newspaper article framed on its cage listed what the vet who'd operated had removed from its stomach: rubber sandals, Coca-Cola bottles, pens, plastic dolls, and pebbles heaved into its trusting, hungry jaws. "Hippopotamus means 'river horse,' Papa said. It's wrong to keep it so dry and hot," I sobbed, overwhelmed with painful empathy. Eustace took me to protest to his friend, Hector Crasto, a City Councillor who sat amid his malodorous cages of white rabbits. Hector and Eustace laughed as I once more burst into tears at the plight of the hippopotamus. Henceforth, the hippopotamus's pool would be filled with water, Hector promised. He would issue orders. And the next time I went to Bombay Zoo, I went straight to the hippo's pool, and there it was, more content, the ripples lap-lapping up to the high-water mark.

On Bombay evenings, Uncle Eustace took me to sit amid acrobatic insects on the verandas of his giggly, gay-spirited friends--fun-loving bachelors and spinsters and the odd couple, who relaxed with nibbles and free-flowing alcohol and banter: Hilda, one leg amputated, the other swollen with elephantiasis; Helen (called Helen of Troy, inevitably) with a white poodle and a crisp pseudo-English accent put on in company, and which gradually faded; Lourdes with hennaed orange hair; Hector, a painter, and jokey Dennis Sequiera, his best friend, who was called, of course, "Dennis the Menace," and who, like Eustace, was inebriated every evening.

Eustace was warmly welcomed in every house, the Crastos, the Rasquinhas, the Vazes, and everyone, knowing him, offered him a drink and in every house, he accepted, his speech slurring as the evening wore on, his eyes drifting–glinting, and far away as the lotus-eaters. "What's your net worth, Eustace? How much have you saved? What man, let us invest it for you," they said as his eyes grew dreamy, benevolent, cat-and-creamy. Or "Can you lend five hundred rupees? Unexpected expense…will return soon." All evening, banter– "Oh come off it, man;" heads bowed in laughter, they pushed his arm, they slapped his back. My cheeks ached with the continual polite smiling at the continual badinage.

Uncle Eustace introduced me with pride and thrilling formality, "This is my niece, Anita. She goes to St. Mary's Convent, Nainital," and "Oooh, an India-famous school!" someone might say with only slightly mock awe, and as befitted someone who went to a posh school, I was, in half-jest, offered a drink, often just *shandy,* beer and lemonade; *toddy,* fermented coconut juice; *feni,* moonshine distilled from cashew nuts; or very sweet homemade wine that I did not think of as alcohol. And in every house, I, a pre-teen, drawled with feigned sophistication, "Oh yes, I think I'll have a shandy." "Say, when." "When!" I said, smart-alecally, as they filled the gag beer mugs past three ounces for a lady, six ounces for a gentleman, almost up to the nine-ounce mark, marked JACKASS. And so, I returned with Uncle Eustace after an evening of carousing, expansive, effusive, in love with the world and everything in it, and most of all with my bubbling *bon mots.*

"Anita!" my mother, grandmother, and Aunt Joyce cried in unison. "Oh," I said airily, swaying—which was not a function of my high-heeled shoes, "I can hold my liquor," an expression I'd picked up in those evenings, "Eustace!" they cried, while he grinned, his mischievous dancing eyes half-closed and far away. *For he on honey-dew hath fed/And drunk the milk of Paradise.*

* * *

At Lent, however, Eustace and his friends, Catholics all, together went on a preached retreat; thought of God, their souls, and the fires of hell; repented, renounced the spirits which brought them such sparkle, and were the bedrock of their friendship; forswore every spirit except the Holy One for the forty days of Lent and forever and ever after that—or least until bubbly Easter.

Eustace's slender, erect father, Stanislaus, also remembered, all too well, the dusty gloom of Ash Wednesday, Holy Day of Fast and Abstinence, first of the Lenten forty. He felt anticipatory hunger pangs well before Shrove Tuesday, when he returned, freshly shriven, to Mangalorean pancakes stuffed with freshly grated tender coconut in a date-palm *jaggery* syrup– which preemptively used all the butter, eggs, and milk in the house, in preparation for a spartan Lent.

As Lent loomed, Stanny said, "Oh Molly, make a few *sannas* for Shrove Tuesday" (fluffy, discus-shaped, steamed rice-flour muffins, which use palm liquor, toddy as a rising agent and have no Western correlative). "Oh, and a little pork *vindaloo* with that, Molly," and (forgetting he had asked for sannas) *"appas, Molly,"* (pancakes made with toddy) "and your mutton and lentil curry, Molly, the *godachi mutli*. And grated coconut and *bimli* (a uniquely tasteless squash—one of India's vegetables, like *ambade* and tamarind, which grow on trees!) And your beef with coconut that goes so well with *bimli*. We'll be fasting all Wednesday, Molly, so please make *pole* (rice pancakes) with it?" he asked, his enthusiasm for feasting before fasting quite Rabelaisian.

And thus fortified, he set his face like flint towards Ash Wednesday, keeping a word-perfect fast, as well he might.

* * *

Uncle Mervyn, a heavy man, heavier every year, physically resembled the Air India Maharaja. His round beaming face had a polished sheen; his large lustrous, slightly squinted eyes sparkled at his own sardonic utterances. Perhaps grounded by his bulk, he was always at home, comfy in his trademark vests or tee-shirt and baggy shorts, yet with the social acceptability of the "self-employed."

51 Chimbai Road: The front door, spirals of wrought iron over wood with flaking paint. (Once, locked out, I had rattled it with impatience, and Aunty Joyce came running saying, "Anita, don't break down our house," disregarding an Indian convention of not reprimanding other people's children. And my mother, for a decade, more, "And what a disgrace, Aunty Joyce had to say, "Anita, don't break our house down"). The door opened onto a foyer where, behind those screens with which Indians, like Japanese, create new rooms, Uncle Mervyn, a self-employed stockbroker, worked. And "worked" was not entirely an overstatement, for, sporadically through the day, Catholic ladies in their immutable Bandra shapeless floral dresses, visited with anxious portfolios inherited from fathers, bachelor brothers, or dead husbands. The post, the postman were objects of sad, strained aquiline eyes, for dividend cheques were tenuous life-lines–comfort hinged on the prompt passage of their cheques through the chancy arteries of the mail. Bandra's bogeys took the shape of bags of post floating on monsoon-flooded streets, washed out from alley refuse heaps into which they'd been dumped on bored and lazy postal days.

A commute down the corridor, "work from home," "set your own hours" are glamorous, alluring lures. Once a month, however, Mervyn, scrubbed and glowing in his dazzling starched terrycot shirt and unaccustomed long trousers, a strand of long hair pulled over his balding head; his huge, hazel eyes bulging with suppressed excitement like his briefcase stuffed with paperwork to be filed in person, and in triplicate–got ready for his tram ride to the Stock Exchange at Bombay, while his mother and sister clucked admonition around him. For though the suburb of Bandra *was* Bombay to us, to my grandparents, inveterate homebodies, the commute from their safe suburb to Bombay, den of iniquity, nest of vipers, sepulchre of the righteous, great Gomorrah, was nasty, fraught, and rare, dreaded in inverse proportion to its frequency.

* * *

When Mervyn's siblings mocked his childhood yearning to become a priest, his secret celebration of improvised masses with missal, bell, candles, censer, and liturgical Latin, he gravitated towards humankind's most common default romance and substitute God: the making of money, obsessively, compulsively—as if to compensate for abandoned dreams.

Food and money were the garb Mephistopheles wore when he appeared to Mervyn. As steaming savoury mirages flooded into memory and imagination, Mervyn dialled one of his genteel women friends who had more time than money. At lunch, for a small fee, his food fantasies lay incarnated before us through the conjurations of Edith, a solemn, middle-aged lady with a neat shoulder-length perm, cat's eyes glasses and tight-sashed, knee-length polyester floral dresses. There lay our favourite Anglo-Indian cuisine: "potato chops;" "pan rolls," "cutlets:" spicy burgers, or light spicy meat puffs.

Mervyn rarely drank water. Instead, he drank Mangola—expensive, sweetened, bottled mango juice—by the crate. When the neighbourhood's illiterate Koli fisher-families sent their sons to the house for help in getting a job or decoding their bank passbook, he'd drawl, "Fetch me a crate of Mangola," his voice full-bodied, resonant, luscious, ripe-fruity, quietly slipping an extra fiver into their hands as a tip, *noblesse oblige.* "The *lakhpati*!" my aunt Joyce exclaimed. "He behaves like a *lakhpati*. Give me what you give them; I'll be a *lakhpati* too." (A *lakh*, a hundred thousand rupees—like a *crore*, ten million—is a uniquely Indian unit, necessary in an inflationary economy. For all Joyce's fulminations, Mervyn, who never worked a regular job, died with several of them, which he left to my mother and Joyce.)

Over lunch, my father and Uncle Mervyn twirled crystal Maharaja-engraved champagne goblets of Mangola and talked about money and investing. I listened—stocks, bonds, dividends of Glaxo, Bombay Dyeing, Reckitt and Colman, Larsen and Toubro... Money, money, money, there's a romance to it.

I felt its excitement as I sat listening: double your money in seven years at ten percent, or in five years at fifteen percent but with more risk. I did mental calculations, marvelling in the miracle of compound interest, hearing the tick-tock of money being fruitful, implacably increasing and multiplying.

Oh, I'd become a millionaire off the abundance encoded in creation for the diligent and imaginative—encrypted in a single apple seed or an egg: farms, orchards, plantations, kingdoms. "I know what, Ma. I'll sell fudge at school; you cook the fudge, and I'll…." "Your head I will!" she said. Okay, then how should I become a millionaire? But each time, I'd back off from this goal and its heady mathematics–so what? For what? Oh, I'd be a millionaire *and* write books, I decided airily. All things are possible: childhood's birthright.

Mervyn's magic: He suddenly appeared with a gigantic brown paper bag from which he flourished chocolate—Krisp (like a Penguin Bar), Five Star (like a Mars Bar), Gems (like M&M's), Caramello, Bournville, Double Decker, Cadbury's Fruit and Nut, which, beaming with the joy of magnanimity, he bestowed on us one by one, *voila,* responding to my little sister's delirious delight—"Wow, *Uncle Merrr-vyn*!"—with an almost eternal "There's more, baby doll!" until finally, almost incredibly, he came to the last of the multiplying loaves, the last fish, and even our gluttonous eyes realised, without sadness, that there was no more. Once, very sweetly for a lifelong bachelor, he took us to Binny's to choose fabric and then to a tailor to have clothes made for us; I remember choosing yellow jeans and a blue denim skirt. Now that they are all gone into the world of light, I see, with sadness, that with hearts that had not yet lived or suffered, we took their kindness for granted—seeing what was comic about Mervyn more vividly than what was thwarted—and kind.

* * *

Mervyn's idols: food, money, and the news. While roosters crowed and muezzins chanted, Mervyn's radios purred as he monitored the world with *The*

Blitz, The Bombay Herald, The Times of India and the morning coffee. Bribery, corruption, politicians and other crooks, and the unnerving rise to power of the Shiv Sena who wanted Bombay renamed *Mumbai* and a Hindustan for Hindus— as if those rooted in the land through race and immemorial residence should belong any less to it because of their faith! Meanwhile, we laughed at the ads, "Breed my Countryman, breed till you cannot breathe," the Air India Maharaja advises while Utterly-Butterly Delicious Amul says, mimicking bhajans, "Hurry Amul. Hurry, hurry."

And while the griefs of the world unfurled through his radio, Mervyn masterminded lavish breakfasts, the meal he conjured up during our visits. From the neighbourhood's only cold storage, the Koli boys fetched, wrapped in white grease-proof paper, the relatively rare luxury meats of my childhood, which we loved: ham, bacon, sausages, salami, luncheon meat, a string of words I now remember like a chant. These were served with "Nana's scrambled eggs," the main thing she personally cooked, fried rich golden in ghee, with onion, coriander, and mint. Eustace surveyed this gastronomic indulgence coolly while, still standing up, he ate, or rather drank his unvarying breakfast—two raw beaten eggs, which I found impossible to swallow despite my great admiration of his jauntiness.

* * *

All morning in his office, cluttered with his cherished menagerie of typewriters, Mervyn fiddled with his expanding universe of shortwave radios, extracting, from their vasty depths, flickering stations: the BBC, the Voice of America, and, most of all, jazzy Radio Ceylon so that he knew the lyrics of ABBA, Cliff Richards, Boney M., or Simon and Garfunkel as well as the coolest girls at school, and walked around the house, humming *The Sounds of Silence* or *I am a Rock.*

And now and again: scoop! He knew, before the newspapers or All India Radio announced it, of the kidnap and massacre of Israeli athletes in Munich in

1972, and, closer to home, on New Year's Day 1978, he heard of the Boeing 747 which crashed on the beach three minutes away from us, and, of course, we scrambled over slippery algae-covered rocks, and fishing nets spread out to dry, arriving at the scene with the rescue workers, and behind the ropes that swiftly cordoned off the treacherous rocks and the sea from the curious and the greedy, watched them haul in wrecked suitcases and bodies and the plucky rubber doll that bobbed above the waves.

* * *

My Aunt Joyce's dress was the perennial deep-frozen length of all Catholic women in Bandra in which, like an enchanted sleeping kingdom, fashions never changed. Their dresses, "frocks" ending just below the knee, a length unchanged from the Raj, though by the sixties, most grown Indian Catholic women in less Westernized parts of India, my father's sisters in Mangalore, for instance, had shed their rather unbecoming dresses for saris,

Aunt Joyce's hair hung lank, her make-up was perfunctory, her figure had thickened; as a young girl, however, Joyce had been pretty. As proposals came from the most eligible bachelors, she sobbed, "But I don't want to leave Mummy." Other proposals came from rich men who, when the Portuguese began to convert our ancestral town of Mangalore almost seven centuries ago, had not, unlike my grandparents, been Brahmins. (At first, the Jesuits who evangelized Mangalore in the mid-sixteenth century converted only Brahmins, the highest caste, to ensure that the new Catholics were the elite. They gave each extended family a Portuguese name to replace its Hindu one; my family were Naiks before they became Mathiases. The old Brahmin families were given names like Lobo, Coelho, Saldanha, Gonsalves, and Rebello, so that even today, surnames are a rough, though not infallible, guide to caste and class (and, anyway, the community remembers). The phrase "old family" has great cachet among Mangaloreans, while "it's a new family" is a patronizing, almost derogatory comment. Old families marry into new families reluctantly, and only when they themselves have come down in the world or the new family has acquired wealth, success, power, or produced beautiful women.

My grandfather, Stanislaus Coelho, rejected all marriage proposals from anyone whose genealogy was less immaculate than his own. (His forebears were wealthy landowning Brahmins before they had been converted to Catholicism; they kept their bloodlines pure by only marrying people from other old, formerly Brahmin families, mostly other Coelhos.) "How can you even consider it?" he said of Joyce's nouveau (very) riche suitor, from a "new" family, originally of a lower caste. "Centuries of *dirt* flowing in his veins!" And so Joyce remained in the house of her youth, a nymph in amber, the taken-for-granted-one who kept the family ticking, who did things for everyone else but for whom no one did anything–nervous, anxious, harassed by the day's Sisyphean worries, whose timidity I remember like a cautionary tale when I shiver on the shores of the great river of experience.

St. Andrew's Church, across the road from their house, loomed over the lane and my grandparents' lives. Each Monday, I counted the Sunday collection with Joyce and her friend Laura at St. Andrew's–tens of thousands of rupees, the mite of widows, paupers, princes, golden lads and lasses… The gleam and chink of money! I attempted engineering feats, building towers of pentagonal five paise coins; hexagonal twenties with Asoka's lions; round rupee coins, and eleven-sided twos.

I counted in paise, my aunt in *annas*, six paise, a superseded unit that my mother and her family still talked and thought in, despite our decimalized post-Independence currency--to the confusion of children and vendors; (similarly and oddly, she called a toilet a commode). And when the Parish needed money, I went with my maiden aunt and her maiden friends to play Housie. With intense concentration, hope and longing, we listened for *jaldi five*, two fat ladies,

88; one and six, sweet 16; all the sixes, 66; hockey sticks, 77; top of the house, 90, and then jubilation—HOUSIE!

* * *

51 Chimbai Road was an old house, its yellowing whitewash moulting flakes. In the narrow strip behind the house and the high back walls, bananas and papayas fell unharvested, their sweetness wasted.

"He never accepted a bribe," my father said of his father-in-law. "And other people go into customs only *for* the bribes,"–deliberately turning blind for cash while smugglers introduced gold, synthetic sarees, watches, perfume, cassettes of western music, juicers, or the coveted "mixie-grinder" into India's protectionist markets.

"And so," he continued, "his colleagues own huge beach houses, but he still rents"—the lower floor of a rambling, coveted, two-storey seaside house.

Their formidable old spinster landlady, Cissy (Cecilia) Valladares, lived in her lair on the upper floor of this house she'd inherited, which—despite Bombay's rent control laws—provided her with a comfortable, predictable, unearned income, and the consequent ironic fate of becoming one of those un/fortunate people blessed or cursed with inheritances and empty, purposeless days.

When the Coelhos talked about her, they metonymically spelt out her name UP so we children wouldn't realise who they were speaking of, but, of course, we did, and so, with traditional Indian good manners, I called her Aunty Youpee, and a new code had to be invented.

She had once blocked my path, her face, a map of warts and wens beneath her Medusa curls. "And what mischief did *you* do that *you* got those?" she pointed to violet-indigo bruises on my tomboy's face. I pointed up in turn and asked, "What mischief did *you* do that *you* got those?"

She gasped, my grandfather gasped, pulling me away, though he, shy, correct, unfailingly polite, could barely conceal his delight. "Anita!" my mother, grandmother and Aunt Joyce cried.

My grandfather said—proudly, "See what answers she gives at five. What answers will she give at twenty-five?" My father laughed.

* * *

Youpee stalked out increasingly infrequently until she no longer could. When I went up with Uncle Mervyn–her sole visitor—to read her the newspaper ("You hoping she'll leave you her money?" Aunty Joyce asked him), the fearsome witch of my childhood lay helpless in her own excrement. Her around-the-clock ayah malingered, squatting in the purer air of the balcony, absently sieving rice, pretending not to hear her faint old woman voice. Her only relatives, three nieces, were invisible. We hollered for the ayah who came and turned her over; the bedsores on her bottom and back were chasms of pink raw flesh, almost reaching the bone.

She died, leaving the sprawling house to her suddenly-visible nieces (that old, strange, stronger-than-water business) who, in the Gotterdamerung that, across India, destroyed so many people's childhood memories, pulled down 51 Chimbai Road—a plummy location, opposite both the beach, and massive St. Andrew's Church, nucleus of the suburb's Catholic social, cultural, and religious life. "Bayside" went up in its stead (making the nieces instant multi-millionaires)–twenty floors of apartments, no room now for quirky mansions with flaking paint. The old order yielded to Lego symmetries, little flats, to the left, to the right, on top of, below each other, two hundred families living in a patch of earth that housed two. And in this world where neither the good nor the evil get exactly what they deserve, the aunt shunned alive, once dead, gave them wealth they could never have dreamed of growing up in sleepy Bandra.

And, as compensation for their torn-down rented house, my grandparents were given a free flat in the posh new Bayside: a seaside residence, like my

grandfather's colleagues in Customs had–through the interventions of providence and the current socialist legislation which protected long-term tenants
against radically raised rents or evictions, though without the lowness, stress,
and subterfuges of dishonesty.

The wages of honesty: not so bad after all.

* * *

Our plans changing from minute to minute, we explored gay Bombay–
the polyglot music of its streets familiar from "Trade," the Indian Monopoly:
Marine Drive, Chowpatty Beach, Cuffe Parade, Churchgate, Flora Fountain,
Apollo Bunder, Malabar Hill. Stylish Bombay, where we bought a year's supply
of churidars, shawls, jeans, *chappals*, nightdresses, jewellery, mini, and then, as
the fashions changed, midi skirts–for it had India's widest, wildest range from
delicate elegance to show-offy garishness.

Bombay, to which all roads led, the country's delight, excitement throb-
bing through it like the Bollywood and Beatles songs whose notes floated out
from little stores with over-the-counter…oh, pretty much any food of the appetite's desiring: north Indian *kulchas* and *bondas*, south Indian *dosas* and *uttapams*,
western Angels and Devils prancing on Horseback, tiny beads of caviar—and
under-the-counter smuggled almost-anything in the warrens of smuggler's par-
adises like Bori Bunder or the covered Crawford market, with its Norman
architecture, and famous frieze, designed by Lockwood Kipling, Rudyard's father, into which my mother, without warning, vanished while my father sighed,
wry, resigned, "An Overpowering Desire has seized her."

Carpe Diem. I got him to let me buy books, secondhand classics I had not
yet ticked off the also-published-by lists at the back of the classics I *had* read
(first oppressions of the heavy weight of unread literature!) while he, liberated,
bought yet another of the penknives he loved, with an ingenious array of just-
in-case-I'm-marooned attachments, or inventive kitchen gadgets that never

worked for long, and doomed coasters with henpecked husband lamentations, *"My wife is my life, my life is my wife. What a wife! What a life!"*

As December unscrolled, scruffy neighbourhood boys gathered at street corners, singing, "Christmas is coming; the geese are getting fat; please put a penny in the old man's hat," as they fanned flickering flames. Pointing at their scarecrow in his faded shirt, they jauntily asked, "A penny for the Old Guy?" Guy Fawkes, I suppose, morphed into the old guy, the old year.

* * *

Eat, visit, shop, explore. Can pleasure pall? By mid-December, it did. My father grew restive. And every year, the same drama.

"Now let's go to Mangalore and see my Ma," my father said with the firmness he rarely mustered. When he did, however, he was—almost—unassailable.

"Mangalore!" my mother said. She was "a Bombayite," proud of her citizenship in the metropolis. *"Never!* I am *never* going to *set foot* in Mangalore again," the sleepy town on the west coast of India where my father's mother and sisters lived and the ancestral hometown of both my parents' families. After the Bombay Port Dock Explosion of 1944, then believed to be Japanese aggression, the "Bombayites" who could evacuate did so. My mother and Joyce, like Blitzed London children, were sent to Mangalore. Which was *not* Narnia. "When we cried in Mangalore and said we missed our Mummy, those Konkani-speaking girls asked, 'And do you miss your Puppy?'"

* * *

My soft-spoken father, Noel, the longed-for first-born son after "a plague of girls," five pretty maids all in a row, had returned after eight years in England with polish and sophistication and a lucrative professional degree--a Fellow of the Institute of Chartered Accountants of England and Wales. As far as his mother, grandmother, and sisters were concerned, any bride must necessarily fall short of his glory.

My mother dissented.

When my mother went on her ill-fated trip to Mangalore as a young bride, she did not dazzle the town; she was not "the belle of every ball." My grandmother delighted to have her gentle, kindly son, now so English and urbane, home again had little time for the young, new wife. My father's elder sisters, Ethel and Winnie, grand dames married into the town's leading families, betrayed no inclination to gush over her. My mother's vanity was piqued. Finding them immune to her charm, she refused to ever visit Mangalore or her mother or sisters-in-law again, winning the Pyrrhic battles between mother and daughter-in-law scripted by centuries of Indian tradition by ignoring as thoroughly as she was ignored (the very best strategy!). "I am a *persona non grata* in Mangalore," she'd say with a cryptic smirk, long before I knew the meaning of the Latin she flourished, or that it was Latin. She did not visit Mangalore or her in-laws again for thirty years.

Every few years: a miracle. My father asserted himself. "Well, if you don't want to go, don't go," he said. "I'm going on my own."

"Pa, I'm going with you," I said desperately. "And I really, really want to see the body of Francis Xavier on the way, in Goa." I wanted to go to Decennial Exposition in 1974 of the miraculously mummified body of Saint Francis Xavier, which the nuns at boarding school had talked about with much excitement. If such a thing were possible, if a four-hundred-year-old body could be preserved incorruptibly, then perhaps there was magic, after all; perhaps there was a God. (Aged eleven, at boarding school, I had shed my faith in God). And my father, always game for explorations of the supernatural or paranormal, whether Padre Pio's stigmata, the charismatic renewal, glossolalia, palmistry, table-tapping, Sai Baba who could materialise holy ash, or a four-hundred-year-old miraculously preserved body, agreed to take me.

"No. No!" my mother said, equally desperately. "You are *not* going to Mangalore. I don't like you meeting relatives. You'll blab family secrets. They'll ask, "Who do you like more, your mummy or your daddy?' and you will say my father, and they'll say why, and pump, and pump, and you are such a donk-- you'll tell them exactly why."

"I'm not a donk!"

"Tell the truth and shame the devil," she sang out gleefully.

"Oh, let her come," my father said quietly. "Or you two will fight all the time."

"Well, she'll be Mary, Mary, Quite Contrary in Mangalore too. She'll say, 'I'm called the naughtiest girl in school.' And they'll say why, and she'll explain– proudly–and there'll be a new series of stories, and..." my mother protested.

"I want to go too," my sister said.

* * *

A conclave late at night, behind closed doors. My parents never argued in front of us, but arrived at decisions mysteriously, the unpleasant ones attributed to our father, our idol, whom we never blamed.

My mother and sister would remain in Bombay. And my father and I were to go to Goa and Mangalore. However, because of the expected throngs of pilgrims, many vaccinations were required before entering Goa, and I was then extremely phobic about needles, dentists, and physical pain. And though I had to have vaccinations for cholera, typhoid, TB, smallpox, the whole slew, annually before leaving for boarding school, that was in March, and this was December, and so, to my father's disappointment, I refused the vaccines, and the trip to Goa and Francis Xavier's miraculous body

But--to Mangalore we went!!

Five generations of Coelhos, my great-great-great-grandfather Diwan Bahadur Pinto, my great-great-grandmother Flora Coelho, my great-grandmother Alice Rebello, my grandmother Molly Coelho, and my mother as a young girl

L to R, my mother, my grandmother Molly, my grandfather Stanislaus Coelho, and my aunt, Joyce Coelho

My grandfather Stanislaus Coelho

My Maternal Uncles, Eustace, Ronny, and Mervyn

to R, Uncle Mervyn, Uncle Eustace, My father, Anita and Shalini

Uncle Ronny restraining me

Shalini and an anguished-looking Anita with our maternal great-grandmother Alice Rebello

Swimming fully clothed at Juhu Beach with Uncle Eustace

Silver Bells and Cockle Shells: Mangalore, My Ancestral Town

Going from Bombay to Mangalore was reverse time-travel, retreating to a more pristine world. We slid through time through the ancient hilly rain forests, luna-moth-green valleys, and the hairpin bends of the Western Ghats. "Look, Pa, look!": black-faced langur monkeys, a slender loris

.

We took a "deluxe" bus, air-conditioned, but every air-conditioned coach was also a "video coach." By day, by night. So while my father and I played interminable, determined games of "Twenty Questions" or "Animal, Vegetable, Mineral," Bollywood movies blared. Widows wailed, abandoned women in white wandered, listlessly singing, "*mera jeevan gora kagaj*," *my life is a blank page*, and coquettish, bright-clad nymphs, high-pitched sopranos, ran around trees, through parks, fleeing from shaggy satyrs called Amitabh or Rishi—all the while singing.

As we prepped for school quiz competitions, my father quizzed me in the style of BBC's Mastermind: "Who painted "The Persistence of Memory"? "Salvador Dali." "What is Bob Dylan's real name?" "Robert Zuckerman. He called himself Dylan in homage to Dylan Thomas," I added gratuitously. "What was the cornucopia?" "The horn of the goat, Amalthea." Later, in an embarrassing epiphany, I suspected my father asked me questions to which he suspected I, who read quiz books, knew the answer.

Then we practised debating, my father setting me topics like those in school– "Which is better, newspapers or television?" "An arranged marriage is better than a love marriage," "Being rich is a pleasure," and five minutes to scribble an introduction, body, and conclusion, and then, certain he'd be immeasurably impressed, over the roaring road and raucous screen, I declaimed my speech.

* * *

Every few hours, the bus pulled into a wayside restaurant, undoubtedly pre-bribed. And since my father spent money in a hay-making way in my mother's absence, I ordered ecstatically, even late at night: *puri pallya*, round deep-fried flatbreads with curried spinach; *masala dosas*, crisp golden, stretching far beyond the plate, and *kulfi falooda*, almond ice cream floating with red jelly, and strands of vermicelli in a pink milkshake flavoured with rose syrup, coloured with cochineal. Sometimes, even the waiter suggested desisting.

My father only ordered coffee. "Order something more, Pa!" He grinned, "I'll see what you leave, *then* I'll order." "Oh, I'll eat *everything*. I'm *ravenous*!" "Huh!"

I gourmandised. Ten minutes later: "I'm full!" "Can't you eat some more?" "*I just can't*," and my father polished off the heaped leftovers, saying as I knew he would, "*Wasting!* When I was a student in England during the War, billboards everywhere showed a plate of half-eaten food. The caption said: 'If you didn't want it, why did you take it?'" Or else he said: "Never waste. One day you may need it and not have it."

Then I was sent to use the toilet and inevitably returned stricken. "Pa, the squat toilet wasn't flushed. There were turds in it. I nearly vomited." "Okay," he said, "Hurry. We'll find bushes." We walked into the scrub by the side of the road with him on guard duty. "You see the advantages of being a man!" he grumbled, as I squealed, "*Paaaa*, is anyone coming?" "I can pee standing up, with my back to the road, and no one will guess what I'm doing." As if *I* needed convincing! "The poor parents!" my father said when he heard of the birth of a girl. "Girls are a terrible thing. A terrible responsibility."

* * *

The bus veered through the precipitous wild green valleys of the Western Ghats. A rambunctious student from Manipal Medical College distributed sugarcane he'd snatched through the bus window from lumbering bullock carts. I crunched the nectary stalks with delight–which faded when my father said the load would be weighed at the journey's end, and the driver, who sat oblivious, switching the magnificent white beasts, would be fined for the deficit. The student organized the English-speaking passengers into riddle-askers, joke-tellers. "Knock, knock." "Who's there?" "Amos." "Amos Who?" "Amos Quito."

Just before the bus left Maharashtra, policemen, rifles in their holsters, boarded, randomly searching luggage. Our hearts stopped. The Scotch–contraband in Maharashtra which was then "dry"–that perennial doomed social experiment.

A drunk man yelled at the officials, who yanked him off the bus. Suddenly sober, he realised he had been arrested, and wept and pleaded with them, touching their feet. They were unmoved. I felt sorry for him and appalled to see his degradation. "They'll take every paise he has," my father said. "What a terrible thing it is to be drunk!"

* * *

Angelus bells pealed and roosters crowed as, at dawn, we entered Mangalore, our God-haunted ancestral town on the west coast of India—a holy town, nuns and priests as common on the streets as secular people, like statue-studded ancient Athens in whose streets, it was said, one was as likely to encounter a God as a man. Mangalore was converted to Roman Catholicism in the mid-sixteenth century by Portuguese missionaries, backed by the power of the Inquisition. Our little town contributed disproportionately to India's nuns and priests, for Mangaloreans have large families, and the nunnery and the seminary were traditional refuges for unmarried women or intellectual men who dreaded "settling down" and the arid busyness of the world of business. They offered security, respect and, sometimes, a career of sorts. There were two thousand nuns and a thousand priests in Mangalore: a proud statistic we often heard, and so the steady, joyful bursts of chapel bells.

Mangalore was lush and pretty, moist, leaf-green, very-green everywhere as if it had just rained, dew seeping through emerald moss on the contorted roots of mango trees and dripping from creepers and purple orchids. The tang of the sea was in the air. Steep, narrow, shady lanes wound between rambling houses surrounded by gardens dense with palm and jackfruit trees, hibiscus, bougainvillaea, canna, and tuberoses. Fruit-laden branches lolled over garden walls, shedding sweet litter: guavas, avocados and mangoes. Fallen knobby custard apples cracked open, spilling their white, sweet, black-seeded flesh.

The mossy old manses had roofs of tunnel-shaped ochre tiles made in the factory, which belonged to my paternal great-grandfather, Peter Paul Lobo. They provided a sober counterpoint to the houses on the outskirts erected by returning emigrants, multistoried monstrosities painted in Disneyland pink, turquoise, and yellow, a flaunting of the fruits of lonely desert toil, built for their families–in the grand tradition of returnee housing, whether in Victorian England or colonial Spain–by the hundreds of Mangalorean working in the Persian Gulf. "Gulf money," one said wryly, passing them. The green hills around Mangalore were terraced with coffee plantations, owned by "the old families," the Coelhos, the Gonsalveses and the Saldanhas, while the sea provided entrepreneurs like my cousin Peter Prabhu with new opportunities: he canned and exported their bounty–crab, shrimp, and oysters.

* * *

In a little black and yellow auto-rickshaw or "bone-shaker," we rattled to "Palm Grove," my grandmother Josephine Mathias's red brick, tile-roofed house, which was large, dark, cool, and rambling. It was secluded in a tree-shaded mosquitoey compound sheltered by high walls; a grove of palm trees swished around it.

A group of Billavas, a Tulu-speaking ethnic group, traditionally toddy-tappers, shimmied up these, small sickles around their waists, to retrieve the tender coconuts she sold them. They parked their bikes in the town's shady nooks, roped cascades of green, smooth-skinned coconuts dangling from either side of the handlebars and back-carriers. Fresh coconut was the rare Indian snack that was unquestionably healthy and unadulterated. A swipe of a machete and a straw; they sold passers-by the cool, clear, nectary coconut juice, the country's purest drink, safer than water. Another swipe halved the coconut, handed to a customer with a chip of its own husk to scoop up the delicate, creamy ambrosial coconut meat.

* * *

We climbed the steps up to the long, shady veranda of Palm Grove, dark and cavernous, its high ceilings and stone floors keeping it cool as a morgue. Its red tiles, like those of many old houses in town, were stamped Messrs. Joseph Lobo and Son, the factory of my Granny's father, Peter Paul Lobo, who left it to his naïve, sweet, very young third wife and widow, my great-grandmother Julianna, twenty-two years younger than him, and just twenty-eight when she was widowed, having borne seven children in her brief years as a wife. The newly-widowed Julianna, baffled and bewildered by the demands of having to run a tile factory as well as bring up her seven children (and the five sons of Peter Paul Lobo's previous wife, Emiliana, who had died young), sold the factory to her nephew, the manager, for "a song"—the factory and the goodwill, as her son Norman discovered when he tried to establish a tile company using his grandfather's name and reputation. "The goodwill? Yes, I signed off on it. He said that meant I had no bad feelings."

When Julianna's debts to my grandfather Piedade Mathias, her daughter Josephine's husband, grew beyond hope of repayment, she signed over her house, Palm Grove, to her son-in-law to cancel them. So, Norman did not even inherit the ancestral home he had expected. Sad, guilty about this, my grandmother, Josephine, invited her younger brother to stay with her in his straitened old age, deriving great comfort from her end being so close to her beginning.

Wiry, ectomorphic Norman was a nimble, spry Old Father William, a familiar sight around Mangalore, as he hopped on and off buses almost until his death at 102. A brusque old man with a savage wit. "How obsequious they were; now, when we pass the paddy fields, they show us their bums,"–he demonstrated! –speaking of land, Granny had lost to her tenant farmers under India's socialist land-to-the-tillers legislation intended to crush the power of the *zamindars*, feudal landowners, who kept peasants in generational virtual serfdom. (A trivial debt at absurdly high interest to be paid off by unpaid labour, never quite wiped out, which meant further borrowing, further labour, a viciously growing debt, inherited by one's children and grandchildren who work without pay to pay off the debt, that two generations later *still* goes up; there are fifteen million "bonded" child labourers in India, working to pay off relatively small sums of money.) Of course, the real feudal landowners, the unscrupulous and bullies with their hired thugs, retained their land through fraud and chicanery. I remember my classmate, Vanita, pulled out of class to doll up in a saree, makeup, and bun of false hair and, assisted by her own portliness, be presented in court as Miss Sabhrawal, independent farmer, thus evading the limits on acreage per family. Meanwhile, the clueless—the cartoonist R.K. Lakshman's Common Man, unversed in the second language of the law—lost their land.)

I dashed towards the dog on the veranda who strained towards me, snarling, steel chain taut, teeth bared. I'd boast that I could gentle even savage *Cave Canem* watchdogs, talking to them at a distance, going ever closer, my outstretched hand just out of biting range, talking gently until their eyes hinted that I could stroke them. But (can any crime be uglier than mutating the natural sweetness of an animal or a child?) Tibby had been deliberately brutalised.

And now memory shrinks as at an impending burn. In the lazy afternoons, Norman, siesta-rested and completely unprovoked, took his walking stick to methodically, savagely, beat the chained cowering dog who, with high-pitched broken-hearted yelps of desperation, helplessly bent his head, screwing his eyes shut in terror as if blindness might shield him from pain. At any moment, the dog could have swerved and bitten the man but did not; humane and brutish are imprecise adjectives. I rushed out, near hysteria; my father held me back, muttering, "It *is* his dog." "*Why?*" I asked the terrifying old man. Norman glared at me and stalked off, chuntering. To brutalise the dog so that, when unchained at night to prowl the grounds, he would–acting on his new-grafted instincts–instantly bite a burglar.

* * *

She sat in the sunlight streaming through the dining room window, a woman thinking; a study in chiaroscuro with her dark sari and her light-skinned, fine-featured sunken face, her brother Norman invariably with her, two old people who looked remarkably alike, both inheriting their paler skin and pendulous ears from their Portuguese grandmother who left Granny an odd, tangible legacy—a porcelain chamber pot brought from Portugal with her name painted on it, Donna Anna Theresa Henriques. Granny remained seated in the dim dining room all day, a frail wraith in a housecoat. She was physically able to walk around her house right into her late eighties, but walking did not interest her, and finally, she no longer could. She never left her home at all, as long as I knew her, not even to go to Mass or visit her children and grandchildren in town.

As she heard my footsteps, Granny called, her voice soft and tremulous with age, "Anita, come here; talk to me,"—uninvited-fairy incantation, petrifaction. I slouched into the dining room. Pale, stern, dark-clothed, she pointed, "Sit there. Talk to me." And I'd be struck dumb, as by a wizard's wand, every thought or memory evaporated. What should I say? My mind froze. *The sedge is wither'd from the lake, and no birds sing.* "Tell me about your boarding school," she said. What about my boarding school? I couldn't think of anything about my boarding school. I sat there, rigor mortis on mind and tongue. After a decent but interminable interval, I escaped.

The air on the verandah felt bright and free. My spirit winged. "Pa," I exhaled, "Let's play Scrabble. Let's play Monopoly." I dived into the game with self-forgetting capitalistic passion. "Noel spends his visit to me playing Monopoly with Anita," his mother said.

And my father said: "What do you mean, "You don't know what to say"? An intelligent person should be able to have an interesting conversation with almost anyone. If all else fails, ask questions."

* * *

And so, I did.

What is your earliest memory, Granny?

Standing in a mulberry field, overhearing a passerby say, "What a beautiful child!" "And that is how I knew I was beautiful." And she was.

Celestial taxation—each blessing: beauty, wealth, great talent has a shadow.

Granny was married at seventeen to a man seventeen years older, as dark-skinned as she was light-skinned or "fair," in Indian English: My grandfather, Dr Piedade Felician Mathias, an ambitious, self-made surgeon who, through the combined financial effort of his entire family—and his own brilliance, sweat and resolve—went to medical school and then, as was typical of upwardly mobile men, married a bride from an old, established family, and pretty in the bargain, light skin being a sought-after trait in an unabashedly "fair"-is-beautiful culture. My grandfather was distinguished, the first Indian Civil Surgeon in the Empire and the first Indian Superintendent of the Stanley Medical College and Hospital in Madras, after whom wards in the Stanley Medical College and the Madras Medical College are still named.

During a phase of teenage snobbery, my father scolded, "Now, now, don't get too snobbish. You don't know my father's family. One of them was a tongawallah. Another was a clerk in Kankanaddy Medical College." He gleefully claimed kinship with the butcher, an apocryphal one we hoped, the baker, the candlestick-maker. At the same time, we screeched in only partially exaggerated horror as he divulged his supposedly lowly paternal origins, "Oh Pa, stoooop."

The marriage was not happy. *Did you like your husband, Granny?* I asked, with curiosity on the verge of rudeness, as her plain-spokeness betrayed the mental softening and sweetening that extreme old age can bring. "No," she said, quite incredibly. "I never liked him. He had a very bad temper. I was always afraid of him," uttering with beautiful, truthful simplicity what, in India, is an almost sacrilegious statement.

This was an observation I'd never heard from any of his fourteen children, who idolised his memory. The official religions of India are deeply, stubbornly, divisive, not so its unvoiced, axiomatic ones: the imperatives of hospitality and generosity; the reverence of wealth and success (an unspoken assumption: "Why be happy when you can be successful?) and, also, the religion of family, which dictates a pretence of affectionate sentimentality towards your blood relatives, a pretence that, of course, they were perfect and, of course, you love them. The religion of family demands that you honour your parents, grandparents, uncles, and aunts; jealously guard family secrets; speak no evil of your blood relations to anyone outside the extended family, and no evil of your nuclear family to anyone at all.

Where did he work?

In the days when "the first" was qualified by Indian, he was the first Indian Assistant Surgeon General in Madras, where he was also the first Indian Superintendent of the Royapuram Hospital and Royapettah General Hospital (leaving traces in a Dr P. F. Mathias surgical ward) and Professor of Surgery at Stanley Medical College.

Piedade captured my father for company during his long days on the Madras docks, where he vetted interminable lines of indentured labourers who, out of desperate poverty and familial love, left India for British colonies, Trinidad, Singapore, Malaya, Burma, Ceylon, Mauritius, Uganda, and Kenya. The physicals were, perforce, perfunctory for long lines of potential cheap labour waited. My father described the diagnoses--Rasping, rattly lungs: suspected TB. Pull down the lower eyelid: too pale, too anaemic. Open your mouth: good teeth, good general health. And vice-versa. A scribe followed. A minute or so a man.

* * *

My grandfather, Piedade Felician Mathias, received two imperial decorations, the Kaiser-e-Hind medal in 1921 and, at the Imperial Durbar in 1929, the OBE, Order of the British Empire. Lolling on the veranda of Palm Grove, I'd read his OBE citation absently, dreamily, "We George Fifth, King-Emperor of Great Britain, North Ireland, and the British Dominions beyond the Seas, Defender of the Faith, to our Trusty and Well-beloved Piedade Felician Mathias, Greetings…" Or something to that effect.

On the day before he left for the Imperial Durbar, he froze. How exactly does one tie a tie? And so, on the day before his exaltation, he humbly went to ask his Portuguese Parish priest to teach him to tie a tie.

A priest in whom he had selective faith. Each time we passed it, my father pointed out the abandoned "haunted" house of his friend and fellow altar boy, Noel Davis, whose sister Jessie was "possessed." Between the Kyrie and the Sanctus, Noel Davis whispered, "Noel, does this happen in your house too? It's terrible! At night, winds blow through our house. Stones fall. Little chalices rain down."

But when the Portuguese Parish priest went to exorcise Jessie, my grandfather snorted, "*That* priest can't cast out demons. He's too fat. You need to be able to *fast* to do that."

In Mangalore, people believed in curses: illness and ill fortune dogging evil, avaricious families who disinherited siblings or cousins. My father told me of his mentor, F.L. Silva (who suggested that he go to England and become a Chartered Accountant), who could not repay money borrowed from his cousins. The cousins had him arrested, and the good man was led, handcuffed, to jail, a broken man even after his release. Within twenty years, *all* those cousins died young in a series of disasters—one in the Quetta earthquake in 1935, one in the Bombay Port Dock explosion in 1942, and one in the crash of Air India's *The Kashmir Princess* in 1955.

* * *

What else do you remember, Granny?

After my grandfather had successfully operated on a Brother of Saint Gabriel, the Order which ran Montfort, my father's boarding school, the Superior visited him, saying: "Oh Dr Mathias, he was invaluable to the Order; how can we thank you? You saved his life."

Piedade replied in the Latin of a thousand masses, *Non nobis Domine, non nobis, sed nomini tuo da gloriam*; "Not to us, O Lord, not to us; but to Thy name give the glory," quoting Psalm 115.

A devout Catholic, he was so soaked in Scripture that when he bled, he bled Scripture. A maid, recommended by the Portuguese Parish Priest, ran away with the gold jewellery which Granny had left on her dressing table, which represented Piedade's life savings, gold being a "safe" investment, certain to appreciate as long as gold remains a status symbol, and women are vain. (In good times, your wife bedecks herself to general feminine envy. In desert times—well, theoretically you could sell the gold, though few do.)

Tell the priest, track her down? Steal time from today's work in a wild gold chase? Dr Mathias shrugged sadly, quoting Job, "The Lord gives, the Lord takes away; blessed be the name of the Lord," and went back to work, slowly replacing the treasure trove.

Shrewdness, foresight, and prudence now became additional themes of Piedade's life, as were faith, hard work, and success in his medical career *and* financially. He invested in land, buying property presciently (one of those surprisingly uncommon people who can translate high IQ into hard cash) in the centre of Mangalore near A. B. Shetty Circle and in Cubbon Road, the posh heart of Bangalore, near both the Residency, now Raj Bhavan, the Governor's mansion; and today's granite *Vidhana Soudha*, State Legislature, land that, like gold, was unlikely to depreciate—or be stolen.

He died, young, at fifty-eight, exhausted by hard salaried medical work and administration (he had three jobs, Assistant Surgeon General of Madras Presidency, Hospital Superintendent, and Professor of Surgery); by his extensive private practice; by managing his investments in gold, land, and houses, and saving for private boarding school and college for his fourteen children. He died intestate while the hastily-summoned lawyer was on the way to the house, leaving sufficient money for Josephine, who remained a widow for the next fifty-three years; for college educations for his sons as well as his daughters (Jessie Pais became one of the community's earliest "lady doctors," while Dora died in an accident while at Medical School); dowries for the girls; start-up funds for the boys; farmland, rental properties, and nearly sixty years of wrangling over them, one case going up to the Supreme Court of India.

Piedade worked God, and God, with mercy and amusement, allowed Himself to be worked. When his private practice dropped, he'd say, aggrieved, accusatory, "Josephine! Are you giving? Give. You are not giving; that is why I am not getting." She gave; people got sick; he bought land, and four houses, including her mother's, three of them investment properties.

Imprinting. As a widow, on the first Monday of the month, Granny had her chair carried out to her palm grove, where a line of "the poor" waited for her. She gave each one a five rupee note and a smile.

"Stop this," her son, Eric, who had taken her in hand, remonstrated as she extricated the staple from yet another wad of fresh fivers: "For you, and you, and you."

"If you must give money, give it to the parish priest to give away. He'll know the truly needy cases." "No, no!" she said. "He'll just give it to his favourites. I'd rather give it to people I know."

"How do you know these people are needy?" he asked. "If they weren't, why would they come?" she retorted with sublime simplicity–and, probably, accurately.

My father's brother, Morris Mathias, the richest of her sons, head of Vijay Mallya's United Breweries International in Singapore and unofficial adviser and emissary of Singaporean Prime Minister Lee Kuan Yew, indulgently sent her a few hundred rupees each month—solely to give away. "Give, Ma, give," he laughed, remembering his father's powerful, paradoxical economy. "The more you give, the more I get."

* * *

Not satisfied with money, Granny compulsively gave the gourmet cheeses and chocolates (her favourite foods) that Uncle Morris sent her from Singapore to her live-in servant Leela's light-skinned, pretty little girl with whom in her old age, she—who had coveted boys and disdained girls—ironically fell in love. ("It's not fair," she'd say bluntly, "that your papa Noel had *two* girls and no boys!")

"The baby needs it more than I do," she said when her son and grandson, who had moved in with her, protested: "They probably haven't even acquired the taste for cheese and chocolates."

Realising that sweet-natured Leela and that adorable toddler might be homeless after her death, reduced to rolling beedis all day (ubiquitous cheap microcigars, "the poor man's cigarette"; Mangalore Ganesh was India's largest brand), she impulsively promised them her ancestral house, Palm Grove.

"Non compos mentis," a couple of daughters discussed a lawsuit, suspecting she would leave her entire one-third share of the property to her most forceful son—as she did! And then they heard of this! Leela refused to leave Palm Grove after Granny's death, maintaining, despite the flourished will, "She gave me the house." All her sons' cajolings or threats could not get the ayah to leave. The police, and *goondas,* thugs, appeared, offering help for a price, but their methods were brutal and often bloody. Leela was finally bought out with a substantial sum. "A wise servant will share the inheritance as one of the brothers:" The Book of Proverbs.

* * *

Did you want so many children, Granny? I asked, skidding on the slippery slope of personal questions. "No," she said simply, Topsy-like. "I *never* wanted so many. I just had them." A rare admission in a culture of gushing and glorying over your children.

Celestial economics, celestial medicine. In the days when amniocentesis must have sounded like a wish-fulfilment fantasy, my grandfather tried to select gender by prayer. At first, unsuccessfully. Ethel, Winnie, Jessie, Dora, Priscilla, five unwanted maidens all in a row, each pregnancy commencing with "PRAY. *Pray* for a boy," and bitterly culminating with "*Another* girl! That's because you did not pray hard enough," and so they did, desperately, and then: eight handsome boys all in a row, the Mangalorean gold standard of blessedness. And my father, in a blessing he carried all his life in his mild, equable, gentle, and good-natured temperament, was the first-born son.

Fourteen children, pepper and salt, some "fair," light-skinned like their mother; others, dark-skinned, and, interestingly, those who physically resembled their mother, my father among them, inherited her temperament and were mild, phlegmatic, scholarly, and urbane, while some of those who resembled their father physically were pugnacious, aggressive, tilting at the windmills of the business world, a little frightening.

* * *

At great expense, Piedade and Josephine sent their children to boarding school, to Montfort School in Yercaud, run by Belgian Brothers, where they received a classical education: Latin, French, Shakespeare, poetry…; the alumni became doctors, lawyers, judges, senior civil servants, especially after Independence. The parents' intention: an alchemical transmutation into Lord Macaulay's "brown-skinned gentleman," which he famously defined as "a class who may be interpreters between us and the millions whom we govern; a class of persons, Indian in blood and colour, but English in taste, in opinions, in morals, and in intellect." My grandmother, however, was disappointed at the slowness of their metamorphosis into brown, or any-skinned, gentlemen. She observed her sons over the dinner table with growing dismay, then wrote a letter of complaint to the Brothers, "They blow into their coffee, they pour it into their saucers, their elbows claim a mile on each side. They are boors." For decades the sons, collectively called "The Bounders," quoted her letter gleefully!

The boors got the haircuts they deserved. Josephine, once a month, lined her fourteen pretty children all in a row, placed a mixing bowl on their heads, and cut their hair like a Gordian knot, shearing every errant curl.

My father, her long-awaited first-born son, faced a different Scylla: His mother could not bear to cut his Absalom ringlets, which curled below his shoulders, stroked by the old and pulled by the young. And so, in the kind of irony which must make God smile, the coveted boy looked girlish!

* * *

From her still point in front of the sunny dining room window, where she gazed at the sunlit backyard pond (near which her four-year-old son, Charlie, had lain mesmerized, watching the lotus, jewelled with droplets, bloom and the bright carp flash, and where his drowned body was found floating limply among the flowers) Granny cooked–in a manner of speaking.

My mother, as a young bride experimenting with the two recommended below-the-belt routes to a man's heart, asked for the recipes my father fondly remembered. "Golden Syrup on toast," he said wistfully. "Treacle on toast." "How do you make Golden Syrup?" my mother enquired. And where in India does one find a treacle well? Neither love nor money could then conjure up Golden Syrup or treacle, for in the first four decades after Independence, India sensibly banned imports of consumer goods to nurture its nascent industries.

"*Golden Syrup?* I boiled sugar in water and fed it to those bounders when they returned ravenous from boarding school," Granny replied. "I called it Golden Syrup, and they were happy." Syrup rendered golden by boyhood's healthy hunger, my father's mythopoeic memory, and the magic of language! Granny would not be drawn into more talk of recipes. "I cook by instinct," she said, a statement my mother mimicked in a hoity-toity, eyebrows-raised, lips-pursed voice.

And so Granny did--by instinct and remote control, summoning the cook, describing a dish from memory and imagination, and prescribing a recipe.

Every few minutes, as the curry simmered, the cook brought her a taste in a small stainless-steel dish. "More salt, more coriander, a little more grated coconut, let it thicken for another, oh…six minutes" until imagination became curry and appeared before us, and we tasted its glory.

* * *

In Granny's house, one slid backwards in time. The water from the backyard well looked yellow and tasted brackish, contradicting the properties of water I'd learnt in chemistry: colourless, odourless, tasteless. Baths were a more fraught enterprise than switching on a geyser at home where the only admonition was "Don't let it overheat, or it will explode and scald you to death," an urban legend, perhaps.

Here, double, double toil and trouble; fire burn, and cauldron bubble. When you wanted a bath, you told the servant, who lit the nest of firewood beneath the smouldering copper cauldron, which fumed and hissed as you dipped your bronze urn, a *chembu* into it, as gingerly (particularly during power cuts) as if that smoke-blackened bathing room were Bluebeard's den, careful not to topple the cauldron or blister your hands on its sides. "The cauldron tipped on Ruthie. Terrible scarring. Her parents will have to pay for plastic surgery, or she'll *never* get married."

The coffee at breakfast was richly sweetened not with sugar as at home but with golden-ochre lumps of *jaggery* or *gur*, raw, unrefined sugar, much like spooning in molasses. My parents were ambivalent about *gur*, formed by pouring boiling hot sugarcane syrup on the dirt floor of country barns to solidify; it had occasional embedded grass, straw, or suspect pellets; at home, my mother severely rationed it.

And with the coffee, *Kube*, cockles in a coconut and jaggery curry. Eating seashells, extricating elusive sea-worms with the tine of a fork from the lovely homes they hefted around—a moralist's object lesson on the misery of possessions—was more trouble than it was worth, much like eating the marrow of mutton bones, "the best part," the old ladies said, as they passed their hair-pins around, with instructions on how to suck or dig out the marrow.

* * *

What are you reading, Granny?

For she always was—the newspaper, a biography of Francis Xavier, per-haps, and each week, cover to cover, the international edition of *Time* magazine which Uncle Morris sent her, her opinions on world politics incisive, shared as freely as her gnomic social maxims. "Don't get a PhD. Nobody marries a woman better educated than they are. If you get a PhD, whom will you find to marry you?" or "Family is more important than the boy. Don't look at the boy so much as the family," or, oddly, exactly what Mother Teresa told me a decade later, "You can't remain single. Get married or become a nun."

Once, as Granny sat reading (an incident which was one of my mother's most reproachful "Your Mother" reproaches), Sister Columba, my mother's beloved eightyish great-aunt, affectionate, gentle, completely sweet, rattled across Mangalore in an uncomfortable "bone-shaker" autorickshaw to see us. The tiny Apostolic Carmel nun in her white and black habit walked up the ve-randa stairs to my grandmother, whose house it, after all, was; arms outstretched, smiling with every evidence of delight, she chirped in the over-accentuated, effusive, mellifluous Mangalorean style, in the high-pitched cooing intonations of feminine social interaction the world over, "Jose–phine, It's An–niie. Do you remember me? We were classmates. It's so good to see you so heal-thy." They had not met for seventy years.

My grandmother looked up, a shade contemptuously, "You've not come to see me. You've come to see Anita and Noel," she said, turned on her heel, and marched in. Sister Columba, a gentle, affectionate, and inoffensive nun, nervously clasped and unclasped her hands. Her small face puckered in hurt and bewilderment. When had she last encountered sheer rudeness? Perhaps never. "Poor thing," my mother said, reliving the scene, each time growing more upset.

But my grandmother was a monolith, simply herself, unyielding, unbending, rarely wasting a smile in social intercourse, except when thoroughly amused. Flattery never escaped her lips, praise rarely. A no-nonsense woman, never squandering a smile on a vacuous joke, dispensing with the falsity that's the lubricant of social life.

* * *

Since successful men married the youngest and prettiest bedfellows they could find, prodigious bearers of children, and nurses in old age, Mangalorean widows were as common as wives. My great-grandmother, Julianna, who had borne seven children in her brief years as a wife, was a widow for seventy-three years, while Granny, widowed at forty-one, with her fourteenth child a newborn, was a widow for fifty-three years!

Wearing the trousers, guarding the inherited bacon—it made one tough. If Granny had ever tolerated foolishness, that indulgence had long been leached out. A rusty old spade was a spade, and—in a culture which valued courtesy, sweetness, graciousness, excellent traits in women—she, though gentle of face and voice, refused to call a spade a silver spoon or a golden rule.

When I fought with my mother, fierce-tongued and ferocious, my father shook his head. "I would never have *dared* to speak to my mother like that," he said. "If she told me to do something, even today, I would obey her." Granny ruled her children with a quiet despotism. "One night, she punished my younger brother, Michael, at dinner by making him kneel on the dining table," my father said. "When she came down to breakfast the next morning, having quite forgotten about Michael, there he was, asleep, swaying on his knees. Assuming she had meant him to kneel all night, he knelt."

But the world breaks all of us, Hemingway wrote, and afterwards, many are strong at the broken places. If we are lucky. When she was in her nineties, her young relative Nina flared up and yelled at her–"My father does so much for you, neglects his own business to look after yours, and you are not grateful." Being shouted at by a descendant struck a poisoned arrow into Granny's heart. It festered as she slipped into Alzheimer's so that, several times a day, she'd tell me, "Nina shouted at me, she said...and I said nothing. I should have said..." Her voicelessness stung her as much as the words.

Aunts and cousins gossiped about how Granny was looted in her old age. "What gold do you have in the bank, Granny? Give it to us. Give me your grandmother's gold swastika necklace for luck," Nina reportedly said. "And this solid silver tea set his patient gave him. And do you have any old crystal?" And then, on moving in, Granny's son chased away her brother Norman whom she had loved for nine decades. "Go and stay with your daughters. Why should our family support you?" he said, reasonably enough, for most of her sons were sending support cheques.

However, losing Norman, this living embodiment of her history and prop to her memory, hastened the deterioration of Granny's memory and will to live until finally, in her nineties, she lay too long in bed and developed perpetual, deep, raw bedsores. And, in one of the odd transformations of old age, she became sweeter, simpler, gentler. I held her hand, stroking it, and said impulsively, "I like you!" "I know you like me," she said. "How do you know?" "Because you are stroking my hand," she pointed out.

Thirty years after her first visit, my mother finally consented to visit her mother-in-law and Mangalore again. My grandmother was now ninety-three, helpless and bedridden. Alzheimer's disease had reduced this unsentimental, unfailingly truthful grandmother to telling my mother that old gushing Indian lie, "You are not like a daughter-in-law, but like a daughter to me." And so, at last, the two women got along.

* * *

We walked through the dark living room with its *de rigueur* shrine on a crocheted tablecloth: a pious assemblage of souvenirs from other people's trips to Rome, Lourdes, Fatima, or our native miraculous pilgrimage spot, Velankanni—cloudy bottles of holy water, silver cameo triptychs of the Holy Family, mortuary cards, and "holy pictures."

The "Sacred Heart" smiled, revealing his thorn-pierced heart. Rainbow lights twinkled around a blue-sashed haloed Virgin who, when cupped in one's hands, glowed, eerie luminous phosphorous in the conjured darkness. The Martian glow of a flame-shaped bulb bathed rosaries with gold and silver beads and a recumbent Infant Jesus of Prague who kicked his silver legs in baby glee.

The most frequent spiritual experience of my Catholic childhood was not the numinous–when the veil parts, you briefly glimpse the face of Christ, and time stands still while you are flooded with joy. That came later. As a child, however, religion meant the intensest boredom. I helplessly calculated the ratio of Hail Marys said to Hail Marys left. The ratio of the Mass said to the Mass which had still to drone on. In fractions, in decimals.

As I walked through Palm Grove, Norman growled from rooms away. "Anita, don't drag your feet." "What a disgrace, him having to scold you so often," my mother later said. "Why do you drag your feet?"

I dragged them to evening prayers at "the family altar" in Mangalore. Each evening, as darkness fell, Norman knelt on the cold stone floor to lead us in the rosary, his head tilted back to gaze at the Virgin, his arms rigidly outstretched, cruciform (an entirely unnecessary, unprescribed show-offy piety; wherever did he get the idea from?) as sixty-six slow rosary beads dripped through his fingers, *Credo, Pater Noster, Ave Maria, Gloria.*

"Hail Mary, full of grace," Norman proclaimed with emphatic gusto and hints of admonishment: "See me, so old; see my reverence. And yours?" Or so

I read his body language as he trawled us through the rosary, present purgatory to abbreviate a future one.

My father knelt too, which he never did at home–unwilling to be shamed by his uncle's dramatic piety–or perhaps because he expected that it was expected. A frown and a frequent downward jerk of his head suggested that I do likewise, which I did not, the embarrassment of conforming to this sanctimoniousness being roughly equal to the embarrassment of refusing to.

"Holy Mary," my father muttered, frowning grimly as he did whenever I was in the vicinity of a nun or a smiling gossip. And so, it went on, Chinese water torture. Mosquitoes buzzed and bit in the darkness. I wanted to bay in exasperation. I wanted to howl. This gabbling of memorized prayers specifically forbidden by Jesus; this superstition; this prayer to Mary, who was not God, imposed on us by others as a sadistic form of control; this rosary, was a criminal waste of time. I angrily felt that throughout my childhood.

Though my grandmother, Josephine, sat primly in her rocking chair, studying her rosary beads, serious and contemplative as a Van Gogh woman, I wondered if she was enduring it as much as my father was, as much as I was, this flamboyant fervency imposed on us by Norman.

* * *

In the gathering darkness of the compound, dhoti-clad men, respectful of Norman's communion with the Almighty, waited. They watched the gaunt man kneel, cruciform, his El Greco face taut. "*Arre Baap.* He must be ninety."

How bland would pastures be without baa-baa black sheep, and how boring cupboards without their skeletons.

An in, an in; Norman claimed he had an in. Everyone's secret fear: that this is *exactly* how the world works, always an inner circle inner-er than your own; the kingdom, the power and the glory circulating through loops closed to you.

Norman said he knew someone who could swiftly get them passports, visas, and jobs in the Gulf, from whence, though scornfully treated by arrogant Arabs, they'd return in aeroplanes uncomfortably overfull with food processors, massive colour televisions and gold jewellery, and having saved for neon houses, their children's education, and their own old age. "But hurry, hurry,"— his friend had only twenty-one openings.

The wise hear "Hurry" and know they should pause. But with shimmering hope, they embark on a frenzy of borrowing and other no-noes as they glimpse the beautiful shore on which they would be rich, and they would be glorious. Of course.

He got twenty-one takers. Who daily, weekly, waited outside the columned porticoes of Palm Grove for updates on their emigration. His mind filled with holy harmonies—*Father, forgive them*, he goes out to meet them after evening prayers, radiant, reproachful, a Lord of the manor to recalcitrant serfs. "O ye of little faith." They wait, clutching hope. Tomorrow and tomorrow and tomorrow.

And who would suspect that octogenarian, validated by his lengthy prayers, his silver hair, and his "good family," who in bank, boardroom, or monastery, serving God or mammon, rose to the top through nature and nurture? I wouldn't have dreamed of suspecting Norman. Neither did they, as they handed over borrowed money. The days became months, interest on the borrowed money they'd handed over to Norman inexorably compounding, compounding. The would-be émigrés suspect; are smooth-talked, white-haired, blue-blooded out of their suspicions–furiously suspect–*know*.

They visited his niece Ethel, a well-known plantation owner, weeping: "How can God let this happen to us?" And "Such a disgrace," my Aunt Ethel said with widened eyes. "One of them committed suicide."

A clerk in the Kankannady electricity board who had handed over the small dowries accumulated during a quarter century of penny-saved-penny-gained, scrimping, shaving, short-shrift thrift begun at the birth of his five daughters. How replace the nest-egg gathered, painful paise by paise? How face beginning again? His body swung metronomically from a ceiling fan.

Then, a copycat suicide. Norman's nephews confront him. *"What* money?" he asks, the injured, sinned-against, his role played so long that he no longer remembered that it *was* a role. (The bare-faced liar and the red-handed thief are as insulted by accusation as the lily-handed.)

Norman warns against tormenting him because God has been for him, visiting strange calamities on past persecutors. But ultimately: "I don't have it." He didn't–he still dressed simply, starched white cotton shirt and trousers; he still skipped off and on buses (continuing until his death at a hundred and two) and ate abstemiously at his sister's table.

But where was the money? Good cop, bad cop, cajoling, threats. Private investigators. I felt as if I were living in my very own Agatha Christie. I over-heard, circuitously questioned, and sat still as the proverbial owl: "The more he listened, the more he knew, and oh, how wise that little owl grew."

He had donated the money to the local cloistered nuns whose prayers, behind high walls, rose like incense as they ceaselessly interceded for the sins of the world!

* * *

My aunts and uncles visited the nuns. "A fool and his money are soon parted," my father lamented when I spent unthinkingly (just as he reflexively said when we saw graffiti, "The names of fools, like their faces, are often seen in public places.")

The nuns were not fools. "But how do you know the money he gave us was *that* money? And anyway, we have spent it." Good cop, bad cop, cajoling, threats to retrieve blood money from the treasury. With no success.

When I left the country, Norman, then ninety-two, was still blood-suck-
ing fresh suckers.

* * *

At last, Christmas. Open air Midnight Mass. My father's sisters arrived,
with lamb cutlets and spicy meat-filled croquettes, called "potato chops,"
freshly prepared by their cooks for their mother. And with small gifts for me.
"She prayed for good Christmas presents last night," my father laughed, while
I hissed "Pa!" as embarrassed as his richest sister, who gave me a single chocolate bar, a gold-foil-wrapped Five Star, with a pink ribbon tied around it. A little
later, I sententiously recycled a just-heard epigram, "The world is divided into
givers and takers." "I'm a giver!" she said swiftly. My father later chuckled,
"Fitzgerald said, 'The rich are the rich because they spend less money.'"

We set off on our morning and evening round of traditional Christmas
visits as the impulse seized us; someone was sure to be in. The people we visited
were affluent and lived on the kind of income generated without dressing up
and leaving your house–money from the ancestral terraced plantations of
cashew nuts, pepper and coffee in the green hills around Mangalore on which
the fortunes of several "old families" were built, or from family factories or
dividends from stocks. ("Has TISCO sent you your dividend?" "I haven't received my dividend from Glaxo," our hosts said; they all invested in the same
blue chips). And what else did we talk about? People, the great continuous soap
opera around us: whose in-laws were making a nuisance of themselves; whose
daughter was "running around" or dangerously "boy-crazy;" the politics of our
relatives' careers; the progress of their diseases; and now and then, juicy scandals—an illegitimate baby; the bipolar mother in "the mental asylum,"
elopements, a florid drunk. Good news, bad news, just news, and running
through it, *schadenfreude*– why doesn't English have a word for it? –barely disguised pleasure derived from the misfortunes of others.

Everywhere: The invisible pressure of people's judgements! Aunt Ethel, the oldest of my father's three regal sisters, kept a car and a chauffeur into advanced old age while lamenting the expense, for she left her house but rarely. (Fixed points of the whirling world magnetise people to themselves; visitors came to her, bringing some gossip, taking some, so that her store constantly grew.) "Sell the car. Dismiss the chauffeur. Take a bus," I suggested, brandishing Alexander's sword. "I *can't* do *that*," he said. "People will say: the old girl has come down in the world."

Aunt Ethel, grandest of the town's grand old ladies, was nicknamed the Grand Duchess by my Uncle Sonny; my grandmother was the Empress, and Aunt Winnie, the Duchess. Her face, a mask of hauteur, tight pursed lips, eyebrows, and nostrils raised in habitual disdain, resembled a sour, severe, ruffed Old Master Renaissance Queen's, say, Velasquez's Empress Isabella. Except for Jessie, a doctor, the fortunes of my father's sisters hinged upon whom they were married off to. Ethel, the only one who married into significant wealth, acquired a coffee estate and a large house through the shortcut of marriage.

The lucky numbers in marriage's lottery, and long habit, gave her the manner of one to the manor born. "Why do people suck up to Aunt Ethel just because she's rich?" I asked my father. "They won't get money off her for all their fawning." "Men praise you when you prosper," he said.

However, her good fortune came, in its insidious way, with a catch: a familiar one–the Indian cliché, the villainous mother-in-law, reputed to be venom-tongued. People whispered: "The horror always lived with them. Ethel never had a proper married life." "That woman!" my grandmother had fretted about the mean potential mother-in-law when the proposal came. "Worry not," the matchmaker reassured her. "She's a sickly old thing. She'll die any day now, and Ethel will have a happy married life."

"In fact, the matchmaker died!" my father said. "Never count on anyone dying. The nastiest, perennially on the verge of death, live the longest out of *sheer spite*, coddling themselves and being coddled by others, while, sometimes, the apparently healthy drop dead in an instant."

* * *

From the egg of inherited coffee estates, Ethel's only son, my cousin, Peter Prabhu, created gaggles of golden geese—canning and exporting the goodness of Arabian Ocean, crab, shrimp, lobster, oysters; buying factories, and eventually constructing a real estate empire: entire neighbourhoods of apartment buildings becoming, at one point, South India's biggest real estate developer. And when, in the universally acknowledged way of single men in possession of a good fortune, he married, Ethel insisted that the bride live with them in the ancestral house, scene of her old travails. My father couldn't get over the folly of it. "I don't know *how* she could do that after what she went through," he said.

But! "The woman who sleeps next to a man has his ear," Aunt Ethel sighed over her dining table, lavish with lobsters (which I had for the first time at her house), oysters, crab curry, and duck *molee* in coconut gravy. The ancient, bitter battle of two women for a man's soul, the younger woman with her ancient biological weapons: youthful beauty, sexual attraction and motherhood, and the older woman with hers: tears, guilt, accusation, and what remains of primaeval bonding and long obedience! But we have it on the highest authority that the meek (the daughters-in-law!) will eventually, temporarily, inherit the earth. A Mangalorean anecdote, perhaps apocryphal: The evil mother-in-law serves herself and her son boiled white rice, giving the daughter-in-law the *kunji*, the broth in which the rice had been cooked. The mother and son look sickly, while the daughter-in-law perversely thrives, growing *thugda*, solid, muscular, and hefty on the gruel–full of the B-vitamins unwittingly boiled out.

Two queen bees? An impossibility. Finally, comes the day of the new queen. Who swarmed. Far away. I listened, I listened to Aunt Ethel's diatribes and ruminations–family politics, wills, lawsuits, the virtues of coffee estates rather than her son's small businesses as cash cows, the importance of investing in gold, "gold is gold," but then later, "land is gold." Money, human relationships, the lowdown on my extended family, the workings of the Mangalorean community, the ticktock of society, these were mysteries to me in the cloister of boarding school, and I listened intently to my aunt's chatter for the world lay before me like a field of dreams, various, beautiful, new, as mysterious as a longed-for, unread book. I used the golden balls of my reading and my own observations to figure out the labyrinth of life, seeing in the three aunts of Maggie Tulliver of *The Mill on the Floss*, the wealthy, formidable Aunt Glegg, doleful Aunt Pullet, and pleasant, quiet Aunt Deane, uncanny parallels to my own three aunts in Mangalore, Ethel, Winnie, and Joyce, while identifying with Maggie, passionate, harum-scarum, an ugly duckling in a too-small duck pond.

* * *

Then to my funny, warm aunt Winnie and her husband, Louis (one of those couples one suspects of a diet as convenient as the Sprats). Louis, plain-spoken, slim, always-smiling, was a shadowy presence quite eclipsed by his large, jocose wife; in memory, he walks, always, a few steps behind her.

Aunt Winnie showed us the whale-bone corsets, like straitjackets, like armour, curiosities of another era, which she wore until she gave up dresses, and the battle with bulges. She now raised her large upper arms and let her nieces and nephews jiggle her rolls of fat.

"Remember when you wore Winnie's dress and rung the front doorbell croaking a request for Mrs Winnie?" Louis asked. My father, who graduated from college in 1937 during the Great Depression, had lodged with Winnie in Delhi while working his first job, clerical, ill-paid—but a job.

Winnie laughed, "And my little Derek did not recognize him and said, "Mummy, there's an old lady at the door, asking for you.""

"And how wicked he was, Anita. When we slept on the verandah on hot summer evenings, he'd wait till poor Louis fell asleep, then flick a wooden cotton reel at the fan.""

My father grinned, a little embarrassed. "And Louis woke, jerking his arms and legs into the air, like an upended spider, saying, "What's that? What's that?"" And then he added, "And I'd wait till he fell asleep, then do it again."

Though Winnie was the only one in the family who did not have a university education, it didn't show. My grandfather, a surgeon, believed in educating women. Ethel and Joyce had degrees in education; Jessie became a doctor; while Dora, died while at Stanley Medical College of a freak accident. Winnie, however, never finished school. She wept all day at boarding school until she was summoned home during middle school, where she lived happily until marriage. In a family in which one or more advanced degrees were a minimum requirement (my grandfather: F.R.C.S., Fellow of the Royal College of Surgeons; my father, a Chartered Accountant FCA, Fellow of the Institute of Chartered Accountants, England and Wales; my Aunt Jessie and Uncle Pat were medical doctors, MBBS and MDs, while Uncle Theo had a PhD) Winnie gaily presented her credentials, JCF, Junior Cambridge Failed.

After Louis died, Aunt Winnie became the lachrymose aunt, bursting into tears at the thought of sweet Louis, and she thought of him often. Oh bereavement, horrid cocktail of guilt, loneliness, and grief, half your self rent from you, flooding you with phantom pain.

And then: archaeology. "Poor Winnie, all the shocks of the family fell on her," Aunt Ethel said. "She was the one who went in and discovered Daddy dead—just after he told her to call his lawyer to, at last, write his will. When your aunt Prissie—she had eyes like yours, Anita—died of sunstroke while swimming, Winnie took the call. When our sister Dora, a medical student, got her stiletto heels stuck in the electric tram tracks in Madras as she short-cutted across them and was crushed to death by the onrushing tram, Winnie was with her and just escaped."

* * *

My father's youngest sister, Joyce, a gifted schoolteacher with a homely, pleasant face, and salt-and-pepper curly hair coiled into a bun, lived in Granny's little tree-enclosed cottage on the grounds of Palm Grove.

She was a favourite among us twenty-six first cousins–interestingly–for she, reserved, dignified, self-sufficient, often abstracted, did nothing to court our affections. Her breezy will o' the wisp manner was like the genie whirling curls from the round-the-clock cigarettes she smoked, and let us cousins puff, so that our first acrid, gagging encounter with nicotine was usually our last. Joyce was, in fact, often preoccupied–with crossword puzzles which she solved obsessively and with books into which she escaped, unable to sleep until she had finished her Graham Greene novel, even when she returned at three a.m. from parties with her beautiful, popular daughter, Veronica.

Joyce was down-to-earth, sensible, with a cool, ironic sense of humour. While the family raged and sputtered in a fraught property battle, Joyce merely chuckled, especially when an irascible, pugnacious Uncle threatened to set the dogs on his stately sisters Ethel and Winnie if they came visiting their mother with queries and reproaches about her will, and (having newly acquired US citizenship) threatened to sue his elderly physician brother, Pat, in the American courts!

Joyce's approach to food was slapdash, her combinations bizarre–canned sardines and strawberry jam. Mackerel and condensed milk. "Mind your own business," she snapped with unusual acerbity when I commented. Food was a subject on which she, customarily phlegmatic, was touchy.

In a family in which women run to fat, Joyce was haggard. Incredibly, her physique had once resembled her stout siblings, Ethel and Winnie. Her brash Jesuit brother, Theo–christened Theophane (the revelation of God!) Archibald, destiny encoded in his name–returned from seminary at Louvain, Belgium, to see her playing tennis in shorts. "Joyce!" he cried. "You look like a fat Chettiar woman!"

With raised eyebrows, her plump sisters told the story in unison, in a rhythmic, emphatic chorus. "She stopped eating rice. Just like that. No sugar. No mangoes. No fruit juice. Just water with a dash of lemon. And dry bread. Soon she was skin and bones. *Tell her,* Anita, tell her to eat. We're *so* worried about her." (Joyce, however, outlived them all, living slenderly until the age of ninety-three, still eating like an abstemious sparrow.)

We visited my father's cousin Thelma who bred chickens. Seeing the flock of white leghorns, I exclaimed, "Oh, you will have *so many* baby chickens." "No, the eggs have to be fertilised for that," she explained patiently. "Oh, how do they get fertilised?" I asked. She looked at my father and smiled a little, almost shy, amused, help-me smile. "Oh!" I realised, embarrassed. And then we visited the nuns and priests to whom we were related: my mother's first cousins, Sisters Marilyn, Marita and Moira, all Apostolic Carmel nuns, and my great-grandmother Alice Rebello's siblings, Sister Columba at the Apostolic Carmel, a mainly Mangalorean teaching order; Sister Marie Agnes at the Cloistered Carmel; and the eldest, Sister Marie Therese at the Home of the Little Sisters of the Poor, at whose growing decrepitude my father was, each year, appalled.

"She looked terrible--wizened," he reported. "Those nuns don't look after her. All her teeth have fallen out, and they haven't got her dentures. How can she eat meat?" His mother, and the old ladies who sat with her in the evenings, listened--with prurient avidity. For with time, the arena of competition shifts from beauty, a "catch" of a spouse, wealth, and success, to one's children's plummy university-spouse-job, to "the one who dies last, and with the most toys, wins." Health, the final arena of competition! And in the rapid-fire questions and veneer-thin concern with which one ancient enquires about another's detached retina, open heart surgery, strokes, diabetes, aneurysms, dementia, you hear the faintest hint of rubbernecking; of ghoulish excitement, perhaps; of pride- "I've escaped;" and fear-"for now."

Sister Marie Therese escorted us, visitors from a sun-bright world, around the grounds and dark wards, pointing out, thumbnail sketching the inmates--old, sick, destitute or disabled. My expected smile felt as awkward as I did. And then on to the blind man, the Sisters of Charity's living sermon. Our Pew sat on the floor in shorts, spindly legs crossed. "Sing," they told him, "Sing." And obediently, he sang in a high-pitched, nasal, slightly cracked voice, the pupils of his eyes rolling, his head tilted at an unnatural angle: *When upon life's billows you are tempest-tossed,/ When you are discouraged, thinking all is lost,/ Count your blessings; count them one by one/ And it will surprise you what the good Lord has done.*

I knew what I was expected to think, and, irritated, I thought it: "Look at this poor blind man counting his blessings, though he has so few. And how much more should I...?"

And then, customary culmination: my father took out his cheque book. The Superior was summoned. Smiles grew wider in the Christmas-eve electricity. The nuns surrounded us, beaming at me as if the benefaction had gold-dusted us.

"How much did you give, Pa?" I asked on our way home. "Two hundred rupees." "Pa! *Two hundred rupees.* And Ma said I couldn't have those high-heeled, embroidered, mirror-worked Rajasthani sandals." My sister's pair were her most treasured possession; her first words, as she came out of anaesthesia after eye surgery, aged ten, were, "Where are my sandals?" "Be quiet, Anita," he said. "You don't need high-heeled, mirror-worked, embroidered Rajasthani sandals. Remember how Grandpa gave *especially* when he needed money? Don't you read the Sermon on the Mount? It's a promise. 'Give and you shall receive, full measure, pressed down, flowing over, for the measure you give is the measure you receive.' Measure for measure is a law of life."

"That's a risky way to get rich," I thought. "Okay," I said, "Okay." Though I still wanted the high-heeled shoes!

My great-aunt, Sister Mary Agnes, was the (first Indian) Prioress of the Cloistered Carmel Convent, whose nuns, cloistered for life, bound by vows of silence, knew much of what went on upstairs and downstairs and in the lady's chamber in all the houses of the town, from the least to the greatest. Their vocation, their only work, was to pray. Mangalore could, of course, pray for herself; professionals were inessential. However, everyone was game for any celestial intervention which might bend the arc of the universe in their favour. So, supported by honey brought by worker bees to the heart of the hive, the nuns lived on divine providence, as birds, bees and lilies do. And the town was unusually prosperous: many successful citizens, its extended families close-knit, generous with loans, jobs, and shelter to their weaker members--so those hidden bees probably did produce palpable sweetness.

They had prayed with and for my parents through their seven-year struggle to conceive, through the birth of a son, that greatest of Indian blessings, through his death three days later, and my birth the next year. I was "the child of their prayers," and as news of my visit swished through silent corridors, a mosaic of brown-swathed faces formed around the grille. Sister Gabrielle, a fat, jolly, French nun whose particular prayer project I was, corresponded with me in idiosyncratic Franglish for years. "Sister, pray, I'm dieting. Again." "I will, but promenade." In my soulful phases, I replied with soulful musings, which were the truth, nothing but the truth, but not, alas, the whole truth. I read her reply written in flourishes and capitals to my father, "You are the Pearl of the Orient," then regretted that spot of showing off when he irritatingly dubbed me Pearly.

The Cloistered Carmel was the repository of the town's secrets, and I, unworthily, inhaled the town's gossip once I learnt the cryptology of the face, the raised eyebrows, the dropped voice, the language of intonation, implication, and ellipses common to religious people. The Portress alone, a nun herself, had relatively untrammelled access to the outer world. (My great-aunt, the Prioress Mary Agnes, joined the Cloistered Carmel in 1903, aged eighteen. When she attended a Convention of Cloistered Carmel Prioresses in 1954, she rode in a car to the train, neither of which she'd seen before!) In my last visit before I left India, the portress, in a startling reversal, startled *me* with her whispered advice, "Never marry a foreigner; they are like dogs running after a hundred bitches"–the wild west of nunnish fantasy.

We visited my grandmother Josephine's brother, Jerome Lobo, a hardy, burly, bearded Jesuit in his eighties, Professor of Latin at St. Aloysius, who had just visited the mummified body of Saint Francis Xavier in Goa, travelling third class, sleeping on a hard wooden bunk (whereas I…a raised eyebrow from my father, an unfinished sentence…) Their sister Catherine, now Mother Ambrose, a Good Shepherd nun, had blood-boiling accounts of the indignities of inter-racial convents. The white nuns made the Indian nuns wear different habits; sit in a separate section of the chapel; undertake the menial chores, the cooking, the laundry, the cleaning, much like lay brothers in medieval monasteries.

* * *

We dutifully paid our Christmas visits to Ethel, Winifred, Rose, Thelma, and Lucy. Mangalorean names changed with each generation. They were once Portuguese: My great-grandparents included Ligouri and Appolina Coelho, Joseph Crispin and Alice Rebello, Peter Paul Lobo and Juliana Saldanha, and Joseph Salvador and Gracia Mathias. Babies were, unimaginatively, given the name of the Parish Priest or the saint of the day, no matter how outlandish or otherworldly: Thrasius, Pulcheria, Balthazar, Blasius, Callistus, Seraphine, Boniface, Bonaventure, Cajetan, and Clothilda.

With the British Empire entrenched, Portuguese names faded, giving place to starchy Victorian ones; fanciful raids on Shakespeare, Chaucer, Greek mythology, or poetry yielded Claudius, Gertrude, Ophelia, Griselda, Christabel, Sybil and Nereus, the old man of the sea. A set of war siblings were impartially named Adolph (Dolphie), Winston and Joseph. Some played a single string, Oswald, Oscar, Orville, and Odile Domingo. Or rhymed: the triplets, Asha, Isha, Usha; the sisters, Meena, Veena, Deena and Neena, or the Pintos–Gilbert, Albert, Humbert, Cuthbert, Egbert, and Norbert. Another set of Mathiases named their children alphabetically, like hurricanes, reluctantly stopping at Quentin, their seventeenth.

Those were the days of prodigious families, mothers and daughters pregnant together, nephews older than uncles. My father's neighbours, the P.G. D'Souzas ("the Blind Pig"), had seventeen children, interchangeable with the fourteen Mathias children. Spotting my uncle Joe at her dining table, Mrs D'Souza said absently, "Joe! You must come and sleep over some time." "I have for the last three days," he said. Neither mother had noticed!

In independent India, Anglicized names like Melroy, Gerson, and Flavia were passé. "Graveyard names!" my father groaned on hearing them. Under Hindu hegemony, many families, discovering or claiming ancestral memories of being Brahmin before their conversion half a millennium ago, replaced their old names, Gonsalves, Mascarenhas, Colaco or Lasrado, with solid Brahminical surnames, so that a Mangalorean Kamath or Prabhu, say, quite likely indicates a Catholic. (An extraordinary number of Catholic families claim descent from Tippu Sultan, the last ruler of the princely state of Mysore, the putative progeny of "hanky-panky" in barns while he fled from the British.)

Hindu first names or nicknames became popular. My sister and I are Anita and Shalini, whereas my parents are called Noel and Celine, and their siblings are Eustace, Mervyn, Ronald and Theophane!! My cousins are Nirmala, Ashok, Malati, Premila, and Sunil though each has a nickname originating in parental endearments, so the inner circle knew that Popsy was Premila; Chicky was Malati; Chippy, "a chip off the old block," was Michael, like his father, while Veronica was Buddie (old woman)–her father Sonny's teasing nickname when she was a gap-toothed six-year-old lasting a lifetime. Now, in the emigration generation, children mostly have "international names," Indian, but transcultural: Tara, Rohan, Sheila, Maya, Neel, Natasha, and, thanks to the Waste Land, Shanti.

* * *

So we visited all the family and friends, loved or hated, with whom we were on speaking terms, arriving unannounced, like the Magi–as was considered good manners. And like the Magi, we brought gifts–not frankincense, gold, and myrrh, but halwa, *pedas,* and news. All morning, all evening, we ate *neurios,* pasties stuffed with sugary coconut; *chucklees,* spicy gram flour deep-fried in bristly snail spirals or beautiful spiral shaped rose cookies as we sat opposite plastic trees, sparkling with neon orbs, wreathed with popcorn or cotton wool snow, celebrating the weather of London, not Bethlehem. . .or Mangalore.

And we talked of many things. Of blue chips, prices, politics, people, a great continuing Ring. "Your friend Liesl–I remember when her mother eloped with that Protestant, a Soanes, with only the clothes she had on. I even had to give her my blouses and petticoats." And in a showily hushed voice. "Your

Bernice's youngest boy; he doesn't resemble Hubert, have you noticed?" "Yeees." "Her lover's from a former princely family," she says. "And your Uncle Patrick. He says the Catholic Church has become "the abomination of desolation" and will only attend Latin Masses in the Tridentine rite, will drive miles to do so."

"And that wicked Mangalorean Judge, that Saldanha, has been arrested for forgery. High time too." "I can't get over how Old Man Mascarenhas inherited his son for marrying his first cousin, and gave Margil to the Apostolic Carmel nuns." And my Uncle S. murmured, pointing at two cousins, "Look at those two bitches animatedly chatter. They hate each other. Bernice stole the other's intended when he came to court her at boarding school. Much good it did her, though."

But, mostly, Götterdämmerung, crepuscular death, decay, doom. "Belinda miscarried. So sad, her mother-in-law forced her to scrub the bathroom floors while pregnant." "He never recovered from his wife's death. On their honeymoon! Stepped into the elevator, expecting to find it there; fell into the shaft, broke her neck."

"Francis just had a heart attack. I'll never forget how he collapsed at his daughter's grand engagement party—you know to that jerk from the States who later dumped her. 'Sug-gar!' he yelled—he's diabetic, you know—and poured the entire bowl into his mouth."

Stories, soap-operatic plots, *Canterbury Tales* swirling around me. All this, good news, bad news, just news, was always in English. Konkani—a hybrid of Portuguese and Marathi only spoken in Mangalore and Goa—is the nominal mother-tongue I neither speak nor understand; neither did my father. Since the nineteenth century, Catholic schools and universities have taught only in English; their students—everyone we visited—spoke it as, or almost as, a first language.

* * *

And food, always food!

"Is your father Mangalorean?" a wedding hostess asked as I got him re-
fills while he chuckled over the lyrics floating from the house where the bride
was bathed in coconut milk for her *roce*, her wedding shower, while her friends
sang sad laments until she burst into tears. Which meant good luck!

"Oh, you poor thing," they sang. "That mother-in-law! When you visit
her, she'll be vegetarian; when she visits you, she'll be "non-vegetarian." Her
visits will be almost eternal. When she leaves, so will your most precious possessions."

"Oh good, he's Mangalorean!" the hostess said, freely loading his plate.
"Then he loves *sarpatel*," Mangalore's signature dish. I felt too shy to explain
that he was a fat-phobic near-vegetarian. I returned with a plate loaded with
fatty, spicy pork, and my father almost wailed. Perhaps influenced by his
brother, Father Theo, who wouldn't touch it, he eschewed pork: free-ranging,
gutter-feeding, its tapeworm spreading meningitis, he feared; its roundworm
causing the recent epidemic of encephalitis.

* * *

> *The witch that came (the withered hag)*
> *To wash the steps with pail and rag,*
> *Was once the beauty Abishag.*
>
> *No memory of having starred*
> *Atones for later disregard,*
> *Or keeps the end from being hard.*

We visited my mother's aunt, Rosie (who seemed too good to be true—
though she was truly good), who smiled broadly, with genuine sweetness, a
woman in whom it was impossible to imagine guile or malice; benevolent, generous, gift-exchanging, to our embarrassment, the little box of sweets we gave
her with a big basket of mangoes from her garden. And then Mangalore feels
like bright Hobbiton.

But many a time, in the age of innocence, I naively walked into the sticky,
tricky parlour of a Black Widow who combats the loss of status, interestingness
and power which age and widowhood bring by weaving a web of whispers; who
smiles and smiles, exuding sympathy and charm, offers little tidbits of gossip
with a conspiratorial air, sucking all of interest about you, about everyone you
know, to then villainously disseminate relationship-wrecking rumours. Do I
sound bitter? I've been bitten. For when I hear my blithe words bloodied, man-
gled, regurgitated almost unrecognizably by a black widow in her treacly web, I
feel that I am in the land of Mordor where the shadows lie, and small towns are
no Shire, but the old sow that eats its farrow.

* * *

Rosie's daughter, Martha, her grin wide, ingenuous, emerged in a house-
coat, the Mangalorean woman's unbecoming at-home garb. She, toothless and
wrinkled, didn't look much younger than her mother; like a baby or a saint, she
was, without artifice, entirely herself. Ecstatic, electrifying gossip about Martha
abounded; in fact, she often told it herself.

"Ah *Baa* (Konkani for dearie). I can tell how shocked you are at how I
look. I will not lie to you, *Baa*. It's because of my diet. I have beer for breakfast
every day, and Mummy sends for a *leetle* whiskey for lunch and rum for dinner.
Just a little."

"But if I don't have that, I feel sick." Martha's sweet-faced Mummy
stood by, like a statue of acceptant love, smiling a somewhat absent smile, as if
she hadn't really heard what was being said, wasn't really there.

My father and I listened, amazed. Martha was (improbably) the first cousin of my mother, whose most frequent expression, like that of her family's, was WWPT, "What will people think?" as she wrung her hands at my every perceived eccentricity of speech, dress, or behaviour.

Virginia Woolf imagines the ignominy and madness that would have cursed Shakespeare's sister were she a writer: "Whenever we see a witch or a mad woman or a suicide, we see a thwarted poet." Martha muttered in her sleep in rhythm and rhyme. She had got into a lawsuit with the bishop who'd asked her to leave the house she rented from him. Sheltering behind tenant-protection laws, she refused.

She wrote doggerel to his minion: "Father Digby is a knave and goon; Father Digby has sealed his doom." "I wanted to write an anonymous letter, baa, but then Baa–I signed it." Hired ruffians appeared, the usual way recalcitrant renters are evicted. "Baa, the walls were splattered with my blood. I lost all my front teeth."

The witch that came (the withered hag)/ Was once the beauty Abhishag... Her cousins told us Martha's story with sadness and bitterness. She was, ominously, the best-natured of the cousins, honest, childlike, full of *joie de vivre*.

Intelligent, vivacious, and charming as a young woman, Martha had been the favourite of her father, my maternal grandfather's brother, Dr Louie Coelho, Professor of Dermatology, famous and revered for treating lepers for free. (He had left instructions for the most spartan of funerals to avoid that guilty one-upmanship with baked meats that can plunge a grieving family into penury and debt—thus giving people "permission" to go and do likewise, to say, "If Dr Coelho's family could...")

When she was young, married, well-connected, and Cabinet Ministers, even the Chief Minister of Karnataka, came to her parties, nuns and priests crowded her. "Come with us to the Chief Minister, Martha," they said. "Come to the Housing Minister. We have a request." She went.

As an honoured guest, she was served alcohol, which (in common with many Mangaloreans) was her Achilles' heel. She drank—to be "dropped" by everyone as her beauty vanished and her marriage, her money and connections, everything but her mother. *No memory of having starred/ Can atone for later disregard/ Or keep the end from being hard.*

* * *

"I'm glad you behaved," my father grinned. "Aunt Rosie's sister, Dotty, was there."

How young men and women giggled about the community's matchmaker, plump, comfortable Dotty, and her little red Domesday Book with every possible stat about every Mangalorean girl or boy who was anyone (or giggled until they needed her services).

And then parental whispers in corners, and Dotty's much-quoted Delphic utterances: "Tell her to lose weight. Or get a US Green Card." "Tell him to find a better job."

Dottie did not charge—"It gives me something to do; I like to help"—but, at weddings, she was a guest of honour, the bride's family gave her expensive lavishly gold-embroidered Kanjeeveram silk sarees, and oh, nothing was too much—as the couple stood before the altar, beaming at each other with joy and wild hope, fully prepared to live happily ever after (which, surprisingly often, they did). And then the new couple rode off into the sunset with pleased punchy Cheshire cat smiles as if it had all been their idea in the first place.

The dragon-guarded strait path to bliss! Destiny hinged on luck as well as on character. Two small-town sisters or cousins: one might marry a successful physician or businessman in the US, say, and file impressive tax returns; her kids are successful. The other's spouse stays put, never realises his ambitions, loses his "small job," then his health, drinks, drifts. Since your spouse partly dictated the course of your life (along with your character and the goodness or darkness of your heart), matchmakers had enormous power.

Algebraic negotiations sought equilibrium between the ideal child-in-law and a realistically achievable one. And as matchmaking got underway, generations of family laundry, clean and dirty, were exhumed from communal memory. Serpentine whispers of doom: "His mother drinks." And she's "a little…"–a discreet tapping of the temples. Drunkenness, mental retardation, instability, and insanity were genetic–everyone believed that.

Desiderata: in "a boy"–good family, money, an upwardly mobile career, "a sweet boy." In "a girl": family, money, "fairness" or a lighter skin colour, beauty; education, sundry accomplishments; "very sweet." Those with the most desirable attributes married their counterparts. Which is probably what would have happened, though less scientifically, had the young people been left to their own devices!!

                                        * * *

Dowry, receiving it, giving it, was banned by the Indian Supreme Court in 1961. Sure!! "The boy's family had all the expense of educating the boy; he'll look after the girl. Why shouldn't the girl's family contribute?" people said. (And if it was pointed out that "the girl" was educated too—a snort, a shrug. That was just the way things are).

No fixed figure. While Ms Plain-Jane's parents might, as she neared the last-chance late twenties, in desperation, offer a farm, it used to be an assortment of jewellery and money, a Fiat, a flat; (now medical clinics, factories, or resorts could be demanded!). There were blatant blandishments: my father told of a jeep ride through coffee estates with his bride-seeking brother: "This will be yours, and this."

However, "the marriage market" was a human transaction, not sheerly a matter of the stock market or stockbreeding, so the best-stocked applecarts of potential mothers-in-law and matchmakers were often upset. An infatuation with a long-lashed Adonis or a girl's beauty and bubbliness might prevail despite the best advice. A double standard: as is universally true, plainness or unattractiveness was more of a handicap for a woman. Our family friends sent their daughter Odette to the Radcliffe Infirmary in Oxford to have her harelip corrected before she entered the marriage market. Her father, escorting her, had the surgery at the same time, though *his* had never mattered: *he* was an engineer. Here, as elsewhere, a woman whose face was her fortune married "up," and a rich woman did better than if her face had been her fortune. A few, including I myself, sidestepped the whole thing and had "love marriages." And "he was caught," everyone says bitterly.

Catholics from the small town of Mangalore have almost exclusively married other Mangaloreans, local or diasporic, since they were converted to Catholicism half a millennium ago. What's more, they marry (often enough their own cousins) within their pre-conversion Hindu caste and snobbily defined class, within which individuals, my husband and I say, can trace multiple relationships. This eugenic mating over centuries–artificial selection in Darwin's terms–has, as intended, disproportionately strengthened desired traits: intelligence, good features, the coveted shades of skin colouring, and, perhaps, the ingenuity, doggedness, flair, and desirousness which produce wealth.

(Of course, as love marriages increase with increasing social freedoms and emigration swells, there will be fewer and fewer arranged marriages; of my twenty-six first cousins, sixteen married out of the community, while only nine, including I myself, married Mangaloreans. Eventually, the Mangalorean community, like the Zoroastrians, another small, inbred community, will probably die out.)

And there was an accidental, inevitable consequence: a community in which "the mad woman in the attic" was not just a literary trope. "*Look up discreetly,*" my father murmured as we passed the mansion of an old, wealthy, respected family.

"Who was *that*, Pa? She wasn't wearing anything…"

"Ssshhh. Maggie's daughter, Margaret. She never mentions her daughter. Neither does anyone else. Though everyone knows. She keeps her locked up, though sometimes she gets to the window and well, you saw."

Outwardly, there was sweet harmony. Outwardly. But often, even in the snootiest families: a missing child, mentally ill like Margaret (whose mother, cutting flowers, alerted by the gaping of passersby, ran upstairs); autistic, or with multiple disabilities (attributed to "birth traumas," so as not to prejudice the marriage chances of siblings) and euphemistically called "spastic," the fruit of genes bruised by five hundred years of a small, much-pooled gene pool.

Most genteel old Mangalorean extended families had their Peter Pan, called Baba or Baby, into middle age, for whom the twentieth century proved too much: a coddled son or daughter, once promising, the community's pride, who, unable to grab the trophies and trophy spouse still lived with Mummy in the bomb shelter of the family home they would eventually inherit. There were, here as elsewhere, sad spinsters and wistful bachelors who somehow missed "two for joy" and square pegs who slipped through cracked round holes and were used as a cautionary tale for the rare eccentric. Beware. Beware.

I too have seen some of the best minds of my generation destroyed. Marlo, my cousin, famous among the nuns and priests of India, promised prayers by many orders of nuns and priests, subjected to every quack and craze, Charismatic healer, yogi, positive thinker; to Gestalt, transaction analysis, psychiatry, psychotherapy, inner healing. A chess champion, proclaimed a genius as the promising young often are; achieving the highest average in the State school-leaving exams, but with one misstep, a failure in compulsory Hindi, which meant a retake–which never happened. Instead, drugs, theosophy, a fling at being a vegetarian rishi in an ashram, dabbling in the occult, deep open-eyed

trances. Some swore he levitated. He looked like Death-in-Life, like one possessed, as he stared out of terrible, blighted eyes, hearing Furies hiss as his
mind's circuits blew and the plagues piled up–frustration, violence, institution-
alization, suicide.

And, in Jamshedpur, the gentle, androgynous Mangalorean, Oliver, on
whom every girl had a crush, long-fringed, long-haired, long-lashed like Paul
McCartney, like the Beatles, whose songs he sang, twangy-voiced, strumming
on his guitar, who went to England on a Commonwealth Scholarship, who
dabbled in drugs, adulterated?, excessive, which whispered words of wisdom,
let it be, let it be, destroyed his mind and the fibre of his character. Study or a
steady job became pipe dreams.

So like others kept afloat by their parents' guilty broken hearts, he vanished behind his newspaper, lived with them until they died, their ironic silver
lining, his immense good nature still evident on his blighted lost-boy face,
whose fine features had grown flabby, for, eventually, character tells its tale.

Once orphaned, he floated around town, a middle-aged wraith, chain-
smoking, chain-drinking tea in grimy *dhabas*, finally growing so dishevelled,
shaggy, sun-scorched and unwashed that, when he tried to visit my parents, the
guard would not let him past the gate.

And I think of another sixties refrain: *And there but for grace, go you or I...*

* * *

Reunited after a month, my sister and I compared notes. While we were
then the only Coelho grandchildren with three bachelor uncles and a spinster
aunt, we were just another two among the twenty-six Mathias grandchildren.
While my Christmas Eve prayers for good presents fell on rocky soil, producing
twenty-five rupees from my grandmother to split with my sister and that Five
Star bar from Aunt Ethel, the trade winds of family love wafted Shalini toys
and cash, clothes and chocolate. To forestall inevitable tears, my father, each
Christmas in Mangalore, flashed a Learian promise, "Ask for whatever you

want, and I'll give it to you." "Four slabs of Cadbury's chocolate, four Agatha Christies, and a Monopoly set!" I stipulated and got them--and then, as if to counteract the spoils and spoiling of Bombay, he forgot to get my sister a present. "But look what *Pa* gave me!" I said, gazing sadly at her presents. "What did Pa give you?" She cried; my mother glared at him and dispatched him to get her a gift, but since we already had Monopoly, he got her a cheaper Indian version, Trade, with Bombay properties, Nepean Sea Drive, Malabar Hill, and Juhu Beach, rather than Fleet Street, Chelsea, and the Strand. "I got Monopoly; you got *Trade*."

And so ended the winter of the matriarchs. I think of these women, my mother, my grandmothers, my great-grandmothers. I wear their jewellery every day, my great-grandmother's ruby earrings, my grandmother's wedding ring and bracelets, and my mother's gold chain and cross. I have too the hair, eyes, and colouring, the IQ and temperament their DNA has given me. A brooding pronouncement in Deuteronomy: "I, the Lord your God, punish the children for the sin of the fathers to the third and fourth generation of those who hate me, but show love to a thousand generations of those who love me and keep my commandments." How might this work naturalistically? According to Lamarck's gospel of hope, your hours in the gym give your future children strong bodies; the books you read elevate their intelligence, as "the forelegs and necks of giraffes have become lengthened through the habit of browsing." Though, of course, Darwin debunked this hopeful–or terrifying–theory, Lamarck described what he observed: that families do transmit acquired traits, appetites for work or food, for religion or the arts, for money, community, or solitude. Your family is the amniotic sea in which you swim. Its ideas seep through you by osmosis–though you may leap out of it like a dolphin, flipper away from it like an antic sea lion, or breech out of it like a whale to sing a high, pure, anguished song. Families hand you a weaving of genes and aspirations, hand-me-down wisdom, prejudices, philosophy, and stories. All your life, you will alternately wrap it around you for security and warmth—or unravel it, to weave with that ancient yarn, a new woman.

The Hollies, My grandparent's home in Cubbon Road, Bangalore

Back row: Uncles Michael, Pat, Theo, Eric and my father
Front row: Aunt Joyce, Uncle Joseph, Aunt Winnie and her son Derek, my grandmother, Uncle Morris and Aunt Jessie

My paternal grandfather, Dr. Piedade Felician Mathias, OBE

Standing, my grandfather Dr. Piedade Felician Mathias OBE. Then, left to right, Eric, my grandmother, Josephine, baby Morris, Dr. Pat Mathias, my father Noel, and Fr. Dr. Theo Mathias.

The Mathias boys, L to R, Theo, Pat, Morris, my father Noel, Eric in white

JOSEPHINE MATHIAS
Passed to Eternal life : 27·7·1985

My grandmothers' Mortuary Card

My great-grandmother Juliana Lobo's 100th birthday.
Top Row, third left, my cousin Margaret Burghagen, Fourth from R, my uncle, Pat, 3rd Uncle Louis, Far right, top, Uncle Eric
Middle Row, 3 rd from L, Aunt Ethel, 5th from Left, my Aunt, Dr. Jessie Pais, cousin, Peggy Gonsalves
Seated, Norbert Lobo, Gerry Lobo, Juliana, my grandmother, Josephine, Uncle Fr. Theo

Excel: Life at Faculty Housing at Xavier Labour Relations Institute

When my father retired from The Tata Iron and Steel Company, Jamshedpur, at the mandatory age of sixty, full of vigour and experience, I, aged fourteen, was at an expensive boarding school, St. Mary's Convent, Nainital, and my sister Shalini was just eleven. He had little wish to retire.

He was, providentially, offered a job as Financial Controller at XLRI, Xavier Labour Relations Institute, a prestigious American Jesuit-run post-graduate business school, one of South Asia's oldest and highest ranked– serendipitously located in Jamshedpur–and with, surprisingly, an increase in salary. My father enjoyed the challenge of his new job, a combination of Chief Financial Officer, Treasurer, and internal auditor—merrily making enemies as he queried fanciful expense accounts. We lived in Faculty Housing on the XLRI campus for eight years.

Jamshedpur, a small town in Bihar, was not an entirely quixotic choice for a Business School. Because of its mother lode of iron ore, it hosted two of India's largest companies, Tata Iron and Steel, TISCO, and Tata Electric Locomotive Company, TELCO, and attracted executives from all over India; few managers were born there! Our sleepy provincial town was a business hub!

XLRI was founded and largely run by missionary priests, Americans from the Baltimore Jesuit province, though as was to be expected from the International Society of Jesus, there were priests on loan, like Spanish Father Arroyo from the Jesuit Gujarat province, a missionary project of the Spanish Jesuits, as well as Mangalorean Jesuits from India's Karnataka Province. (The Jesuits, like the Catholic Church, were an early multinational!). Though XLRI was then largely staffed by American priests, my father's Jesuit younger brother, Father Theo Mathias, was the Director during the eight years that we lived there. My father held Theo up to us as an exemplar of productivity and perfection. "Lolling?" he'd say if, on coming home for lunch, he found me sprawled on his bed, desultorily scanning the newspaper or *Time* magazine. "Wasting time? I don't think Theo ever wastes even five minutes." I grimaced guiltily (but over the decades have developed a similar but even intenser horror of wasting my time.)

East and West! Culture shock--all the time. Good-natured Father O'Brien noticed his student had a *mundan,* shaved head, a custom of conservative Hindus mourning relatives.

"Hey, Ravi," he slapped him on the back with easy American friendliness. "How are you doing? And why have you shaved your head?"

"My mother died," the student said mournfully.

"Great, great!" Father O'Brien absently patted his shoulder and walked on, his mind already on other things.

The genial American Jesuits on campus, Fathers Keogh, McGrath, Moran, Tome, and Guidera, referred to Theo as "your kid brother" when they spoke to my father, which amused us; both dignified gentlemen were in their sixties. "Here comes Noel and his harem," the American priests sang out as they saw my father walk through campus with my mother, sister and me in tow. "XYZ," they'd say, eyeing his fly, which mystified my absent-minded father till he worked out it meant "Check Your Zip."

* * *

When we were invited to dinner at the Jesuits' house, peacocks strutted, manifesting iridescent moons—they were pets, food, mewling watchbirds, and five a.m. alarm clocks! Heartmeltingly sweet caged rabbits provided free and delicious meals; the house was guarded by magnificent pure-bred Alsatians, parents of our Brutus.

Some of the priests were left-wing, radical, and I listened, open-eared and fascinated, as they openly criticised the Vatican for censoring Hans Kung and explained Liberation Theology. These gentle, idealistic men had come to India, probably expecting to serve the poor, but often piqued, frustrated and restless, found themselves educating ambitious go-getting business managers-to-be while valiantly hoping to transmit Christ's kindly vision to them, so it might trickle through society, like salt, like light.

I used to attend the weekday student masses on the XLRI campus. The winds of the Sixties–a post-Vatican II liberation–had reached India. The Latin Masses I remember from my earliest childhood–a complete travesty and disgrace in a country where few knew Latin–had given way to English masses for the English-speaking and Hindi masses for the rest. We sat on the floor on cushions and sang toe-tapping folksy songs, accompanied by guitars–"Make God your guru," "Honey in the Rock," "He is my Everything," a far cry from the soulful, formal hymns of my German-run boarding school in the Himalayas. We gustily sung protest songs against Vietnam and for Civil Rights, "Kumbaya" and "Blowing in the Wind,"–oblivious of their origins.

* * *

XLRI offered an MBA in Industrial Relations and Business Management, drawing students from all over India, and even Sri Lanka, Bhutan, Nepal, Iran, Malaysia, and Nigeria to Jamshedpur. It was ranked fifth among India's eight hundred business schools.

Since fewer than one percent of applicants were accepted, Professors on the admissions committee, as my father was every year, were offered myriad bribes. My father scanned the letters and then flung them in the wastepaper basket. I retrieved one. "*Why are you torturing me?*" and then, "Okay, I can offer an additional five thousand rupees." Wealth, emigration to the US, better marriage prospects for men, a cheaper dowry for women–a lot hinged on the right education.

My father's secretary, sorting his mail, snorted, "This bloody fool thinks he can draw green hearts on the envelope and get into XLRI."

"Show me!" my father said uneasily. And then, shyly, "It's my daughter!" Attempting to assert my individuality at boarding school, I used brilliant fountain pen inks: turquoise, emerald, bright pink, and magenta, idly covering the envelope with hearts.

* * *

Living in Faculty Housing on the XLRI campus as a teenager provided more cultural and intellectual stimulation than usual in a small Indian town, particularly when XLRI hosted Kaleidoscope, an annual national inter-collegiate cultural festival. Student teams from all over India competed for a few frenzied days–music, debating, drama, and quiz competitions, based on the BBC's Mastermind; elocution competitions: strutting forth purple passages of poetry or prose; and "Just a Minute" impromptu oratorical competitions in which one was given, well, just a minute to argue a point, starting the instant a topic was announced. (I introduced this to boarding school and was rather good at it.)

We watched *Of Mice and Men* at XLRI performed by a visiting American theatre troupe; edgy productions like Peter Shaeffer's *Equus*, and a chilling production of Agatha Christie's *Ten Little N***ers* by XLRI students, who then probably did not realise that the word was uniquely offensive, and interestingly, the American priests didn't tell them. When I loved a play, I asked my father to get a typescript off the students and took it up to boarding school, where I directed them as fundraisers for our Social Service League, which I ran—Moliere's *The Miser* when I was fourteen and *Overtones* by Alice Gerstenberg when I was fifteen. *Overtones* has feral scowling secret shadow-selves voice sharp thoughts, while the public social selves blandly smile; it shaped my perceptions of social life.

Unusually for Indian libraries then, XLRI's library was well stacked with American classics, absent from both the local Club libraries and from my school library, which had–almost entirely–British authors. Besides, being on faculty in an American-run institution enabled my father to borrow books for me through inter-library loan from the United States Information Service in Calcutta, and he did. This was the era of the Cold War; we received *Sputnik* from Russia, on cheap paper, with hagiographic stories of the childhood of the sainted Vladimir Ilyich Lenin, and a glossy magazine *Span* from the USIS, with absorbing profiles of American writers like Eudora Welty, Isaac Bashevis Singer, Flannery O'Connor, and Katherine Ann Porter. I yearned to read them all.

I read T. S. Eliot for the first time in a volume borrowed from the XLRI library, mesmerised by the rhythm and resonance of the words, long before I understood the poems. I memorised the poetry of the Jesuit Gerald Manley Hopkins; like Eliot, he spoke to me, pulse to pulse. I was learning the magic language of poetry. I read, with relief, St. Augustine's *Confessions*, enchanted by his sense of the dual plots in our lives. "You acted with malice," he addresses the teachers of his youth, "but God was active too, shaping it all for good."

I also read the American writers the priests suggested, sobbing through the visceral last scene of *The Grapes of Wrath*. One winter, I checked out the complete plays of Eugene O'Neil, Tennessee Williams, Arthur Miller, and then Ibsen from the XLRI library, reading play after play. When I was home from boarding school, I read rapidly, a book a day effortlessly, lying on my bed, on my stomach; eating up the novels of E.M. Forster, D.H. Lawrence, and Aldous Huxley in the Club and XLRI library, besides my old favourites, Jane Austen and Thomas Hardy. Durga, who had moved with us to live in the servant's room provided, did all the cooking and cleaning; I had no domestic chores. There was no television; except for the three movies we saw each week at the Clubs, I had nothing to do but read, genius when I could find it, the mediocre– Morris West's The Shoes of the Fisherman!–when I could not.

During the three-month winter vacation from boarding school, I checked out *The Hundred Greatest Speeches* and memorised some of the great American speeches for elocution competitions at boarding school: Frederick Douglass "What to the Slave is the Fourth of July,": *Fellow citizens, above your national, tumultuous joy, I hear the mournful wail of millions;* "The Gettysburg Address," and Martin Luther King's resonant, living, "I have a dream." Decades later, I remember them; their rhythms beat in my veins.

* * *

The students hosted marketing festivals to road-test new products, guinea-pigging their relatively affluent and educated visitors into market research in the form of games. My mother played intently and came home having won tote bags of Nivea Cream, Ponds Talcum Powder, Head and Shoulders Shampoo, and Britannia biscuits. My father watched from a distance, quietly amused.

We often had students, faculty, and the Jesuit priests from the Business School over for dinner, and, unconsciously, during those eight years on the campus of a business school, the romance and magic of business and wealth-generation seeped into my poetic consciousness. I borrowed the books the students read in their Organisational Behaviour course from the XLRI library— introductions to psychology, pop psychology and Transactional Analysis: *I'm Okay; You're Okay; Games People Play*, or "*Why Am I Afraid to Tell You Who I Am?*" and listened intently to conversations on business, wondering if I'd be good at creating one, or if I were too bookish to do so. I do own my own business now; perhaps those years in faculty housing of a Business School indirectly led me to think creatively in business as in writing; to see both poems and wealth-creation ideas blushing unseen everywhere.

* * *

The bright, charming Catholic students invited us to dance with them at Christmas parties and bestowed our first kisses on us. Coolness was prized, being "hep" or "a hep cat;" those who tried too hard were called "pseuds." (In retrospect, there was probably little difference between them.)   While XLRI had foreign students from all over Asia and the Middle East, there was only one African, a Nigerian called Charlie. Charlie really, really fancied Indian woman. Undaunted by repeated, sometimes horrified rebuffs, he assiduously proposed marriage to fellow students, stenographers, and telephone operators. My father's secretary burst into his office in tears, wailing, "Charlie asked me to *marry* him." The entire college community would now tease the latest love object…until Charlie proposed to someone else.

My mother once invited Charlie to lunch with other students. He talked about women, marriage, and weight! In Nigeria, brides were sent to fattening parlours before their wedding day, he said, for being hefty was sexy, a status symbol. My family claimed Charlie looked straight at me as he said that. I was five feet two and weighed a hundred and sixteen pounds (very much a normal weight!) though my parents, who wanted me to weigh a hundred pounds, constantly nagged me about it. They teased, "Well, you *could* diet, or you could marry Charlie."

* * *

Autorickshaw drivers and rickshawmen called the secluded leafy campus of Xavier Labour Relations Institute, set in a sylvan setting on the outskirts of town, *"Jayber-Laber."* "Jayber-Laber, please," we said. To the English-speaking, it was XLRI, or serendipitously, XL, *Excel*, a much-milked acronym.

The Jesuits built faculty housing in an enclave adjoining the University; as with our house at Tata Steel, the apartment came with the job and was surrendered with it. Throwing in housing helped employers attract talent in a developing economy in which banks did not offer mortgages. (The provident middle-class saved and bought houses with cash, after retirement; many never did.)

I liked strolling on the quiet, peaceful road which encircled Faculty Housing—two storied apartments, each assigned to two families, on one side, and brilliant, red-flowered flame of the forest and bottle brush trees on the other. Each house had two balconies; oases where I sat and gazed at the fiery parasol of the Royal Poinciana trees across the road.

The faculty and staff of XLRI worked together during the day and lived a few yards apart in the evenings; almost every family housed domestic help in their allotted single room for servants–a maid or a cook and their family, who hung out with other families' servants in their off-hours. What was whispered in living rooms, virally transmitted through the servants, reached the rooftops where families relaxed in the evenings. Any illusion of privacy was, well, illusory.

During his hours off, our cook Durga sat in the sun outside the campus gates with other off-duty servants and the Gurkhas, indomitable Nepalese watchmen who guarded XLRI and the Jesuit residence. He returned with juicy gossip–which faculty members were at war with each other; whose wife was going quietly insane in the privacy of their house; whose secretary was shamelessly flirting with her boss—who, in one instance, was a priest! And perhaps our secrets left the house by the same channels through which other people's secrets entered it!

* * *

Moving from a large, bright, airy twelve-roomed house with an additional outdoor kitchen, a garage, and quarters for two servants to a three-bedroom apartment with no private garden was a huge transition. Our flat in XLRI was significantly smaller and was laid out on a more open floor plan than most Indian houses with a combined living room and dining room (which, as a child, I used to consider a sign of poverty!). The apartment was compact: two ensuite bedrooms, a small study for my father, a living-dining room, a kitchen, two balconies, and a single room for the cook downstairs.

I felt cabined, cribbed, confined, finding it too small, dark and garden-less; poems I'd learned didn't course through my mind, nor did I sink as deeply into the dream-world of a book as I did in the much larger house with a huge garden. The apartment afforded markedly less privacy to read and think than our previous house--and my mother pined for a garden, having grown her own flowers, fruit, vegetables and herbs all her married life. There was little solitude, little space to dream. My spirit and imagination flower in larger gardened spaces.

While an acre of garden encircled our Tata Steel house with an oasis of privacy, at XLRI, we were assigned the top floor of the apartment building. There were *neighbours beneath us.* According to campus tradition, families on the upper floor used the rooftop terrace to relax or to eat dessert in the cool of the summer evening and to sit and read in winter, soaking up the sun. We hung out laundry; spread shrimp, pork, ginger, and vegetables on dishcloths to sun-dry for pickles, and, on sweltering summer nights, even slept on the terrace; it func-tioned as an extra room. The people on the lower floor traditionally had the small garden to hang out their laundry, and to cultivate.

Eating from the garden was a way of life for us—crisp freshly-picked let-tuce, radish, tomatoes, or peppers for breakfast layered in cheese sandwiches, and fresh vegetables for salads, curries, and homemade mint and coriander chutney. On seeing cultivatable land lie overgrown and unused right beneath our windows, my mother's green thumb itched. She had our cook dig out a little plot and plant vegetables, herbs, flowers, mulberries bushes and banana trees. The little garden bloomed.

The faculty wife downstairs, Mrs Gupta, an overweight, sloppily dressed, very dark-skinned woman, was a recluse, made strange and half-crazed by lone-liness within her yellow-walled house. Less educated than her respected professor husband (as often happens in arranged marriages where parental life savings "buy" a better-educated husband, whose salary would, perhaps, support both sets of parents in old age), she was out of her depth in the University environment. Though this indolent, eccentric, unhappy woman rarely stepped outside her house and had done precisely nothing about planting a garden in all the years they had lived there, she was furious to see my mother plant a garden on what, by campus tradition, was *her* land.

One day, as my mother was pruning and harvesting, Mrs Gupta rushed out of her house with a packet of seeds and flung them over the hard, unbroken, weed-choked ground, almost dancing in her rage like the multi-armed goddess Kali over battlefields. "Mrs Mathias," she yelled. "This is *my* garden. See, I am using the garden. See, I am planting my seeds."

There were interventions. Both soft-spoken dignified husbands managed the families' foreign policy, and my mother was given half the garden in which she densely planted flowers, vegetables, herbs, papaya, banana, and mulberry trees, and perennial fruiting shrubs like roselle. The Guptas, it was agreed, could use the terrace too, though being reclusive, Mrs G. never did—for then we might have seen her. In the eight years we lived there, I caught sight of her just once.

The families then co-existed, an uneasy truce, confining themselves to barbs. When I returned from boarding school, and my mother and I were left alone while my father was at work and my sister was at school, the decibel level soared. Bored of seeing to household tasks, perhaps resentful of my happy total immersion in a book, my mother walked into my room to see what I was doing. Within minutes, we were both screaming. When my father returned for lunch, my mother and I rushed to him, the first at the door having the first shot at a recitation of woe. "I was quietly sitting reading, and she burst in and said, "You are sitting so badly. Durga can see your knickers." And I said, 'Well, I'll close the door.' And she said, "I won't have closed doors in this house."" And my father sighed, exasperated, "I *told* both of you to stay in your own rooms!" On encountering my sister as they entered the building, Professor Gupta said dryly, "I *hear* your sister's home." And so, he must have.

* * *

The next salvo in the war of the neighbours: Mrs Gupta hired a "jungli" (as the indigenous Adivasi forest dwellers who belonged to the scheduled or "backward tribes" in official parlance then, were called in Bihar) to dig her half of the garden, and prepare the hard, compacted, rocky, never cultivated laterite soil for planting. This was iron country; the red earth was riddled with *murram*, pellets of iron ore. He laboured, day after day, from dawn to dusk. And when, each evening, he presented himself at her door for payment, she inspected the plot and said, "No, it's not deep enough; it's not wide enough."

The hungry, tired man continued the exhausting digging with the silent, accepting air of a crushed, sad animal, afraid of quitting and not being paid for the work he had already done. However, when she kept commanding, "Dig deeper. It's not deep enough. I will pay you when it is finished," our cook Durga advised him to quit. "She'll *never* pay you," he warned. And, sorrowfully and reluctantly, the man finally did leave. Never paid. It was the first time I observed someone who made a game of exploitation.

Mrs Gupta never did have a garden. Little was planted on that cruelty-cursed earth, and little grew. Her half of the yard was soon weedy, overgrown, and neglected, but it was hers, and she had it.

The faculty flat came with an outdoor room for a servant. Mrs Gupta let hers to a woman who, well… Durga said men on motorcycles came at night, stayed a while, and then left. During the day, Mrs Gupta worked that woman-- no fixed hours or half-day off as our servants had. Sweep, scrub, cook, wash up, do laundry, iron. But when she said, *"Ma, hum jata hai,"* "Ma, I'm going," the parting greeting of the servant going off duty, Mrs Gupta replied, "Wait.

Massage my feet. Massage my daughter Kalpy's feet; massage my daughter Archy's feet," keeping her and on, exploiting the woman's vulnerability.

* * *

Somewhat ironically for a university which taught Industrial Relations and Business Management, XLRI had a strike–endemic in India, a common way to negotiate wage increases or better work conditions.

"Labour," the staff: secretaries, telephone operators, and clerks, struck against "Management," the administration–the Jesuits, including my uncle, Father Theo Mathias, the Jesuit Director, and some faculty, such as my father, the Financial Controller.

Some American Jesuits ("bleeding-heart liberals!" my father snorted) sided with the staff. This was to be expected, given their temperament and politics; they had come of age in the sixties; they were forgiven by the other priests. An Indian Jesuit from Mangalore, however, also sided with the staff, to be cool, to court popularity, the other Jesuits said in disgust; and he was never forgiven. (Eventually, he was moved to the University of Detroit, and his archenemy, the fiery Spanish Jesuit who sided with the administration and considered this betrayal of his Jesuit brothers inexcusable, was moved to St. Joseph's, Philadelphia. To the Jesuits, the world was a chessboard.)

The strike was a game for the students. It had an air of gaiety and unreality, an unexpected foretaste of big-boy life, making solemn armchair ethicists of them. The students sided with Labour—the charms of the underdog whom you don't have to feed! They were playing at being liberal, but this would change once they became management, my father snorted. The more radical people were in youth, the more conservative they became at the scent of money, he said, recollecting the idealistic hot-air talk of the young Indians he knew in London in the forties and early fifties. "All those Indians in England, talking about socialism and communism! They're now the pillars of the Indian establishment!

The more a young man trumpets his disdain for money, the more avaricious he becomes in middle age."

* * *

We felt besieged during the strike, waking up to see the air released from the tires and long gashes in the silver paint of my Father's beloved Fiat. He insisted that my sister and I stay home during the strike, fearful that students or strikers, recognising us, might call out something rude. Also, he didn't want us to see the posters.

However, since keeping secrets was never my father's forte (and I struggled too!), he eventually mentioned that posters with insults including, "Director, get rid of your inefficient retired brother," were plastered all over campus. Too punctilious to be inefficient, and pernickety about the strictest honesty, my father was, if anything, too competent. (I would say that, wouldn't I? but it's true!). As he had at Tata's, he challenged creative accounting and imaginatively padded expense accounts. "And he's billed us for a stay at the Oberoi Sheraton when I know for sure he stayed with his brother-in-law! And *six* meals a day? Five I could accept." And so, he discovered the truth of Emerson's saying, "He who has a thousand friends has not one to spare; he who has an enemy shall see him everywhere."

* * *

I was surprised to hear my father say that he prayed every day, for I thought I was the only member of the family who really prayed.

"*You pray?*" I exclaimed. "What do you pray for?"

"I pray for you and Shalini and Dan."

My father detested Dan, an unpleasant clerical worker who was the ringleader of the strike, taking advantage of the gentle, fair-minded, generous, and out-of-their-depth American Jesuits to demand concessions unusual for India. Dan was responsible for those offensive posters.

"For us and *Dan?*" I was offended. "Why *Dan?*"

"Because Jesus said we should pray for our enemies," he said, adding hastily, "Not just our enemies!"

Ah, never underestimate the spirituality of your parents!

My Uncle Father Theo Mathias SJ

My father at Anghien, Belgium at his brother Father Theo's ordination. The Cardinal who ordained Theo is between the brothers.

The Naughtiest Girl in the School: Sacred Heart Convent, Jamshedpur

I started preschool aged three, the norm in academically competitive India, at Misses Jhinghan's Preschool. My mother often recounted a story from this period reproachfully: the time Indira Gandhi, the Prime Minister, visited Jamshedpur, and both Misses Jhingan went to the airport to catch a glimpse of her but asked my parents to keep me home, saying that the *ayahs* could manage all the other children--but not me!

And then, for five tumultuous years, I attended a Catholic girls' school, Sacred Heart Convent, run by the Apostolic Carmel, an order founded in Mangalore, my ancestral hometown, and staffed by Mangalorean nuns. I went to Lower Kindergarten, aged four, in my blue cotton school uniform and Bata shoes, my brown canvas satchel stuffed with a white slate pencil and a bright beaded abacus, ecologically and economically sound school supplies. Whenever I saw her, my first teacher, Mrs Millie D'Cruz, a little, plump lady from Goa always dressed in knee-length one-piece dresses, told me tales of myself. In a fit of temper, I had grabbed another child's lunch and thrown it into the drain. Teacher Millie then informed me that she had thrown *my* lunch into the drain, a Mosaic morality which so outraged me that I slapped her. She giggled, still shocked; she had hidden it in the closet to teach me empathy, consequences…

* * *

Since I was a finicky, distractible eater, my mother sent the *ayah* to walk across town to my school at recess, carrying my freshly-packed lunch in a tiffin carrier, a cluster of five tin containers bound by a metal clasp. The ayah was to ensure I worked through the sandwiches of home-cured salt pork, corned beef, or tongue before I got to the homemade sweet in the lowest container, a piece of fudge, halwa or burfi–though I habitually reversed the order, and the ayah never told.

In between working through layers of my tiffin, I bounced around with the others, all of us chanting, hopefully and impractically, *"Ching-Chong China-man, Chow, Chow Chow/Kutta bolta bow-wow-wow/ Billie bolta meow/Anda bolta butt,"* (Dogs bark, cats meow, eggs crack like our Chinese enemies). There were border skirmishes between India and China in 1967, and these jingoistic chants displayed our impotent patriotism.

Aggressive kites circled overhead as we ate. One swooped down, terrifyingly, and snatched my tongue sandwich.

"What did it take?" everyone asked. "Tongue," I said.

"Tongue?"

"Cow's tongue," I said, a succulent delicacy.

The thought of eating a sacred cow filled my Hindu classmates with revulsion--which paled beside the notion of eating its *tongue*.

"Chee-chee-chee," my classmate squealed (which roughly translates as yuck-yuck-yuck) and ran away, almost gagging. I pursued her, holding my slice of pink cured tongue, chanting, "Cow's tongue, cow's tongue," threatening to touch her with it. More and more girls shrieked and fled, the recess degenerating into chaos as I chased the running girls, shouting, "Cow's tongue, cow's tongue."

"Anita Mathias, what are you doing?"

"Trying to touch the girls with tongue, Sister."

"Who told you to do that?"

I considered. "The Devil?"

Wrong answer. "Mr Mathias, Mrs Mathias, she said *the Devil* told her to…."

Never answer rhetorical questions: I was slow to learn that.

"Why did you do that?" the nuns kept asking.

"Well," I sometimes said, answering laterally, "so-and-so did it too" (a typical response of Indian children).

"If so-and-so jumps into the well, will you jump into the well?'

"No, Sister."

* * *

Another unanswerable question the nuns kept asking: "Why are you so naughty when your sister is so good?

With childhood naivete, I pondered the question. Since I had contracted amoebic dysentery, which had killed my baby brother Gerard in three days, I had had an emergency baptism in the hospital performed by my mother's cousin, Father Aloysius Coelho, a saintly, down-to-earth Jesuit who, unlike most Jesuits who taught in fee-paying schools and colleges, worked with indigenous Adivasi tribal people, in Gujarat. My sister, however, had been baptised by the Bishop of Jamshedpur and had a lavish baptism party, the Bishop and numerous priests and parishioners filling our house and garden, a roast piglet as the centrepiece, its eyes glistening.

"Because she was baptised by a Bishop, and I was baptised by a priest?" I guessed, having absorbed my parents' fine-tuned consciousness of social and ecclesiastical hierarchy.

The sycophantic nuns, of course, reported this to our Bishop, Anglo-Burmese Lawrence Picachy, a Jesuit. At his next pastoral visit to the school, he summoned me to the parlour. "You can't be baptised twice," he said, "but I *can* give you a special episcopal blessing." Which he proceeded to bestow on me.

"*Two* blessings! That's better than one baptism, even by a Bishop," he said. "Now you have to be "gooder" than your sister because you have not only been baptised by a priest but been blessed by a Bishop." (And a decade later, when I was a novice at Mother Teresa's convent in Calcutta, and he, the Cardinal of Calcutta, he told the story to the assembled four hundred novices and nuns—attributing my sudden virtue to that special Episcopal blessing.)

While some teachers were fond of me, one, a sadistic Parsee spinster, Teacher Subhadra, was certainly not. When, in a fit of temper, I angrily threw a stone at one of her favourite Parsee girls, she made me stand still and had that girl throw a stone at me–stone-age justice! I remember the terror of it, standing there, waiting to be stoned.

When I entered the First Standard, aged six, I was reading entire Enid Blyton novels while my classmates were learning to read simple sentences in the Radiant Reader. Schoolwork bored me as it did for the next six years until I had a brilliant, loving, inspiring teacher at boarding school, Sister Josephine. I could not focus on memorising the juiceless material. Teacher Lily, a mild, sweet-natured Chinese Catholic, sat on a little raised teacher's platform, her legs parted. Once, when I was bored, I crouched down, looked up, and announced, "Teacher Lily has purple polka-dotted knickers." The class tittered. The teacher flushed. "No, they're not," she cried, to even louder, nervous giggles.

The next day, Sister Veronique, the Principal, swept into the classroom and asked me to gather my books and follow her to the second standard classroom. I had received a "double promotion"– an academic honour which confers an aura which endures throughout one's schooldays: an exceptional student who got to skip a school year.

Double promotions reduce boredom by marginally increasing the academic challenge (though I was still bored and remained so for years) but set you back in sports since physical development doesn't coincide with intellectual leaps--a blow to self-confidence I never overcame so that I despised and tried to avoid physical activity for decades after that (but no longer!). Emotionally, one will probably be more immature and less self-controlled than one's new peers (and I was). Besides, you are no longer the star of one class but the baby of the next–but with the burdensome reputation of genius. Academically, they weaken your weakest subjects.

After my double promotion to the second standard, while my new class-mates were reading short chapters from their Hindi readers, I was still practising the Hindi alphabet–the complex curly-wurly Devanagri script with thirteen vowels and thirty-three consonants is not easy–and so I was far behind my class especially since, unlike most of the other students, we did not speak Hindi at home. I tackled Hindi with resentment, disdain, and insecurity, which persisted until we read serious literature in High School, plays by Kalidasa, novels and stories by Premchand, and, in Hindi translation, the novels and stories of Rabindranath Tagore. In Maths, similarly, I moved in a day from simple addition and subtraction to long division and advanced times tables, and so I feared and disliked Maths, disrupting classes.

I greedily read through the literature anthology, *The Radiant Reader* and the ethics textbook on the first day of Standard Two, and then my textbooks in History, Geography and Science, after which I lost interest; they were easy to read but boring to memorise, as we were expected to do for tests. And they were far less interesting than my favourite much-reread books at home--*Little Women, Heidi, The Swiss Family Robinson,* and *The Three Musketeers.* Sometimes feeling intensely bored, I simply walked out of class, marched into my sister's classroom, and led her and her friend Marukh by the hand to the playground, where we happily played.

I did take spelling tests seriously, for my parents equated bad spelling with being stupid and uncultured, and, whether by practice or instinctively, I learnt how to spell a new word almost at a glance, unconsciously breaking words into syllables. Poetry and literature I loved, almost unconsciously reading and rereading a poem or prose passage I loved until I had it almost "by heart," a habit which remains. I was praised as a precociously gifted writer because of my essays—though this was unearned! My mother wrote an essay on the set topic, stylised purple writing, overwriting, full of fancifulness and flourishes, and, memorising easily, I memorised it, regurgitating it on the test, getting high marks, consolidating that easy-come-by reputation of genius. For the rest, I found handwriting practice, repetitive homework, and studying for the constant tests exasperating, so I did not do them, resulting in terribly undistinguished marks, or perhaps I was marked down for unformed handwriting and unruly behaviour.

During our First Holy Communion preparation, we were given a picture of a Sacred Heart, speckled with little hearts, which we were to colour in when we had made "an act," a little voluntary sacrifice or random act of goodness– denying ourselves a sweet, say, or picking up a dropped scrap of paper.

My chief memory of communion preparation, which we shared with the local Jesuit boys' school, Loyola, is chasing a quiet boy called George Kuruvilla, the first person I knew called George, down the school corridors, singing, "Georgie-Porgie, pudding and pie/Kissed the girls and made them cry," which made *him* cry, especially when everyone else chanted, "Shame, shame, poppy shame; all the girls know your name."

I confessed this when I made my First Confession. My father wrote out my "sins," preferring to control what I told the priest. I memorised these and recited, "Forgive me, Father for I have sinned. This is my first confession, and these are my sins. I quarrelled, fought, and called bad names..." a catalogue I mechanically, unthinkingly repeated until, with relief, aged twenty-one, I shed the carapace of Catholicism forever.

In my First Holy Communion photograph, I stand scowling in my white lacy dress, my veil askew, looking pigeon-toed and bow-legged as my father mourned I was, holding a lighted First Communion candle awry, while my father frowns at me, ready to squash any nascent mischief.

There were some kindly teachers: the plump, light-skinned Art teacher, Mrs Wadia, a Parsee who benevolently smiled at me over her cat eye glasses and invited Shalini and me to spend the day at her house, where we painted on cups and handkerchiefs with acrylic paints, along with her sweet unmarried daughters, Yasmin and Perin, who lived with her.

I adored my gentle Third Standard teacher with the romantic name of Sister Desiree, a petite, soft-spoken nun with distinctive light hazel eyes. (Eleven years later, when I was a novice at Mother Teresa's convent in Calcutta, working in Kalighat, the Home for the Dying, she visited, and I recognised her immediately because of those eyes!) She taught us about shadows in science, short and bulky, long and lanky, fair-weather guardian angels, following you while the sun shone. "I am your shadow, Sister Desiree. Where you go, I will go," I announced. And I did so, running out of class to shadow her when I saw her pass, following her in breaks, until, suddenly conscious of me, she'd giggle, "Oh Anita."

Sister Desiree taught singing, the hour commencing with copying down the lyrics from the blackboard into our exercise books–excruciating boredom. I could not force myself to do so but instead took out and ate my packed lunch. Finally, my mother, who loved singing, promised me a piece of homemade fudge, "milk toffee," per song transcribed. I boasted of this promised toffee in the sky to Sister Desiree, though my resolve vanished when it came to copying down the songs.

When I went home that evening, my mother unpacked my school bag, grumbling, "I bet you haven't copied even one song. As usual,"–then went silent. Every single song we had learnt all year was there, tidily written: "How much is that doggy in the window?" "My Bonnie lies over the ocean", "Row, row, row your boat," "Bits of paper," and "I wish I lived in Monkey Land." My astonishment equalled hers, and I received a whole plate of milk toffee, full measure, flowing over. I never confessed that I had not copied them down myself, though looking back, obviously, my mother had spotted the grown-up handwriting and, obviously, Sister Desiree had taken pity on my desire and inability, and wasn't there was something godlike about those slivers of grace that ran through a period of life that I experienced as traumatic, turbulent, and chaotic, and have mostly blocked from my mind?

My third standard Hindi teacher was called Miss Kispota, an Adivasi name which amused my father, who muttered absently, "If you want to kiss, kiss Pota." I bounced around the playground that Monday, chanting, "If you want to kiss, kiss Pota," which seemed very funny and faintly obscene to my seven-year-old contemporaries in a culture in which kissing was censored on screen and never beheld in public.

She heard me.

"I have taught for seventeen years, and never have I come across such a *gundi ludki*," she screamed at me in Hindi, translated as "dirty girl," dirty having ethical connotations in Hindi, as in those Dutch still lives in which cleanliness is next to godliness. My father laughed heartily when I reported this, adding *"Itna gundi ludki"* to his collection of my "famous last words," while my mother, unamused, said, "Noel, why must you say these things in front of her? Anita, why must you repeat family jokes?"

My father invented a capacious nonsense rhyme to affectionately tease my sister, Shalini: *"Shalini, Balini, Big Fat Shalini,/ High-Bald, Low-Bald, Bald-headed Shalini."* It could be used with any name, I realised. The senselessness of it tormented the victim, who suspected a hidden meaning she did not understand.

With an awed but riveted crowd of little girls behind me, I followed Sister Veronique, the Principal, rapping, "Veronique, Beronique, big fat Veronique, high-bald, low-bald, bald-headed Veronique." She spun around.

Unlike Shalini, she *was* large and, it was rumoured, was like all nuns shaven bald beneath her veil.

"What did you say?" she demanded. A little cowed, I repeated the chant.

"What a filthy rhyme! Who taught it to you girls?"

"My father," I said.

* * *

"You are a square peg in a round hole," my father mourned. "Everybody has heard of how naughty you are; who will marry you?" My father's colleague Mr Pannikal, whom we called Mr Parkles, remembered how I told him my solution: "Don't worry, Pa. I will marry someone from Canada. Nobody will have heard of me there" --in Canada, the country of my mother's penfriend, Barbara Redlich.

Reputations are potent things, the accidental often misinterpreted. The senior class, organising the school's fancy dress competition, asked us what we wanted to go as. "A fairy," I said, visualising myself with iridescent, diaphanous wings. "Nothing doing!" my mother said. "Your head, I am making wings! We have red gum boots; we have a red hooded coat. Go as Red Riding Hood." And so, the announcement, "And now, Anita Mathias, as a fairy." And I trudged on as Red Riding Hood to gales of laughter and my own mortification.

One of my childhood's nebulous question marks: I woke one morning with abdominal pain so crippling that I could not walk but had to crawl to the bathroom; I was rushed to the hospital. I had been chosen to present a bouquet of flowers to the Papal Pro-Nuncio, who was visiting Jamshedpur from Rome, and, being devastated to miss it, was driven in an ambulance to the airport where I sat in a wheelchair until the moment when I stood up to present the bouquet.

I was scheduled for surgery for appendicitis, but as the nurse appeared with a terrifyingly fat syringe of purple anaesthetic fluid, I leapt out of bed and raced down the hospital corridors, the nurse huffing after me, holding out the syringe and half-smiling. At which proof of vigour, I was ignominiously discharged to the chagrin of my mother, who had rather relished the drama, attention, and being the almost-heroine of the hour, and maintained that I did indeed have appendicitis and needed surgery and was only discharged because I had fled in that most cowardly fashion. "And you refused to share your hospital bed with me; you said "No, sleep on the sofa," and I had to wait till you fell asleep and then slip in."

The great adventure of my childhood was trying to run away, like Enid Blyton's children, The Adventurous Four, The Famous Five, and The Secret Seven, who got deeply, thrillingly lost and encountered benign adults and benevolent, dim Bobbies, solved crimes, apprehended thieves, discovered uninhabited islands, and gained glory. I ran away with my friend Dany Dias to a leper colony, like my favourite literary character, Maggie Tulliver of *The Mill on the Floss,* who ran away to the gypsies and was fed aromatic rosemary-flavoured rabbit stew. We were fed *laddoos* by the lepers and sat talking until we were discovered there by our horrified parents, for Langra, a lame boy the Diases helped, led us there at our request, then returned to tell on us!

I once took my sister by the hand to run away from home, but we had barely left our street when our parents, returning, saw us and retroactively rescinded the prize of the puzzle book I had been promised for being good at the dentist, gentle Dr Piroshaw, an irrational injustice that rankled for years, for my mother rarely bought me books. I remember sitting there, hoping that she would tell Dr Piroshaw that I was six, which seemed terribly grown-up, and resolving not to whimper while my cavity-ridden teeth, wages of our diet of sweets at three meals a day, were drilled, the very sound of the drill filling me with terror.

Whenever the watchman left his post at the gate of Sacred Heart Convent, I ran away and crossed the road to the peace and timelessness of the Catholic graveyard. It was like stepping into eternity. (On the way, I bought bright red ice lollies from the pushcart parked outside the school, using the five paise my mother had given me to buy the broadsheet *Soldiers of God*–leaflets on cheap paper with Bible stories and pep talks to encourage us to become little "soldiers of God." My mother blamed every urinary tract infection on these illicit purchases.)

I wandered among the graves, reading the names of people I'd heard of, mentally calculating heartbreak in the birth and death dates of children who had died young, as well as in the long lives of singleness and widowhood. What large families! I read the book of the graveyard, trying to identify the names–English, Anglo-Indian, Mangalorean, Goan, Keralite, Tamilian, Adivasi or tribal, many with generic, ancient Catholic saint names, Praxedes, Euphrosia, Thrasius, the saint of the day often. I read the effusive tributes to husband, wife, and child. Everyone who had died was such a walking saint, I noticed sceptically. See, here was the grave of Neville, the son of Mrs Millie D'Cruz who had drowned at Riversmeet, the spot now evoking much Catholic dread. *Dust thou art, and to dust thou shalt return…* The graveyard was a realm of deep peace, despite the noise of city streets, cars, and scooters. Eventually, I was missed, discovered, and led back to school; there was trouble, but still, the quietude and the sips of solitude and eternity lured me back to the graveyard.

I had to go to the Principal's Office each evening before I went home and record everything naughty I had done that day, the turbulence and adrenalin-flooding of home manifesting in school too. Some sheets survive. I'd darted up, grabbed something off each girl's desk, an eraser, a sharpener, a pencil, and sprinted through the classroom, depositing them at random on someone else's desk, singing, *"I sent a letter to my love, and on the way, I dropped it. Someone came and picked it up and put it in his pocket."* Everyone jumped up and dashed around the classroom, trying to retrieve their stuff. There was pandemonium. I sat down and smiled.

The free-floating anger I felt at home, often appeared at school. I remember being infuriated by a tall, well-built classmate, Rita, several inches taller and many pounds heavier than I, and, surrounded by other girls, throwing her down on the floor, flinging myself on top of her, throwing her glasses off her face, grabbing her hair, and…memory draws a blank. Most of my mischief, though, was unpremeditated and impulsive. I wandered up to the roof-top terrace of the school at recess, then leapt down onto the narrow parapet above the first-floor classrooms and shouted to the sea of blue-clad girls below me, "I am the Queen of this school." The blue sea screeched, pointing upwards, "Sister, Sister, Anita Mathias is on the roof." Teachers joined the throng, nuns in their white habits and black and white wimples. Giggles, shrieks. I peacocked in this moment of elevated glory, me up there, on the ledge, at the highest point of the school, the crowds massed beneath me. "I am the Queen of this School," I proclaimed again in a mood of exaltation. The bell rang; no one went into class. "Anita, come down immediately," Sister Veronique shouted. But I had lost my nerve and was unable to hoist myself back up to the terrace from which I had so gaily leapt and, looking down, plunged into vertigo and panic. I stood there, grinning feebly at the shrieking crowd until a ladder was found, and a servant climbed up, grabbed me, and carried me down. The girls crowded around me, the heroine of the hour. No one had guessed my terror.

When sent to stand outside the class as a punishment, I jumped up on a bench and made faces through the window. Everyone giggled, pointing. Seeing the teacher make for me, I jumped down and bolted the door from the outside. The bell rang for recess, and everyone banged on the door and the windows facing the corridor, shouting, "Open the door, open the door," but I sat outside, so goody-goody, saying, "Teacher had locked the class in because they have been *so* naughty." Meanwhile, the teacher and students rushed to the other side of the first-floor classroom and shouted down to the children in the playground: "Help, help. Anita Mathias has locked us in. Someone unlock the door." But they were not heard through the racket of girls at recess, and, eventually, I got hungry and unlocked the door to get my own lunch

I was once sent to the Principal's office with an Anglo-Indian girl called Mercy Green over some mischief. Sister Veronique turned all her fury on Mercy Green, and I felt guilty and scared, for I had been the instigator. "Why did you do it, Mercy Green?" she asked, "Why?" while putting her chastising ruler between the little metal buttons of Mercy's flimsy blouse, spaced too far apart in economy, carelessly pulling one button undone, then two, revealing her flat eight-year-old chest. I was horrified.

I probably got away with so much because of my family--my father, a senior executive at Tata's, which dominated that company town, was the school's honorary treasurer; his brother Father Theo Mathias, S. J., was on the board of the All-India Council of Christian Higher Education, the Xavier Board, and later Director of the well-regarded XLRI; my mother's cousin, Father John Prabhu, the Provincial, in charge of the Jamshedpur Jesuit province, and my mother's first cousins, Sisters Marilyn, Marita, and Moira, were respected nuns in the Apostolic Carmel, the order which ran Sacred Heart Convent.

* * *

However, just before my ninth birthday, I was told two things—firstly, that I had been expelled from Sacred Heart Convent. "She doesn't respect anyone at Sacred Heart," my mother reported Sister Veronique's complaint. "Not a nun, not a teacher, not a girl, not an *ayah*." And then, in the fairy tale way that the best things in my life have often risen phoenix-like from what should have been the worst things, I learnt, to my high delight, that I was to go to boarding school, to Saint Mary's Convent, Ramnee Park, run by German and Irish nuns in Nainital, an exquisite hill-station in the foothills of the Himalayas. I looked at the Prospectus: girls in blazers and pixie caps throwing snowballs at each other, pine trees and mountains in the background. My father, who, aged eight, had been sent to a European-run hill station boarding school, Montford School, Yercaud, had decided to give me too a snobby and coveted experience and an excellent education.

"No getting expelled from Ramnee," my father and my Uncle, Father Theo Mathias, said. "Or it's Gobichettapallyam for you." A decidedly unclassy boarding school in Tamil Nadu, apparently, probably a mythical one. "Gobi-chetta-pallyam, Gobi-chetta-pallyam," my father and Uncle said, roaring with helpless laughter, probably remembering a childhood in-joke.

"Or Madhupur," my mother said with quiet enjoyment, which somehow sounded a meaner place.

My mother promised me presents (bribes!) of my choice if I did well in my Fourth Standard Final Exams, fourteen prizes if I stood first, thirteen if I stood second, twelve for third, and so on. I gleefully composed my eccentric list—a bicycle if I came first (though, in fact, unlike my sister, I only learnt to cycle as an undergraduate in England); a prism because I had read of the triangle that shattered white light into all the colours of the rainbow. *The Apocrypha*, which I imagined was a book of mysterious wisdom, full of fearful and wondrous dragons, because of the picture from it in my *The Mill on the Floss*, and, besides, I liked the strange, ominous sound of the word (that most of the Apocrypha was right there in my Catholic Bible, I did not know). A Dunlopillo, like my mother's. Sundak sandals, rubber, waterproof, very comfortable, and new on the market. The list inched down, ever more modestly, to a bar of Cadbury's chocolate for coming fourteenth, which I indeed did. I had told my teacher Berna D'Cruz about this list, though my high excitement and longing did not translate into studying harder–or at all, (for I then could not make myself do what bored me!) At the end of the year, however, I found I had magically jumped from forty-second place to fourteenth, chased again by grace.

And so, to boarding school, I went, aged nine. My childhood was over. I had to stand on my own two feet and make all my decisions myself, with no one to advise or comfort me. I grew up rapidly and achieved an emotional independence and self-sufficiency, which have stood me in good stead while also learning much about reading people, surviving, making friends, and thriving. Thriving!

However, on hearing I was going to Enid-Blyton-land, I stood on tiptoe, peeking into the future in high excitement. An adventure, an adventure, more than I asked or dreamed of asking for.

Also by Anita Mathias …
Wandering Between Two Worlds: Essays on Faith and Art
Anita Mathias
Benediction Books, 2007
152 pages
ISBN: 0955373700

In these wide-ranging lyrical essays, Anita Mathias writes, in lush, lovely prose, of her naughty Catholic childhood in Jamshedpur, India; her large, eccentric family in Mangalore, a sea-coast town converted by the Portuguese in the six-teenth century; her rebellion and atheism as a teenager in her Himalayan boarding school, run by German missionary nuns, St. Mary's Convent, Nainital; and her abrupt religious conversion after which she entered Mother Teresa's convent in Calcutta as a novice. Later rich, elegant essays explore the dualities of her life as a writer, mother, and Christian in the United States--Domesticity and Art, Writing and Prayer, and the experience of being "an alien and stranger" as an immigrant in America, sensing the need for roots.

The Story of Dirk Willems: The Man who Died to Save his Enemy
Anita Mathias
Benediction Classics, 2019
18 pages, Full colour.
ISBN: 9781789430448

The religious wars of the Reformation had heroes and villains. There were giants like Luther and Calvin, and quieter unsung heroes. Five hundred years later, one of these stands out: the Dutch Anabaptist, Dirk Willems, who sacrificed his life to save his enemy.

Francesco, Artist of Florence: The Man Who Gave Too Much
Anita Mathias
Benediction Books, 2014
52 pages (full colour)
ISBN: 978-1781394175

In this lavishly illustrated book by Anita Mathias, Francesco, artist of Florence, creates magic in pietre dure, inlaying precious stones in marble in life-like "paintings." While he works, placing lapis lazuli birds on clocks, and jade dragonflies on vases, he is purely happy. However, he must sell his art to support his family. Francesco, who is incorrigibly soft-hearted, cannot stand up to his haggling customers. He ends up almost giving away an exquisite jewellery box to Signora Farnese's bambina, who stands, captivated, gazing at a jade parrot nibbling a cherry. Signora Stallardi uses her daughter's wedding to cajole him into discounting his rainbowed marriage chest. His old friend Girolamo bullies him into letting him have the opulent table he hoped to sell to the Medici almost at cost. Carrara is raising the price of marble; the price of gems keeps rising. His wife is in despair. Francesco fears ruin.

* * *

Sitting in the church of Santa Maria Novella at Mass, very worried, Francesco hears the words of Christ. The lilies of the field and the birds of the air do not worry, yet their Heavenly Father looks after them. As He will look after us. He resolves not to worry. And as he repeats the prayer the Saviour taught us, Francesco resolves to forgive the friends and neighbours who repeatedly put their own interests above his. But can he forgive himself for his own weakness, as he waits for the eternal city of gold whose walls are made of jasper, whose gates are made of pearls, and whose foundations are sapphire, emerald, ruby and amethyst? There time and money shall be no more, the lion shall live with the lamb, and we shall dwell trustfully together. Francesco leaves Santa Maria Novella, resolving to trust the One who told him to live like the lilies and the birds, deciding to forgive those who haggled him into bad bargains--while making a little resolution for the future.

About the Author

Anita Mathias was born in India and lives in Oxford, England. She has a BA (Hons.) and an MA in English from Somerville College, Oxford University, and an MA in English/Creative Writing from the Ohio State University.

Anita has won a Literature Fellowship from the National Endowment for the Arts, an Individual Artist Fellowship from the Minnesota State Arts Board, and fellowships from The Jerome Foundation, The Vermont Studio Centre, The Sweet Briar Writers Colony, and The Virginia Centre for the Creative Arts. She has published in The Washington *Post, London Magazine, Commonweal, America, The Christian Century,* The *Virginia Quarterly Review, The Journal, Notre Dame Magazine, Contemporary Literary Criticism,* and *The Best Spiritual Writing* anthologies. Anita has blogged for Tearfund in Cambodia, and has won awards for her blogging and tweeting at the Premier Digital Awards, London.

Anita blogs at anitamathias.com. Her books include *Wandering Between Two Worlds (2007)* and *Francesco, Artist of Florence* (2014).

Printed in Great Britain
by Amazon

14965705R00210